Essential Readings ON Vocabulary Instruction

Compiled and introduced by Michael F. Graves

INTERNATIONAL
 Reading Association
800 BARKSDALE ROAD, PO BOX 8139
NEWARK, DE 19714-8139, USA
www.reading.org

IRA BOARD OF DIRECTORS

Barbara J. Walker, Oklahoma State University–Stillwater/Tulsa, Tulsa, Oklahoma, President • Kathryn Au, SchoolRise LLC, Honolulu, Hawaii, President-elect • Patricia A. Edwards, Michigan State University, East Lansing, Michigan, Vice President • Adelina Arellano-Osuna, University of the Andes-Mérida, Mérida, Venezuela • Carl Braun, University of Calgary, Calgary, Alberta, Canada • Maryann Manning, University of Alabama at Birmingham, Birmingham, Alabama • Donald J. Leu, University of Connecticut, Storrs, Connecticut • Taffy E. Raphael, University of Illinois at Chicago, Chicago, Illinois • D. Ray Reutzel, Utah State University, Logan, Utah • Janice F. Almasi, University of Kentucky, Lexington, Kentucky • Marsha Moore Lewis, Duplin County Schools, Kenansville, North Carolina • Rizalina C. Labanda, Sts. Peter and Paul Early Childhood Center, Laguna, The Philippines

The International Reading Association attempts, through its publications, to provide a forum for a wide spectrum of opinions on reading. This policy permits divergent viewpoints without implying the endorsement of the Association.

Executive Editor, Books   Corinne M. Mooney
Developmental Editor   Charlene M. Nichols
Developmental Editor   Tori Mello Bachman
Developmental Editor   Stacey L. Reid
Editorial Production Manager   Shannon T. Fortner
Design and Composition Manager   Anette Schuetz

Project Editor   Wesley Ford

Cover   Linda Steere

Copyright 2009 by the International Reading Association, Inc.

All rights reserved. No part of this publication may be reproduced or transmitted in any form or by any means, electronic or mechanical, including photocopy, or any information storage and retrieval system, without permission from the publisher.

The publisher would appreciate notification where errors occur so that they may be corrected in subsequent printings and/or editions.

Library of Congress Cataloging-in-Publication Data

Essential readings on vocabulary instruction / Michael F. Graves, editor.

    p. cm.

  ISBN 978-0-87207-806-2

  1. Vocabulary—Study and teaching.   I. Graves, Michael F.

  LB1574.5.E877 2009

  372.44—dc22

2009015766

Contents

Fostering Word Consciousness

Teaching English-Language Learners

Teaching Vocabulary in Content Area

The Four-Part Program

About the Editor

Michael F. Graves is Professor Emeritus of Literacy Education at the University of Minnesota, Minneapolis, USA, and a member of the Reading Hall of Fame. His research, development, and writing focus on vocabulary learning and instruction and comprehension instruction. His most recent books include *Teaching Individual Words: One Size Does Not Fit All* (2009), *Fostering Comprehension in English Classes* (with Raymond Philippot, 2009), *Teaching Reading in the 21st Century* (4th edition, with Connie Juel and Bonnie B. Graves, 2007), *Reading and Responding in the Middle Grades: Approaches for All Classrooms* (with Lee Galda, 2007), and *The Vocabulary Book: Learning and Instruction* (2006). His work has also appeared in journals including *American Educator, Child Development, Educational Leadership, The Elementary School Journal, Journal of Adolescent & Adult Literacy, Journal of Educational Psychology, Journal of Reading Behavior, Middle School Journal, Reading Research Quarterly, Research in the Teaching of English,* and *The Reading Teacher.* He has served as a consultant for a range of government, nonprofit, and commercial agencies and organizations; as editor of the *Journal of Reading Behavior* and associate editor of *Research in the Teaching of English*; and as a member of the editorial review boards for *Reading Research Quarterly, Journal of Reading Behavior, Research in the Teaching of English,* and the yearbook of the National Reading Conference.

Introduction

Michael F. Graves

Forty years ago, Petty, Herold, and Stoll (1967) began their book-length review of the research on vocabulary instruction by emphasizing the importance of word knowledge:

> The importance of vocabulary is daily demonstrated in schools and out. In the classroom, the achieving students possess the most adequate vocabularies. Because of the verbal nature of most classroom activities, knowledge of words and ability to use language are essential to success in these activities. After schooling has ended, adequacy of vocabulary is almost equally essential for achievement in vocations and in society. (p. 7)

Unfortunately, after completing the review, Petty and his colleagues were forced to conclude that while vocabulary is tremendously important, "the teaching profession seems to know little of substance about the teaching of vocabulary" (p. 84).

Today, that situation has changed markedly: Compared with the case 40 years ago, the importance of vocabulary is now even more widely recognized. Moreover, and more important, we now have a huge store of data that supports our belief in the importance of vocabulary. Those data are described in reports such as that prepared by the U.S. National Reading Panel (National Institute of Child Health and Human Development, 2000), *Reading for Understanding* (RAND Reading Study Group, 2002), and *Improving Adolescent Literacy* (Kamil et al., 2008); in scholarly collections such as those of Hiebert and Kamil (2006), Wagner, Muse, and Tannenbaum (2007), and Farstrup and Samuels (2008); and in reviews of research such as those by Graves (1986), Beck and McKeown (2001), Blachowicz and Fisher (2000), Baumann, Kame'enui, and Ash (2003), and Graves and Silverman (in press). We certainly do not know everything there is to know about vocabulary and vocabulary instruction. But we do know a great deal! This resource is designed give you that information in a convenient and accessible form so that you can design, plan, and implement the best vocabulary program possible for your classroom, school, or district.

The remainder of this introduction is divided into two parts. First, in the Overview section, I discuss the importance of vocabulary, the number of words children need to learn, the vocabulary deficit that some children face, the nature and importance of having a comprehensive and multifaceted vocabulary program, the comprehensive and multifaceted program described in this resource, the contents of this book and its companions in the IRA Library: Vocabulary package, and resources for additional study. Second, in Guide to the Readings, I give overviews of each of the readings and suggest approaches to working with them.

Overview

The Importance of Vocabulary

As I just noted, we know a huge amount about vocabulary and vocabulary instruction. The findings of more than 100 years of vocabulary research include these:

- Vocabulary knowledge is one of the best indicators of verbal ability (Sternberg, 1987; Terman, 1916).
- Vocabulary knowledge contributes to young children's phonological awareness, which in turn contributes to their

Essential Readings on Vocabulary Instruction, edited by Michael F. Graves. © 2009 by the International Reading Association.

word recognition (Goswami, 2001; Nagy, 2005).

- Vocabulary knowledge in kindergarten and first grade is a significant predictor or reading comprehension in the middle and secondary grades (Cunningham & Stanovich, 1997; Scarborough, 1998).
- Vocabulary difficulty strongly influences the readability of text (Chall & Dale, 1995; Klare, 1984).
- Teaching vocabulary can improve reading comprehension for both native English speakers (Beck, Perfetti, & McKeown, 1982) and English-language learners (ELLs; Carlo et al., 2004).
- Growing up in poverty can seriously restrict the vocabulary children learn before beginning school and make attaining an adequate vocabulary a challenging task (Coyne, Simmons, & Kame'enui, 2004; Hart & Risley, 1995).
- Less advantaged students are likely to have substantially smaller vocabularies than their more advantaged classmates (Templin, 1957; White, Graves, & Slater, 1990).
- Learning English vocabulary is one of the most crucial tasks for ELLs (August, Carol, Dressler, & Snow, 2005; Goldenberg, 2008).
- Lack of vocabulary can be a crucial factor underlying the school failure of disadvantaged students (Becker, 1977; Biemiller, 1999).

How Many Words Do Students Need to Learn?

The vocabulary learning task is enormous! Estimates of vocabulary size vary greatly, but a reasonable number based on the work of Anderson and Nagy (1992), Anglin (1993), Miller and Wakefield (1993), Nagy and Anderson (1984), Nagy and Herman (1987), Snow and Kim (2007), Stahl and Nagy (2006), and White et al. (1990) is this: The books and other reading materials used by school children include more than 180,000 different words. The average child enters school with a very small reading vocabulary, typically consisting largely of environmental print. Once in school, however, a child's reading vocabulary is likely to soar at a rate of 3,000–4,000 words a year, leading to a reading vocabulary of something like 25,000 words by the time he or she is in eighth grade, and a reading vocabulary of something like 50,000 words by the end of high school.

The Vocabulary Deficit of Some Children

I have already noted that some children of poverty have a serious vocabulary deficit, but this important finding deserves elaboration. The most compelling evidence comes from Hart and Risley's (1995, see also 2003) longitudinal study of the vocabularies of 1- to 3-year-old children of professional, working class, and welfare children. Hart and Risley's results indicated that welfare children had vocabularies about half the size of their middle-class counterparts and that similar differences persisted into the school years. There is also evidence that having a small vocabulary is a very serious detriment to success in reading (Becker, 1977; Biemiller, 1999; Chall & Jacobs, 2003). These two facts make it especially important to find ways to bolster the oral and reading vocabularies of students who enter school with small stores of words. For similar reasons, bolstering the English vocabularies of ELLs is critically important (American Educational Research Association, 2004; August et al., 2005; Folse, 2004; Goldenberg, 2008; Nation, 2001).

A Multifaceted and Long-Term Vocabulary Program

The importance of vocabulary, the number of words that children need to learn, and the vocabulary deficit faced by some children all argue for creating robust and comprehensive vocabulary programs, programs that are multifaceted, long-term, and can assist all students—children who enter school with relatively small vocabularies, ELLs with small English vocabularies, children who possess adequate but not exceptional vocabularies, and children who already have rich and powerful vocabularies and are prepared for the challenge of developing still more sophisticated and useful vocabularies—in developing the vocabularies that they need to succeed in school and beyond. Over the past 20 years, I have worked to develop such a program, which is described in some detail in *The Vocabulary Book* (Graves, 2006). The program has received a good deal of support. It was reviewed favorably in the report of the RAND Reading Study Group (RAND Reading Study Group, 2002), used by Baumann and Kame'enui (2004) as a framework for their vocabulary book, endorsed by Blachowicz, Fisher, Ogle, & Watts-Taffe (2006), used in a slightly modified form by Stahl and Nagy (2006) in their vocabulary book, validated in a recent study by Baumann, Ware, and Edwards (2007), and serves as the instructional framework for a five-year research project funded by the National Institute of Child Health and Human Development and the Institute of Educational Sciences (August & Snow, 2008).

The program has four components: Providing Rich and Varied Language Experiences, Teaching Individual Words, Teaching Word-Learning Strategies, and Fostering Word Consciousness. In the next several paragraphs, I briefly discuss each component and the rationale behind it.

Providing Rich and Varied Language Experiences. One way to build students' vocabularies is to immerse them in a rich array of language experiences so that they learn words through listening, speaking, reading, and writing. In kindergarten and the primary grades, listening and speaking are particularly important for promoting vocabulary growth. Most children enter kindergarten with substantial oral vocabularies and very small reading vocabularies. Appropriately, most of the words in materials they read are words that are in their oral vocabularies. For this reason, young children will not learn many new words from reading. Where they will learn them is from discussion, from being

read to, and from having their attention directly focused on words. In the intermediate grades, the middle grades, and secondary school, listening and speaking continue to be important. Students of all ages and ELLs as well as native English speakers need to engage frequently in authentic discussions—give-and-take conversations in which they are given the opportunity to thoughtfully discuss meaningful topics.

Increasingly from the intermediate grades on, reading becomes the principle language experience for increasing students' vocabularies. If we can substantially increase the reading students do, we can substantially increase the words they learn. Anyone interested in increasing students' vocabularies should do everything possible to see that they read as much and as widely as possible.

Teaching Individual Words. Another way to help students increase their vocabularies is to teach them individual words. To be sure, the size of the vocabulary that students will eventually attain means that we cannot teach all of the words they need to learn. However, the fact that we cannot teach all of the words students need to learn does not mean that we cannot and should not teach some of them. Fortunately, research has revealed a good deal about effective—and ineffective—approaches to teaching individual words. Vocabulary instruction is most effective when learners are given both definitional and contextual information, when learners actively process the new word meanings, and when they experience multiple encounters with words. Said somewhat differently, vocabulary instruction is most effective—and most likely to influence students' comprehension—when it is rich, deep, and extended. At the same time, because there are so many words to teach, not all of them can receive rich, deep, and extended instruction. Thus, there is a need both for rich, deep, and extended instruction on some words and for less robust, introductory instruction on others. In *The Vocabulary Book* (Graves, 2006), I suggest different methods (some more robust and more time consuming and some less robust and less time consuming) for different learning goals. These goals include teaching students to read words already in their oral vocabularies, teaching new labels for known concepts, teaching words representing new concepts, and clarifying and enriching the meanings of already known words.

Teaching Word-Learning Strategies. A third approach to helping students increase their vocabularies is to teach word-learning strategies. One widely recommended strategy is that of using context. As Sternberg (1987) has forcefully pointed out, "Most vocabulary is learned from context" (p. 89). If we can improve students' abilities to use context to glean word meanings, they will markedly increase their vocabularies. Using word parts to unlock the meanings of unknown words is another widely recommended strategy and doing so is well supported by research. If students can use their knowledge of prefixes, suffixes, and roots to recognize the various members of word families—for example *indicate*, *indicates*, *indicated*, *indicating*, *indication*, and *indicator*—the number of individual words they need to learn is significantly reduced. Using the dictionary and similar reference tools is a third recommended approach, and many students need assistance in more effectively using these tools (Graves, Juel, & Graves, 2007). Finally, many English words have Spanish cognates. For ELLs who are Spanish speakers, learning to use cognates can be a powerful word-learning strategy.

Fostering Word Consciousness. The last component of the four-part program is fostering word consciousness. The term refers to an awareness of and interest in words and their meanings. Word consciousness involves both a cognitive and an affective stance toward words, and integrates metacognition about words, motivation to learn words, and deep and lasting interest in words (Graves & Watts, 2008).

Students who are word conscious are aware of the words around them—those they read and hear and those they write and speak. This awareness involves an appreciation of the power of words, an understanding of why certain words are used instead of others, and a sense of the words that could be used in place of those selected by a writer or speaker. It also involves, as Scott and Nagy (2004) emphasize, recognition of the communicative power of words, of the differences between spoken and written language, and of the particular importance of word choice in written language. And it involves an interest in learning and using new words and becoming more skillful and precise in word usage.

With something like 50,000 words to learn and with most of this word learning taking place incidentally as students are reading and listening, a positive disposition toward words is crucial. Word consciousness exists at many levels of complexity and sophistication, and it can and should be fostered among preschoolers as well as among students in and beyond high school.

This Resource and Its Related Components

In addition to this overview and introduction, this book includes 14 articles and book chapters grouped around each of the four parts of a comprehensive program—providing rich and varied language experiences, teaching individual words, teaching word learning strategies, and fostering word consciousness—along with additional readings on teaching vocabulary to ELLs, teaching vocabulary in content areas, and a field test of the four-part program.

Also available is the IRA Library: Vocabulary collection that includes this book along with two others selected particularly to complement the readings: One that I have already mentioned, *The Vocabulary Book* (Graves, 2006), describes the four-part program in detail; the second is William Nagy's *Teaching Vocabulary to Improve Reading Comprehension* (1988), a terrific little book on providing rich and deep instruction on individual words.

This book and the related IRA Library: Vocabulary package contain a lot of information on vocabulary—really all you need to plan, design, and implement a powerful vocabulary program. But if you want to reach even deeper levels of knowledge, here are four recent books I particularly recommend: Baumann and Kame'enui's

Vocabulary Instruction: Research to Practice (2004) is a collection of chapters dealing with teaching individual words, teaching word-learning strategies, and fostering word consciousness. Beck, McKeown, and Kucan's *Bringing Words to Life: Robust Vocabulary Instruction* (2002) is a detailed account of how to create one type of vocabulary instruction, robust instruction on individual words. Stahl and Nagy's *Teaching Word Meanings* (2006) presents a detailed description of a comprehensive vocabulary program very much like the one in *The Vocabulary Book* (Graves, 2006). And my *Teaching Individual Words: One Size Does Not Fit All* (Graves, 2009) presents an expanded version of the program for teaching individual words first presented in *The Vocabulary Book*, emphasizing that different words, different goals, and different contexts require quite different teaching procedures.

Guide to the Readings

In the remainder of this introduction, I describe the two books included with this one in the IRA Library: Vocabulary package and then go into depth about the articles and book chapters included here. I also offer some suggestions for studying the readings.

The Books

My publication *The Vocabulary Book* (Graves, 2006) describes the comprehensive vocabulary program that provides the framework for the readings included here. Chapter 1 is an introduction very similar to this one. Chapter 2 is a review of research. Chapters 3 to 6 describe the four parts of the multifaceted program. Finally, Chapter 7 presents classrooms portraits of the program in action in a first-grade classroom, a fourth-grade classroom, a middle school classroom, and three high school classrooms.

If you decide to work with *The Vocabulary Book* (Graves, 2006) as well as this book of essential readings, I would recommend studying the former first. You can read quickly through Chapter 1, however, because you have already been introduced here to most of its information.

Chapter 2 will take more time and effort. I suggest studying it with a colleague or group, taking some notes, and discussing or writing some comments on research findings that you were not aware of or find particularly important for practice. For Chapters 3 to 6, I suggest making a record of suggested activities that you already use, activities that you plan to use, and activities that were not suggested but that you come up with while reading. As always, it would be beneficial to work with a colleague or colleagues. For Chapter 7, the classroom portraits, I suggest critiquing the portrait for the age group that you teach.

William Nagy's slim volume, *Teaching Vocabulary to Improve Reading Comprehension* (1988), examines approaches of teaching individual words that focus on increasing students' comprehension of selections containing the words taught. However, it is much more than a cookbook of activities. Instead, Nagy notes that his purpose is to provide teachers with knowledge about "how and why one can choose and adapt vocabulary-related activities in order to maximize their effectiveness" (p. 2). Nagy begins by noting that much vocabulary instruction fails to produce comprehension gains because it does not foster in-depth word knowledge, points out that by themselves both definitional activities and contextual activities are inadequate to the task, but then notes further that a combination of these two types of activities can produce the sort of in-depth knowledge needed. Then, in the longest section of booklet, Nagy describes qualities of effective vocabulary instruction—integration, an emphasis on concepts, repetition, and meaningful use—and provides detailed descriptions and examinations of teaching methods illustrating these qualities. After this, Nagy explains that not every unknown word needs to receive in-depth instruction because texts include redundant information and students will learn words incidentally from the texts they read. Nagy next argues that students need both explicit instruction on a limited number of words and lots of opportunities for wide reading in which they will encounter myriad words in myriad contexts. Finally, he notes that explicit instruction should include in-depth work on a small number of words and briefer instruction on other words.

Although *Teaching Vocabulary to Improve Reading Comprehension* (Nagy, 1988) includes only 42 pages, it contains a wealth of important and useful information. I have read it and studied it on three separate occasions separated by several years, and I continue to learn from it. So I definitely recommend multiple readings. Reading it with a colleague or group will give you the needed opportunity to discuss and ponder what you read. Additionally, I want to point out that while Nagy discusses only a two-pronged program here, in his newer and considerably longer book, *Teaching Word Meanings* (Stahl & Nagy, 2006), he considers a multifaceted program much like that emphasized in *The Vocabulary Book* (Graves, 2006) and this resources.

If you are using this book as part of the IRA Library: Vocabulary collection, I suggest reading Nagy's booklet at the same time that you read the articles in this book on teaching individual words.

Exploring the Readings in This Book

Providing Rich and Varied Language Experiences. Steven Stahl and Katherine Dougherty Stahl's "Word Wizards All! Teaching Word Meanings in Preschool and Primary Education" considers approaches for both providing rich and varied language experiences and for teaching individual words. The authors begin with an eloquent and convincing explanation of the power and control young children gain as they learn words. "To expand a child's vocabulary," they note, "is to teach that child to think about the world." Next, they discuss the gaps in vocabulary that some children have and the consequences of having those gaps. After this, they discuss how word knowledge develops—bit by bit over time (something Steven Stahl also discusses in "Words Are Learned Incrementally Over Multiple Exposures," which is included later in this book). In the next several sections, the authors discuss the importance of talking to children, of carefully selecting the right words to teach, and of using techniques like interactive

oral reading. Then, they emphasize that written texts are a particularly rich source of vocabulary, and that the language of school differs from that of many homes and will require some special attention. After that, they suggest several methods for directly teaching words. Finally, the authors suggest that in addition to teaching words to children, we need to build children's curiosity about words and their excitement in learning words.

This is not a difficult article, and it contains a good deal of information that you will find elsewhere in this resource. But it is a terrific piece to help you solidify the knowledge you have, and it presents a really convincing case for the importance of vocabulary. I suggest that, while you read it, you take some notes on the authors' arguments for the importance of vocabulary. Then, as you work through the other readings, consider the connections between what you find in this article and what you read in the other parts of this resource.

The next reading, Andrew Biemiller's "Teaching Vocabulary: Early, Direct, and Sequential," is brief, straightforward, and carries a very important message. Biemiller notes that an increased emphasis on phonics has not resulted in gains in reading comprehension and that what is missing is a parallel emphasis on vocabulary, particularly in kindergarten and the primary grades. Next, he argues that children do not need to learn all that many words, perhaps 12,000 or so root words by the end of high school. His estimate of the size of the task of learning vocabulary differs from mine and from many of the authors represented in this book. Despite this difference of opinion, Biemiller's recommendations for practice are much the same as others'. He recommends directly teaching a number of words and teaching word-learning strategies like the use of word parts and context to infer word meanings. And he recommends that a substantial teacher-centered effort is needed to promote vocabulary growth, particularly in kindergarten and the primary grades.

You will find the article a quick read and one that suggests some definite actions to take. I believe that an effective way to deal with it is to read through it once, and then read it a second time. During or after this second reading, jot down some ways in which you can take advantage of Biemiller's insights in your own vocabulary teaching.

Isabel Beck and Margaret McKeown's "Text Talk: Capturing the Benefits of Read-Aloud Experiences for Young Children" describes an approach carefully designed to foster both comprehension and vocabulary growth during read-alouds for kindergarten and primary-grade children. The authors begin by noting that although reading aloud is probably the most highly recommended approach to fostering language and literacy in young children, doing so does not always produce strong effects. They then discuss the types of texts and the kinds of talk that are likely to produce the greatest benefits and some of the problems with read-alouds they observed when visiting classrooms. Their observations revealed that children often responded on the basis of pictures or background knowledge and that teachers often asked questions requiring only one-word answers that did little to foster comprehension of the text as a whole. Their solution is Text Talk, a specific approach to read-alouds that employs fairly sophisticated texts, suggests criteria for initial questions and follow-up questions that will get students talking and grappling with text, and teaches a small number of fairly sophisticated words, introducing them after students have read the text and dealing with the words in some depth.

Just as the Text Talk procedure is designed to give children plenty to think about during a read aloud, the Text Talk article will give you plenty to think about as you read it. One way to approach the article is to read it carefully, paying particular attention to the sorts of texts Beck and McKeown suggest using, the sorts of comprehension questions they suggest asking, the types of words they suggest teaching, and procedures they suggest for teaching the vocabulary. If you are using the IRA Library: Vocabulary collection, you can then reread the section on interactive oral reading in Chapter 3 of *The Vocabulary Book* (Graves, 2006), compare the methods suggested there with Text Talk, and decide which approaches or combination of approaches you will use for reading aloud. Also, for a formal study of Text Talk, take a look at Beck and McKeown (2007).

Teaching Individual Words. Camille Blachowicz and Connie Obrochta's "Vocabulary Visits: Virtual Field Trips for Content Vocabulary Development" describes a clever plan for creating virtual field trips that can get students excited about vocabulary and at the same time teach key content words. Blachowicz and Obrochta first discuss the educational and motivational value of field trips. Then, they list the characteristics of field trips that make them so effective. After this, they explain the solid body of theory and research on effective read-alouds and active teaching that grounds the Vocabulary Visits activity. Next, they describe the steps in planning a Vocabulary Visits unit. These include identifying a topic, five or more thematically oriented informational texts, and some keywords, and constructing a poster to focus students' attention on the unit theme and the words to be learned. Then, they explain how the unit proceeds. Steps here include having students list the words they know about the topic and put them on the poster, taking a simulated field trip using the poster, reading each book aloud and having students give thumbs up when they hear any of the target words, adding keywords to the poster as necessary, and doing a variety of extension activities.

Probably the best way to get familiar with Vocabulary Visits is to try it out. Although the procedure was developed for first graders, I suspect you could use it through at least the third grade and could modify it for older students. As you read about the procedure and work with it, you'll notice that it includes several parts of a comprehensive vocabulary program: In addition to teaching individual words, it provides students with rich and varied language experiences and promotes word consciousness. I think two or so Vocabulary Visit units over the course of a year would do a lot to stimulate interest in words. Finally, if you would like to see a formal study of Vocabulary Visits, take a look at Blachowicz and Obrochta (2007).

In " 'Extraordinary,' 'Tremendous,' 'Exhilarating,' 'Magnificent': Middle School At-Risk

Students Become Avid Word Learners With the Vocabulary Self-Collection Strategy (VSS)," Martha Rapp Ruddell and Brenda Shearer describe their student-centered, motivational approach to building students' vocabularies. After several illustrations showing the sophistication of the words students choose to study and students' enthusiasm for selecting words themselves, Ruddell and Shearer discuss their initial encounters with the approach. Next, they note its theoretical foundations, citing social constructivist, transactional, and activity theories as supporting the approach. The authors then discuss how the large number of words to be learned makes finding efficient ways to teach words and creating interest in words and motivation to learn them so important. After this, they describe the VSS approach, the study they did to validate it, and the results of the study.

As is the case with Vocabulary Visits, the best way to get familiar with VSS is to try it out. Or you can try a variation of it you create. Doing so is well worthwhile. Certainly, student selection is not the only approach to use; there is plenty of room for you as a teacher to identify words to teach. But involving students in word selection some of the time is a great way to build motivation, word consciousness, and independence. After all, teachers will not always be there to select words to be studied.

In the very brief "Words Are Learned Incrementally Over Multiple Exposures," Steven Stahl makes this crucial point about the nature of word learning noted in his title, and does so with some really telling examples. Although he and Katherine Doughtery Stahl made the point more briefly in "Word Wizards All," described earlier, it is worth the amplification it gets in this article because we often forget this fact when teaching vocabulary. After directly stating that we learn a little about a word each time we encounter it, Stahl goes on to discuss levels of word knowledge, the fact that we need both definitional information and repeatedly meeting a word in context to learn it well, and the fact that words have either slightly different or very different meanings in different contexts.

As you read the article, pay attention to both the main points and the telling examples. Then, ask yourself what the incremental nature of word learning means for teaching.

Margaret Ann Richek's "Words Are Wonderful: Interactive, Time-Efficient Strategies to Teach Meaning Vocabulary" details six procedures for initially teaching or reviewing vocabulary. She begins the article with arguments for the importance of vocabulary and a discussion about how vocabulary should and should not be taught, arguments that you are undoubtedly familiar with by this point in your reading. Then, she describes two procedures for initially teaching words. One of these is Semantic Impressions, in which student write a brief text using words from a narrative they are about to read. The other is Word Expert Cards, a procedure in which each student takes responsibility for becoming an expert on several words and students then share their expertise. These very detailed descriptions give you a real sense of how the techniques work. Next, prompted by the fact that words are learned incrementally (as Stahl explained in the article that precedes this one), Richek describes four procedures for reviewing words already taught. She titles these Anything Goes, Connect Two, Two in One, and Find That Word. Finally, Richek notes that these procedures can be used in various content areas and at various grade levels.

I suggest two things to do in dealing with this very practical set of ideas. First, take a look at Tables 1 and 2, which describe the Semantic Impressions and Word Expert Card procedures, and create similar step-by-step directions for the other four procedures. Second, try out one of more of the procedures in your classroom and jot down some notes on the results.

Teaching Word-Learning Strategies. Thomas White, Joanne Sowell, and Alice Yanagihara's "Teaching Elementary Students To Use Word-Part Clues" is one of the most useful articles on vocabulary ever published because it identifies the 20 most frequent English prefixes and the 20 most frequent English suffixes. Although there are many other lists of prefixes and suffixes, no other list provides such a definitive set of affixes to teach. Moreover, as the authors point out, these 20 prefixes and 20 suffixes are all that you need to teach. After presenting their lists, the authors go on to warn about some confusion that prefixes can create, describe a prefix lesson, and suggest which prefixes should be taught at which grade levels. They then describe a procedure for teaching suffixes—which, because the meanings of suffixes do not need to be taught to native English speakers, is quite different from the procedure for teaching prefixes. Next, they present data showing the effectiveness of their teaching methods. Finally, they argue that systematic and direct teaching is necessary, a position with which I strongly agree.

Read the article carefully. It is short but packed with useful information. Pay particular attention to the lists of prefixes and suffixes. Copy them and put them some place where you will have them close at hand. If students do not know these prefixes, which will help them unlock the meanings of many new words, or cannot remove suffixes to reveal root words, they need instruction. Also, many ELLs will need instruction on the meanings and function of English suffixes. For additional information on teaching prefixes and suffix removal as well as the general approach I recommend for teaching all word-learning strategies, see Chapter 5, Teaching Word-Learning Strategies, in *The Vocabulary Book* (Graves, 2006).

Michael Kieffer and Nonie Lesaux's "Breaking Down Words to Build Meaning: Morphology, Vocabulary, and Reading Comprehension in the Urban Classroom" packs a lot of useful information into just a few pages. It begins with a brief review of the literature on the importance of developing a rich vocabulary, of the small vocabularies of some children in urban and low-income schools, and of the relationship between vocabulary and reading comprehension. Next, it discusses ways of closing the vocabulary gap, giving precedence to a multifaceted program like the one I have been describing. After that, it outlines some fundamentals of English vocabulary. Then, it describes a small descriptive study of fourth and fifth graders' morphological knowledge, which showed that morphological knowledge was related to reading comprehension, that

the relationship was stronger for fifth graders than for fourth graders, and that it was as strong for Spanish-speaking ELLs as for native English speakers. The article also suggests what sorts of shifts between root words and derived forms tend to cause students difficulty, as well as suggesting some prefixes, suffixes, and roots worth teaching. Finally, it presents and discusses four principles for effectively teaching morphology.

As I said, Kieffer and Lesaux pack a lot of valuable information into a brief space, and getting everything possible out of the article will take some study. The article would be worth outlining, studying as a group, and taking some fairly detailed notes on. You could also take a critical look at each of the principles for teaching morphology and discuss them with your colleagues. Finally, having read this, the White et al. article, and the chapter "Teaching Word Learning Strategies" in *The Vocabulary Book* (Graves, 2006), you should be able to make a decision about where and how work with word-learning strategies fits into your classroom and school.

Fostering Word Consciousness. In "Developing Word Consciousness," Judith Scott and William Nagy make several very important points about the nature of word consciousness and present some practical approaches to fostering it. The authors introduce the chapter by noting that word consciousness is not a frill or something done just for fun; instead, it is a vital part of getting students to take responsibility for their own word learning. They also point out that while we can think of word conscious as one of four components of a vocabulary program, it is important that work in word consciousness be integrated into the other parts of the program rather than occurring in isolation. And they note that in the chapter they will focus on two aspects of word consciousness: (1) students becoming aware of the difference between spoken and written registers and (2) the powerful role of word choice in written work. After this, they define word consciousness, noting first that it is a special sort of metalinguistic awareness—the ability to reflect on and manipulate linguistic units—and second that it involves knowledge and beliefs about word learning such as that knowing a word means more than knowing a definition. They next emphasize the importance of word choice in written language. Then, they discuss the approach to word consciousness taken in The Gift of Words, a project that Scott and several elementary teachers worked over a number of years. After this, they point out that word consciousness can only be developed with students who have deep knowledge of words, make the important distinction between teaching new labels for known concepts and teaching new concepts, and suggest some approaches to teaching concepts. In concluding, they note that word consciousness is essential for sustained vocabulary growth, that it is essential for effective writing, and that it contributes to reading comprehension.

Scott and Nagy's article does two things: It makes many useful points about word consciousness, and it presents some specific ideas about fostering word consciousness through writing. One way to work through the chapter is to make a list of the general points it makes, try out the authors' approaches to fostering word consciousness in writing, and then devise some ways of your own to foster word consciousness in writing.

"For the Love of Words: Fostering Word Consciousness in Young Readers" by Susan Watts-Taffe and myself begins with several anecdotes illustrating word-consciousness activities in various contexts. The article then defines word consciousness, noting that it "involves both a cognitive and an affective stance toward words" and "integrates metacognition about words, motivation to learn words, and a deep and lasting interest in words." In other words, helping students become word conscious means getting them really interested and excited about words. Building such interest and excitement about words, the article argues, is not a minor matter. With the number of words students need to learn and the importance of vocabulary to success in school, becoming interested and excited about words is crucial. After this, the article describes a six-part framework designed to act as a scaffold as teachers create word-consciousness activities for their classrooms and provides examples of each of these six types of activities. The six parts of the framework are (1) creating a word rich environment, (2) recognizing and promoting adept diction, (3) promoting word play, (4) fostering word consciousness through writing, (5) involving students in original investigations, and (6) teaching students about words.

This is a straightforward article and an easy read, and it will not require much study. What I would suggest is to read it through one time, and then do these follow-up activities. First, choose one of the activities described in the article, use that activity in class, and then debrief by either discussing how the activity went with colleagues or journaling on how it went. Second, select one of the six categories of word consciousness activities, create your own activity that falls within that category, try that out, and debrief.

Teaching ELLs. Lori Helman's "English Words Needed: Creating Research-Based Vocabulary Instruction for English Learners" is a brief review of relevant research coupled with specific suggestions for instruction in keeping with that research. The topics Helman discusses include vocabulary research with English learners, connections between vocabulary research and second-language teaching principles, choosing words to teach, choosing teaching activities for different grade levels, integrating vocabulary into all areas of the curriculum, modifying instruction for students with various levels of English proficiency, and materials that support vocabulary learning. The chapter is packed with important and useful information, and I recommend it highly. I do, however, have one caution I'd like to make. Helman recommends that instruction should be in depth, going beyond definitions to include multiple meanings, finding synonyms and antonyms, and engaging in higher-order thinking. As I explain in *The Vocabulary Book* (Graves, 2006) and *Teaching Individual Words* (Graves, 2009), there is no doubt that in-depth instruction is more effective than briefer instruction, but with the task of learning 50,000 words by the end of high school, some instruction needs to be brief. I also want to stress that, while Helman's article is the only reading included here that focuses exclusively on ELLs, most of ideas suggested in this resource are as useful for ELLs as they are for students who speak English as their first language. As experts like August et al. (2005) and Goldenberg (2008) have noted, most of what we know about teaching native speakers also applies to ELLs.

As I said, Helman's chapter is packed with valid and useful information. It will require some serious study. I recommend both outlining it and taking detailed notes on each section. If you are working in a group, there is plenty of information to warrant a jigsaw approach, with each of half a dozen or so teachers becoming an expert on one section of the article and leading the discussion on that section. Finally, with so many approaches and activities described here, it might be a good idea to choose a small number—say, two or three—to focus on at first.

Teaching Vocabulary in Content Areas. In "Teaching Vocabulary Through Text and Experience in Content Areas," Marco Bravo and Gina Cervetti take a close look at this challenging teaching task and offer some principled solutions. They begin by documenting the importance of vocabulary in content areas such math, science, and social studies. Next, they outline some of the challenges that content area vocabulary presents. These include that content texts include a copious number of challenging words, that much content area vocabulary is abstract, and that content texts include many words with multiple meanings. Still another challenge is that content vocabulary includes many words that represent new concepts and therefore require very sturdy instruction. Although vocabulary instruction in content areas presents challenges, it also presents important possibilities. As the authors point out, these include multiple and varied exposures to individual words, opportunities to teach words as thematically related concepts, and the potential for multimodal experiences. Based on these considerations, the authors make several research-based suggestions for instruction: Select words carefully, focusing on high-utility words in the discipline, discipline-specific words representing important concepts, and words that represent related concepts; provide multiple exposures to keywords; connect unknown words to known ones; and involve students in varied domain-related experiences.

Bravo and Cervetti have written a clear, concise, and well organized article, and the major points come through clearly. To engage deeply with the ideas presented, I suggest identifying a content area chapter in social studies, science, or math; selecting a small set of words to teach for that chapter; creating instruction in keeping with the authors' principles; and, if possible, trying out your instruction in a classroom.

The Four-Part Program Underlying This Resource. " 'Bumping Into Spicy, Tasty Words That Catch Your Tongue': A Formative Experiment on Vocabulary Instruction" is appropriately the final article in this collection. It is particularly fitting as the closing document because in it James Baumann, Donna Ware, and Elizabeth Carr Edwards describe a study testing out the four-part program that provides the framework for this resource. They describe their implementation of the program over the period of a year in Donna's fifth-grade classroom, with James and Elizabeth assisting Donna in developing the instruction, teaching some of the lessons, and collecting much of the data. What you will find here is a rich instantiation of the program—activities to provide rich and varied language experiences, teach individual words, teach word-learning strategies, and foster word consciousness. The instruction, as you will see, is faithful to the four-part model yet incorporates unique elements that fit Donna, her teaching style, her students, and their needs. Several aspects of the instruction seem particularly worth noting. There are a lot of activities. They are varied. They deeply involve students. And they include a great deal of writing, something Donna sees as vital to her approach to literacy instruction. The results are impressive. Quantitative data showed that students' expressive vocabularies improved more than would be expected, that students initially low in vocabulary particularly benefited from the instruction, that students used far more words in their writing following the program than they had at its beginning, that parents rated their children's vocabulary size and interest in words higher at the end of the program, and that students rated their interest in reading, writing, and vocabulary higher at the end of the program. Qualitative results indicated that students used more sophisticated and challenging words, that their interest in vocabulary increased, that students demonstrated use of word-learning tools and strategies independently, and they engaged in word play.

Baumann, Ware, and Edwards's article presents great news for educators who want to help students build their vocabularies. Effective vocabulary instruction is possible in real classrooms with real students, and the four-part framework presented here is a powerful and practical guide for planning such instruction. This book of essential readings along with the related texts in the IRA Library: Vocabulary collection will provide you with the information you need to plan powerful instruction. Your task now is to use that information to create and deliver that instruction.

Author Note

Parts of this chapter are taken from Graves, M.F. (2008). Instruction on individual words: One size does not fit all. In A.E. Farstrup & S.J. Samuels (Eds.), *What research has to say about vocabulary instruction*. Newark, DE: International Reading Association.

References

American Educational Research Association. (2004). English language learners: Boosting academic achievement. *Research Points: Essential Information for Educational Policy, 2*(1), 1–4.

Anderson, R.C., & Nagy, W.E. (1992). The vocabulary conundrum. *American Educator*, Winter, 14–18, 44–47.

Anglin, J.M. (1993). Vocabulary development: A morphological analysis. *Monographs of the Society for Research in Child Development*, Serial No. 238, *58*.

August, D., Carlo, M., Dressler, C., & Snow, C. (2005). The critical role of vocabulary development for English language learners. *Learning Disabilities Research & Practice, 20*(1), 50–57. doi:10.1111/j.1540-5826.2005.00120.x

August, D., & Snow, C. (2008). *Vocabulary and assessment for Spanish-speakers* (VIAS). Program grant supported by Grant Number P01HD039530 from the *Eunice Kennedy Shriver* National Institute of Child Health and Human Development.

Baumann, J.F., & Kame'enui, E.J. (Eds.). (2004). *Vocabulary instruction: Research to practice*. New York: Guilford.

Baumann, J.F., Kame'enui, E.J., & Ash, G.E. (2003). Research on vocabulary instructing: Voltaire redux. In J. Flood, D. Lapp, J.R. Squire, & J.M. Jensen (Eds.), *Handbook on research on teaching the English language arts* (2nd ed., pp. 752–785). Mahwah, NJ: Erlbaum.

Baumann, J.F., Ware, D., & Edwards, E.C. (2007). Bumping into spicy, tasty words that catch your tongue: A formative experiment in vocabulary instruction. *The Reading Teacher, 61*(2), 108–122. doi:10.1598/RT.61.2.1

Beck, I.L., & McKeown, M.G. (2001). Text talk: Capturing the benefits of read-aloud experiences for young children. *The Reading Teacher, 55*(1), 10–20.

Beck, I.L., & McKeown, M.G. (2007). Increasing young children's oral vocabulary repertoires through rich and focused instruction. *The Elementary School Journal, 107*(3), 251–271. doi:10.1086/511706

Beck, I.L., McKeown, M.G., & Kucan, L. (2002). *Bringing words to life: Robust vocabulary instruction*. New York: Guilford.

Beck, I.L., Perfetti, C.A., & McKeown, M.G. (1982). The effects of long-term vocabulary instruction on lexical access and reading comprehension. *Journal of Educational Psychology, 74*(4), 506–521. doi:10.1037/0022-0663.74.4.506

Becker, W.C. (1977). Teaching reading and language to the disadvantaged—What we have learned from field research. *Harvard Educational Review, 47*(4), 511–543.

Biemiller, A. (1999). *Language and reading success*. Cambridge, MA: Brookline Books.

Blachowicz, C., & Fisher, P. (2000). Vocabulary instruction. In M.L. Kamil, P.B. Mosenthal, P.D. Pearson, & R. Barr (Eds.), *The handbook of reading research* (Vol. 3, pp. 503–524). New York: Longman.

Blachowicz, C., & Obrochta, C. (2007). "Tweeking practice": Modifying read-alouds to enhance content vocabulary learning in grade 1. In J. Worthy, B. Maloch, J.V. Hoffman, D.L. Schallert, & C.M. Fairbanks. *56th Yearbook of the National Reading Conference* (pp. 111–121). Oak Creek, WI: NRC.

Blachowicz, C.L.Z., Fisher, P.J.L., Ogle, D., & Watts-Taffe, S. (2006). Vocabulary: Questions from the classroom. *Reading Research Quarterly, 41*(4), 524–539. doi:10.1598/RRQ.41.4.5

Carlo, M.S., August, D., McGlaughlin, B., Snow, C.E., Dressler, C., Lippman, D.N., et al. (2004). Closing the gap: Addressing the vocabulary needs of English-language learners in bilingual and mainstream classes. *Reading Research Quarterly, 39*(2), 188–215. doi:10.1598/RRQ.39.2.3

Chall, J.S., & Dale, E. (1995). *Readability revisited: The new Dale-Chall readability formula*. Cambridge, MA: Brookline Books.

Chall, J.S., & Jacobs, V.A. (2003). The classic study on poor children's fourth-grade slump. *American Educator, 27*(1), 14–15, 44.

Coyne, M.D., Simmons, D.C., & Kame'enui, E.J. (2004). Vocabulary instruction for young children at risk of experiencing reading difficulties: Teaching word meanings during shared story book reading. In J.F. Baumann & E.J. Kame'enui (Eds.), *Vocabulary instruction: Research to practice* (pp. 3–10). New York: Guilford.

Cunningham, A.E., & Stanovich, K.E. (1997). Early reading acquisition and its relationship to reading experience and ability 10 years later. *Developmental Psychology, 33*(6), 934–945. doi:10.1037/0012-1649.33.6.934

Farstrup, A., & Samuels, S.J. (Eds.) (2008). *What research has to say about vocabulary instruction.* Newark, DE: International Reading Association.

Folse, K.S. (2004). *Vocabulary myths: Applying second language research to classroom teaching.* Ann Arbor: The University of Michigan Press.

Goldenberg, C. (2008). Teaching English learners: What the research does and does not say. *American Educator, 32*(1), 8–11, 14–19, 22–23, 42.

Goswami, U. (2001). Early phonological development and the acquisition of literacy. In S.B. Neuman & D.K. Dickinson (Eds.), *Handbook of early literacy research* (pp. 111–125). New York: Guilford.

Graves, M.F. (1986). Vocabulary learning and instruction. In E.Z. Rothkopf (Ed.), *Review of Research in Education* (Vol. 13, pp. 49–90). Washington, DC: American Educational Research Association.

Graves, M.F. (2006). *The vocabulary book: Learning and instruction.* New York: Teachers College Press; Newark, DE: International Reading Association; Urbana, IL: National Council of Teachers of English.

Graves, M.F. (2009). *Teaching individual words: One size does not fit all.* New York: Teachers College Press; Newark, DE: International Reading Association.

Graves, M.F., & Watts-Taffe, S.W. (2008). For the love of words. Fostering word consciousness in young readers. *The Reading Teacher, 62*(3), 185–193.

Graves, M.F., Juel, C., & Graves, B.B. (2007). *Teaching reading in the 21st century* (4th ed.). Boston: Allyn & Bacon.

Graves, M.F., & Silverman, R. (in press). Interventions to enhance vocabulary development. In R. Allington & A. McGill-Franzen (Eds.), *Handbook of reading disabilities research.* Mahwah, NY: Erlbaum.

Hart, B., & Risley, T.R. (1995). *Meaningful differences in the everyday experiences of young American children.* Baltimore: P. H. Brookes.

Hart, B., & Risley, T.R. (2003). The early catastrophe: The 30 million word gap. *American Educator, 27*(1), 4–9.

Hiebert, E.H., & Kamil, M. (Eds.). (2006). *Teaching and learning vocabulary: Bringing research to practice.* Mahwah, NJ: Erlbaum.

Kamil, M.L., Borman, G.D., Dole, J., Kral, C.C., Salinger, T., & Torgesen, J. (2008). *Improving adolescent literacy: Effective classroom and intervention practices: A practice guide.* Washington, DC: National Center for Educational Evaluation and Regional Assistance.

Klare, G.R. (1984). Readability. In P.D. Pearson, R. Barr, M.L. Kamil, & P.B. Mosenthal (Eds.), *Handbook of reading research* (pp. 681–794). New York: Longman.

Miller, G.A., & Wakefield, P.C. (1993). Commentary on Anglin's analysis of vocabulary growth. In J.M. Anglin, Vocabulary development: A morphological analysis. *Monographs of the Society for Research in Child Development, 59*(10), 167–175.

Nagy, W.E. (1988). *Teaching vocabulary to improve reading comprehension.* Newark, DE: International Reading Association.

Nagy, W.E. (2005). Why vocabulary instruction needs to be long-term and comprehensive. In E. Hiebert & M. Kamil (Eds.), *Bringing scientific research to practice: Vocabulary* (pp. 27–44). Mahwah, NJ: Erlbaum.

Nagy, W.E., & Anderson, R.C. (1984). How many words are there in printed school English? *Reading Research Quarterly, 19*(3), 304–330. doi:10.2307/747823

Nagy, W.E., & Herman, P.A. (1987). Breadth and depth of vocabulary knowledge: Implications for acquisition and instruction. In M.C. McKeown & M.E. Curtis (Eds.), *The nature of vocabulary acquisition* (pp. 19–35). Hillsdale, NJ: Erlbaum.

Nation, I.S.P. (2001). *Learning vocabulary in another language.* Cambridge, UK: Cambridge University Press.

National Institute of Child Health and Human Development. (2000). *Report of the National Reading Panel: Teaching children to read: An evidence-based assessment of the scientific research literature on reading and its implications for reading instruction* (NIH Publication No. 00-4769). Washington, DC: U.S. Government Printing Office.

Petty, W., Herold, C., & Stoll, E. (1967). *The state of knowledge about the teaching of vocabulary.* Urbana, IL: National Council of Teachers of English.

RAND Reading Study Group. (2002). *Reading for understanding: Toward an R&D program in reading comprehension.* Santa Monica, CA: RAND Education.

Scarborough, H.S. (1998). Early identification of children at risk for reading disabilities: Phonological awareness and some other promising predictors. In B.K. Shapiro, P.J. Accardo, & A.J. Capute (Eds.), *Specific reading disabilities: A review of the spectrum* (pp. 75–119). Timonium, MD: York Press.

Scott, J.A., & Nagy, W.E. (2004). Developing word consciousness. In J.F. Baumann & E.B. Kame'enui (Eds.), *Vocabulary instruction: Research to practice* (pp. 201–217). New York: Guilford.

Snow, C.E., & Kim, Y. (2007). Large problem spaces: The challenge of vocabulary for English language learners. In R.K. Wagner, A.E. Muse, & K.R. Tannenbaum (Eds.), *Vocabulary acquisition: Implications for reading comprehension* (pp. 123–139). New York: Guilford.

Stahl, S.A., & Nagy, W.E. (2006). *Teaching word meanings.* Mahwah, NJ: Erlbaum.

Sternberg, R.J. (1987). Most vocabulary is learned from context. In M.G. McKeown & M.E. Curtis (Eds.), *The nature of vocabulary acquisition* (pp. 89–105). Hillsdale, NJ: Erlbaum.

Templin, M.C. (1957). *Certain language skills in children, their development and interrelationships.* Minneapolis: University of Minnesota Press.

Terman, L.M. (1916). *The measurement of intelligence.* Boston: Houghton Mifflin.

Wagner, R.K., Muse, A.E., & Tannenbaum, K.R. (2007). *Vocabulary acquisition: Implications for reading comprehension.* New York: Guilford.

White, T.G., Graves, M.F., & Slater, W.H. (1990). Growth of reading vocabulary in diverse elementary schools: Decoding and word meaning. *Journal of Educational Psychology, 82*(2), 281–290. doi:10.1037/0022-0663.82.2.281

Word Wizards All!
Teaching Word Meanings
in Preschool and Primary Education

Steven A. Stahl and Katherine A. Dougherty Stahl

The research of Hart and Risley (1995) found significant gaps in vocabulary knowledge among young children, demonstrating a need to address vocabulary knowledge in preschool and primary aged children. Most vocabulary development in those years will come through adults reading storybooks to children. We suggest a few approaches that might improve vocabulary learning from listening to storybooks. We also suggest that some approaches validated on older children, such as semantic mapping and Venn diagrams, can be adapted for younger children.

Consider the power that a name gives a child. Now this is a *table* and that is a *chair*. No longer are they merely things that one must crawl around. Having a name for something means that one has some degree of control. The child can say *milk* and get some to drink, or *eat* and get a cracker or some baby food. As children get more words, they get more control over their environment. To move from *eat* to *cracker* or *bottle* or *cookie* or *fruit*, from *milk* to *juice*, allows the child to better communicate wants and needs, and to have a better chance of having them fulfilled.

As the child learns new words, the child can further classify the environment. The child can go from gross categories—things that sit on the floor, things that one can get nourishment from—to more precise labels. A child's ability to name establishes the ability to form categories (Nelson, 1996). As knowledge about the named item increases, the word may be transferred to related situations. This pattern is true for first vocabulary and extends to each new or expanding knowledge domain. Language and reading both act as the tools of thought to bring representations to a new level and to allow the formation of new relationships and organizations.

This process does not end in early childhood, but goes on and on as long as the person continues to learn. To follow the *juice* example to *orange juice* to the various kinds of juice available (*fresh squeezed, no pulp, from concentrate*) in your local supermarket may be absurd, but a good deal of the process of knowing about your world is learning the categories and subcategories of objects and actions within that world. For example, Berlin and Kay (1969) examined color naming in peoples all over the world. They found that most advanced or industrialized civilizations

Reprinted by permission of the publisher from Stahl, S.A., & Dougherty Stahl, K.A. (2004). Word wizards all! Teaching word meanings in preschool and primary education. In J.F. Baumann and E.J. Kame'enui (Eds.), *Vocabulary instruction: Research to practice* (pp. 59-78). New York: Guilford.

had more words for colors. Very primitive societies may have terms for only *dark* and *light*, slightly more advanced societies may add one for *red* until we get to very advanced societies with a panoply of color names.

Even if one cannot argue that having as many color names as we do allows for the development of a Renoir or a Monet, having more words enables one to think more precisely about one's environment and to manipulate that environment. Classification, the basic mental process underlying naming, is important not only in naming but also in summarizing (Kintsch & van Dijk, 1978), inferencing (Anderson & Pearson, 1984; Trabasso, 1981), among other things. To expand a child's vocabulary is to teach that child to think about the world.

This chapter will discuss the teaching of word meanings to children from pre-kindergarten to grade 2. This is an area that is not widely researched, but vitally important.

Gaps in Vocabulary Knowledge

Given the importance of the words we know, it is distressing that there are large gaps in vocabulary knowledge, beginning in the preschool years and persisting through the elementary school years, and probably beyond. Hart and Risley (1995), in a troubling study, found that children from advantaged homes (i.e., children of college professors) had receptive vocabularies as much as five times larger than children from homes receiving Aid to Families with Dependent Children (AFDC). They found that children in AFDC homes had concomitantly fewer words spoken to them, with more words spoken in imperative sentences and fewer in descriptive or elaborative ones. Their picture is that of a widening gap between well-off and poor, one which threatens to grow with time.

These differences in vocabulary knowledge, even in the young years, can influence children's reading throughout the elementary years. Dickinson and Tabors (2001) found that children's word knowledge in preschool still had significant correlations with their comprehension in upper elementary school.

Another study, of elementary school students, found a gap in word knowledge persisting through the elementary years. White, Graves, and Slater (1990) examined the reading and meaning vocabularies of children in first through fifth grades in three schools—a largely white suburban school, an inner-city school with mainly African American students, and a semi-rural school enrolling largely Pacific Island children. They found that both reading vocabulary and meaning vocabularies grew rapidly over the school years, with meaning vocabularies growing at an estimated average of 3,000 words per year. This average, though concealed large variations, with estimated vocabulary growth ranging from 1,000 to 5,000 words per year. The reading and meaning vocabularies of children in the suburban school grew more rapidly than those in the two schools serving low-income children.

In contrast, Biemiller and Slonim (2001), who examined children's growth in word meanings between grades 2 and 5, found that children in the bottom quartile learned more words per day (averaging 3 root words) than did children in the upper quartile (averaging 2.3 root words per day). They suggested that children in the lower quartile had more words to learn, so, given the same exposure to words in school, were able to learn more. However, children in the lowest quartile still knew only as many word meanings by grade 5 as a typical fourth grader, because they started so far behind in second grade. Biemiller and Slonim suggested that vocabulary instruction should begin earlier to close the gap.

The vocabulary gap between children of different socioeconomic status can be conceived of as a Matthew Effect (Stanovich, 1986). The term *Matthew Effect* comes from the Book of Matthew, in which it is foretold that the "rich get richer and the poor get poorer." Stanovich suggested that children who are more proficient readers tend to read more and read more challenging materials than children who struggle in reading. Because most words that children acquire are learned from reading them in context (Kuhn & Stahl, 1998) and because proficient readers read more challenging materials, those which contain rarer or more difficult words, they tend to learn more of those words, enabling them to read yet more challenging materials. Thus, the gap between proficient and struggling readers grows each year.

Gaps in Experiences

Hart and Risley (1995) also found that parents of lower SES children spoke significantly fewer words to their children than did the professional parents. Part of this was attributable to discourse patterns. Parents of children receiving AFDC tended to use more imperatives, or commands, and fewer elaborated explanations than did the professional parents. The fewer words also may have reflected the more limited resources available to the parents of AFDC children (Nunberg, 2002).

To expand children's vocabularies, then, one must not only provide more words for children to learn, through expanding the number of words used when speaking to children, but also expand children's experiences. After all, the words have to label something. These experiences do not have to be firsthand experiences. There are many things that we know about without having seen them directly. For example, we have a clear idea of what dinosaurs look like (or at least what scientists have posited that they look like) and had such an idea even before seeing the movie *Jurassic Park*. Children learn from television, the movies, and descriptions in books. What is important is that they have experiences with a wide variety of concepts.

How Word Knowledge Develops

The philosopher W.V. Quine (1960, cited in Woodward, 2000) presents the basic problem in word leanring. In his example, a linguist sees an aboriginal point to a rabbit and hears the native say *gavagai* just as the rabbit runs by. What does *gavagai* mean? Does it refer to the rabbit, to the act of running, to some characteristic of the rabbit such as its color, or to something else, such as dinner? The essential problem of attaching words to concepts is that, because each concept has multiple dimensions, the learner must choose which aspect of the word is referred to.

Because young children are presented with many examples in the context of words they do not know, often with a single exposure, they cannot know which aspect of the context to attend to. We are most interested in how words are learned in storybooks, but the process should be similar in other settings.

In one model (Stahl, 1991), when a word such as *gavagai* is first encountered, the hearer creates a phonological representation of the word. Because the hearer has not encountered this word before, this phonological representation is not connected to any stored semantic or syntactic information. The hearer might assume that the term refers to the whole object, *rabbit*, but this is not necessarily so. Smith (2000) suggests that children initially learning words have a predisposition to assume that words refer to objects as wholes. They use overall shape as an initial definition. However, the linguist would realize that this is just a guess and that *gavagai* might refer to any aspect of what was seen. Thus, the linguist would store all aspects of the experience. Piaget (1990) describes a young child who pointed to a dog through a window. His mother labeled it *chien* (dog). The child for a short time used the word to describe any object seen from the window, only gradually learning to accurately label *dog*.

Children also often overgeneralize words during this initial learning. Thus, *daddy* refers to any male, *dog* to any animal, and *cookie* to anything cookie-shaped or the cookie jar (Woodward, 2000). The process of word learning is not only learning what the word refers to but also constraining the use of the word to actual examples.

As the word is encountered repeatedly in different contexts, the linguist will be able to constrain the possible meanings. Thus, if *gavagai* is next used to refer to a sitting rabbit, the possible aspect of running is removed. If it is used to refer to another animal of the same color, the linguist may conclude that it refers to that color. In this view, a word is learned by repetitive exposure in context. For each exposure, the child learns a little about the word, until the child develops a full and flexible knowledge of the word's meaning. This will include definitional aspects, such as the category to which it belongs and how it differs from other members of the category, but this knowledge will be implicit and not conventionalized, as in a dictionary definition. It will also contain information about the various contexts in which the word was found, and how the meaning differed in the different contexts. Schwanenflugel, Stahl, and McFalls (1997), working with older children, found that children's learning from context seemed to fit this model. They were able to document the gradual growth of knowledge about a word after a single exposure in context. Other studies have found that children gradually learn words from both reading (e.g., Nagy, Anderson, & Herman, 1987) and from listening (e.g., Elley, 1989).

This model of word learning is a fairly passive one. As children are exposed to words, they gradually pick up information about words they encounter. This model ignores the importance of children's agency in word learning (Bloom, 2000). However, children will learn more words from context only if they attend to them. Bloom argues that words must be relevant to children, that is, they must describe something that children are interested in for word learning to occur. In addition, the words need to describe states that children have experienced and need to communicate. According to Bloom, without engagement in a world of ideas and concepts, children will not develop a rich knowledge and use of language. This engagement occurs in a supportive and motivating atmosphere.

These needs will not be met, however, if the words required for expression are not available. Hart and Risley (1995) found that children in AFDC homes were not exposed to the same quantity of language as children from advantaged homes. Regardless of the child's cognitive capacity and need to express those cognitive states, the child's vocabulary will not grow unless the words are available in social and interactive settings. Further, they were given more imperatives and fewer opportunities for elaboration. Parents in the advantaged homes gave children more *motherese*, or repetitions with expansions. For example, Hart and Risley (1999) cite the following example:

A parent asked a 23-month-old, "What happened to Marlon?" When the child did not answer, the parent gave a hint, "What does he have on his arm?" The child said, "Cast." The parent confirmed, "A cast," and returned to "What happened to his arm?" The child said, "Cast." The parent then supplied the answer she would expect (and the child would be able to give) at 36 months old, "Yes, the cast is on because he broke his arm. He fell and broke his arm." (p. 103)

In this and other examples, parents elaborate on children's knowledge and expand it. This expansion moves from the child's knowledge and expands it.

Talking to Children

One aspect of expanding the vocabulary of children should be to talk to them. It is striking not only from Hart and Risley's (1995, 1999) work that there are wide variations in how much adults talk to children. For children to develop rich vocabularies, they need to have many interactions with adults. It is from these interactions that they will develop the words they need to negotiate their world. Huttenlocher, Haight, Bryk, Seltzer, and Lyons (1991) found both the total volume of words and the number of different words mothers spoke to children significantly influence the child's vocabulary learning.

"Goldilocks" Words

It is not enough to just throw big words into conversations with children. This does not seem to be effective in improving children's vocabularies. Juel (2002) observed children in various kindergartens. She found that the one teacher who used the most rare words in her lessons was among the least effective in aiding children's vocabulary growth. Her interpretation is that the children could not understand the rare words because they did not have enough conceptual knowledge to understand the new words. Instead, they disregarded them.

Beck and McKeown (2003) suggest teaching what they call Tier 2 words. These are words that are in general use, but are not common. Tier 1 words would be common words, such as common sight words and simple nouns and verbs. Tier 3 words are words that are rare, limited to a single context, or represent concepts that young children might not have such as *cogitate*, *amble*, or *photosynthesis*. Tier 2 words include words such as *dome*, *beret*, *wade*, *nocturnal*, *accountant*, *chef*, *amble*, and *emerge*. We call them "Goldilocks" words, words that are not too difficult, not too easy, but just right.

There is evidence that children learn words in a similar order. Biemiller and Slonim (2001) found that the order of vocabulary acquisition was similar between children, with high correlations in word knowledge between children. That is, children will learn a word like *stride* before they learn *amble*. Their findings suggest that words grow in complexity and that children cannot learn a more complex word without learning the simpler words. Thus, we should make sure that the words we are teaching are of appropriate complexity. This sounds harder than it is. In natural conversation, mothers and teachers seem quite able to get the right level, if they keep their ears open to how the children are responding to them.

Talk Around Words

The type of talk around words is important. That example of motherese cited above is a good example of what effective teachers and parents do to expand their children's vocabulary. In that case, the parent started with what the child knew and expanded it through a series of questions. This type of expansion through questioning seems effective in helping older children learn new words encountered in context.

deTemple and Snow (2003) suggest that nonimmediate and cognitively challenging talk is effective in helping children develop newe word meanings. Nonimmediate talk is talk that goes beyond what is in front of the child that enables the child to make connections to past experiences, to analyze information or draw inferences, or to discuss the meaning of words. Mothers' use of this type of talk was found to relate to their children's later performance on vocabulary measures (deTemple, 1994). deTemple and Snow (2003) use storybook reading for examples of this type of talk, but it can be done when talking about things that one encounters on a walk or on a trip. It can be of a "What's that?" kind of discussion, as in the following. In this segment, a mother and her 3-year-old son were reading *The Very Hungry Caterpillar*.

Mother: What's that (pointing to the sun)?

Child: (Shrugs.)

Mother: What's that? What make you hot?

Child: I don't know. Huh?

Mother: What make you hot?

Child: (Shrugs.)

Mother: The sun don't make you hot?

Child: Mmhm. (Nods.)

Mother: It make you real hot (nodding)?

Child: Mmhm. (Nods.)

(deTemple & Snow, 2003, pp. 21–22)

In this segment, the mother tries (unsuccessfully) to get her son to use the word *sun*. When he was unable to say it, she gave a defining characteristic (very hot) and then provided the word for him.

In cognitively challenging talk, the adult tries to get the child to extend her or his thinking about the topic. Such talk not only expands vocabulary knowledge, in terms of the numbers of words known, but also the depth of that knowledge.

Mother: That's a tusk see? It's white. Know what Domingo?

Child (Domingo, age 5.11 years): Hmm?

Mother: Hunters kill these elephants for that.

Child: Why?

Mother: Because they want it for, um, well, they use it for different things. I think um some museums buy them and I don't know about museums but I know that they kill the for this white um.

Child: There's no tusk on these elephants though.

Mother: See? That one's bigger so some of them die because of that. That is sad.

Child: I wish there was not such things as hunters and guns.

Mother: I know it me too. Oh there's a herd. That's a lot of them. See how they walk?

Child: Ma here's ones that's dead.

Mother: I don't think he's dead! Well we'll find out. "They use their tusks to dig" Oh see he's digging a hole! "They use their tusks to dig the salt...."

Child: Hmm.

Mother: Let's look and see if there's another page you might like. It's ivory! The tusks are made of ivory. And they can make things with these tusks and that's why some animals, they die, hunters kill them.

Child: No wonder why they have hunters.

Mother: Yeah that's sad.

Child: I'm never gonna be a hunter when I grow up.

(deTemple & Snow, 2003, pp. 23–24)

The talk in this excerpt shows how a mother can take an experience as a springboard to new concepts. In this case, the mother begins by pointing out the *tusk*, then expands it to the uses of the tusk by the elephant and by the hunters, finally ending on an emotional reaction to hunting. The richness of the language expands the child's knowledge of the word *tusk*, by connecting it to *hunting*, *digging*, etc.

Just talking is important. However, it is equally important to have something to talk about. This means that adults (teachers and parents) need to consciously provide experiences that expand children's horizons. These experiences might include trips around one's neighborhood, to the grocery store (to talk about all those varieties of orange juice), to the park, the zoo, or any other place that gives the child new experiences or a chance to expand on older experiences.

Where the Words Are

Most vocabulary learning, however, comes from books. Storybook reading is the most powerful source of new vocabulary, including those academic words that are valued in school discourse. Books are literally "where the words are." Hayes and Ahrens (1988) examined the vocabulary used in a variety of sources. The average difficulty of a typical children's book ranks above that of either a children's or an adult television program and above that of a typical conversation between two college-educated adults. The number of rare words per 1,000 in children's books also ranks above that of television programs, adult conversation, and cartoon shows. Even a book like *Curious George Gets a Job* (Rey, 1947), intended for first graders to read and younger children to listen to, contains relatively rare words, not only *curious* by *cozy*, *dizzy*, *wound*, *scold*, *attention*—just from the first 20 pages.

Stanovich (2000) and Cunningham and Stanovich (1991) have found that exposure to books, as measured by author recognition or title recognition measures, can account for a great deal of the variation in vocabulary knowledge among children and adults. In their studies, they looked at exposure specifically to books, but we believe that the same effect would hold true for exposure to all verbal language, written or spoken. As Hart and Risley (1995) found, increased exposure to a breadth of words will lead to increased words in a child's vocabulary.

Neuman and Celano (2001) examined the availability of print resources in low-income and middle-income communities. They found striking differences in the availability of print resources between these communities. For example, in one middle-class community, there were 13 venues selling children's books with 358 titles available. In a contrasting low-income community, there were 4 venues with only 55 titles available. Thus, the gap that begins with differences in the richness of language continues through differences in print resources available.

If we are to decrease the gaps between children, we should start where the gap begins, in the preschool or at least the primary grades. By addressing the gap early, we might be able to diminish some of the differences between children later on in school, allowing more children to succeed in school.

The Language of School

All words are not valued equally. Instead, what we want children to learn is the language of school. For many children, this is a foreign language (Nagy & Stahl, in press). This language of school includes words that are used in school, but not necessarily in one's homes or neighborhoods.

Olson (1977) makes a useful distinction between utterance and text. *Utterance* refers to the conversational language that often contains sentence fragments, reliance on deixis (e.g., "over there") and other contextualized referents, a reduced vocabulary, and a shared knowledge base between speaker and hearer. Utterance tends to be a relatively restricted form of language, capable of communicating in the here and now, but dependent on a shared context for communication. *Text*, on the other hand, is relatively autonomous, contains more complex sentence forms, uses a more complex and exact vocabulary, and makes fewer assumptions about a shared knowledge base. It is text that is the language of school.

Although we use the term *text* usually to refer to written text, in Olson's (1977) notion, Text[1] could be written or oral, as long as it contains the autonomous and elaborated language typical of written text. One could argue that the college professor parents in Hart and Risley's (1995) study were speaking in Text, with more full sentences and rarer, more academic words, even to their preschoolers. Children's books are also Text, containing more formal language, especially rarer vocabulary words. We will call this *academic vocabulary*, because this is the vocabulary of school. Children need to be exposed to Text, both spoken Text as in the rich utterances of Hart and Risley's professor parents and reading written children's books, in order to learn the language of schooling.

Children without the exposure to Text can be predicted to have difficulties in learning academic vocabulary. And, again, there are wide disparities in the amount of Text that children are exposed to. Adams (1990) estimated that she spent at least 1,000 hours reading storybooks to her son prior to his entrance into first grade. In contrast, Teale (1984) observed children from low-income homes and saw an average of 2 minutes per day with a projected average of 60 hours prior to first grade. Teale did not observe any storybook reading in the majority of homes in which he observed. The differences between the exposures given to the children studied by Teale and Adams's own child can be assumed to have profound effects on children's learning, including the learning of word meanings.

One solution to the problem posed by Hart and Risley (1995) would seem to involve increased reading of storybooks to children. This is not the only solution. Storybook reading might occur 45 minutes to an hour per day. Children need to be in an environment rich in vocabulary in order to learn words. This involves having children involved in elaborated interactions that involve academic vocabulary. In addition to reading storybooks, some direct teaching of word meanings will help.

Of special note should be alphabet books. Although we do not think about alphabet books when we think about vocabulary teaching, many alphabet books are well suited for that purpose. There are animal alphabet books, machine alphabet books, bird alphabet books, and so on, which can be a wonderful source for new words. Even ordinary alphabet books have surprise words that will help children's knowledge of word meanings to grow.

Direct Teaching in Early Childhood Classes

For older children, Stahl and Fairbanks (1986) found that teaching word meanings significantly improved children's vocabulary knowledge as well as improving the comprehension of texts containing the taught words. For older children, such vocabulary teaching is done before reading a story, as in the directed reading activity. For younger children, the teaching might be done before a book, in a picture walk (Fountas & Pinnell, 1996), but it also might be done after reading or apart from reading entirely. We will discuss several activities that might be used to teach word meanings in K–2 classes.

Text Talk

Beck and McKeown (2001, 2003) suggest an interchange with young children called Text Talk. Text Talk is an approach to read-alouds designed to promote comprehension and language development. It involves the selection of texts that exhibit an event structure and enough complexity to prompt discussion and higher-level thinking. The strategic use of open-ended questioning encourages children to explain, elaborate, and formulate their own questions surrounding the text. Salient features of Text Talk have to do with the way background knowledge and vocabulary are addressed as part of the read-aloud. Background knowledge discussion should be limited to that which is directly related to the text. "Birdwalking," or encouraging elaborations that are only tangentially related to the text, has been found to disrupt the comprehension process and distract students from the text itself. Extensive vocabulary work follows each story. The meaning of three or four words is given, with examples of how each word is used. Children are encouraged to generate their own sentences for each word immediately after reading, and an incentive chart records each child's use of the words over time. An example of a dialogue in Text Talk about the word *absurd* follows.

> **absurd:** In the story, when the fly told Arthur he could have three wishes if he didn't kill him, Arthur said he thought that was absurd. That means Arthur thought it was silly to believe a fly could grant wishes. When something is absurd—it is ridiculous and hard to believe.
>
> If I told you that your teacher was going to stand on his/her head to teach you—that would be absurd. If someone told you that dogs could fly—that would be absurd.
>
> I'll say some things, and if you thiknk they are absurd, say: "That's absurd!" If you think they are not absurd, say: "That makes sense."
>
> I have a singing cow for a pet. (absurd!)
>
> I saw a tall building that was made of green cheese. (absurd!)
>
> Last night I watched a movie on TV. (makes sense)
>
> This morning I saw some birds flying around the sky. (makes sense)
>
> If I said let's fly to the moon this afternoon, that would be absurd. Who can think of an absurd idea? (When a child answers, ask another if they think that was absurd, and if so, to tell the first child: "That's absurd!") (Beck & McKeown, 2003, p. 165)

The discussion extends the meaning of the word as encountered in the story. From a single encounter, it is unlikely that children would gain much information about the word. This "text talk" both gives the child a rough definition of the word and extends its use into other contexts. Including both types of information was found to be characteristic of vocabulary instruction that improved children's comprehension (Stahl & Fairbanks, 1986). In addition, the discussion requires children to not only listen but also generate new knowledge about the word ("Who can think of an absurd idea?"). Generating new understandings is also important in word learning. Through generation words become more memorable. And all this interaction, as with the interactions around storybooks described earlier, leads to more vocabulary learning (Beck & McKeown, 2003).

Picture Walk

A picture walk is a guided reading book introduction in which the teacher goes through the pictures methodically, carefully supporting children's predictions about the text. Although we stress the use of picture walks for vocabulary development, they are used more broadly than just for vocabulary. Picture walks are based on the work of Marie Clay and her descriptions of an effective book introduction for novice readers (Clay, 1991, 1993; see Fountas & Pinnell, 1996, for more explicit descriptions). These conversations typically occur as the teacher and students preview each page or few pages of the new book before reading. The pictures are used as a catalyst for discussion of what the book is likely to be about. The picture walk does not have a specific set of procedures. It is used flexibly and in response to the students' needs and the challenges of a particular text. Teachers follow a few guidelines to ensure that students have a successful, independent first reading of the text.

- The introduction is conducted as a conversational social interaction around the text.
- The conversation prompts student engagement in activating background knowledge and experiences that relate to the text.
- The teacher provides an overview of the plot, theme, or important ideas.
- Children's attention is directed to text structure and language structure.
- Teachers use the book's language structure and vocabulary in the conversation about the book.
- Teachers may direct attention to using letter–sound relationships in one or two places in the text.

The extensiveness of the introduction depends on the expected challenges caused by context or text readability. A few vocabulary words may be introduced during the story introduction and conversation. The teacher selects vocabulary that the particular group of students may need introduced or developed. Unlike a vocabulary workbook page taught prior to reading, the discussion and the illustrations help situate the vocabulary in the story context. After reading the students and teacher might include the new vocabulary in their discussion or writing activity.

Word Wizard

The Word Wizard activity was designed by Beck, Perfetti, and McKeown (1982) to sensitize children to a wide range of words and to provide encouragement and incentive for the repeated use of new vocabulary. Individual classroom teachers apply the Word Wizard ideas in a variety of ways. In some classrooms, interesting words from class read-alouds, including Text Talk, are posted on a vocabulary word wall. A class poster contains the children's names along the side and the words along the top. When the children use the vocabulary in their conversations or written products, they receive a check on the poster. They may also receive a check for noticing the word in a new book, conversation, or elsewhere. The student with the most checks at the end of a designated time period becomes the Word Wizard.

In one second-grade class, Wednesday was word day, and each child brought in an unfamiliar or interesting word that he or she had heard or read during the preceding week. The Word-of-the-Week (WOW) sheet included the intereresting word, where it had been heard or seen, the meaning, and the word in a sentence. The words were posted on a vocabulary word wall. Again, a poster was used to reflect the students' names and the weekly words. Checks were given, as in the original example. Each Wednesday both the children who had received the most checks and the children who had contributed the words with the most checks since the previous Wednesday ate lunch with the teacher in a special section of the cafeteria. Rewarding the contributors resulted in a wider range of student participants receiving the special lunch. It also resulted in the selection of sophisticated words that were likely to be used in conversation rather than obscure words that were difficult to apply in classroom conversations.

Teaching Children to Classify

As discussed at the beginning of the chapter, classification is a basic mental process, one that underlies vocabulary knowledge as well as other cognitive processes. Teaching children to classify can be done as early as preschool. An activity such as "Which one does not belong?" forces children to think about concepts in terms of their attributes. For example, you can give children as young as preschool age pictures of a bird, an airplane, a cat, and a kite and saks them which one does not belong. Then ask them why they chose what they chose. In this case, you want children to verbalize that a bird, an airplane, and a kit fly or are in the air, while cats do not fly.

A little more advanced activity is a type of sorting game. A teacher can take a flannel board divided into two sections, and a group of children sorts pictures into two groups. Sample categories might be farm animals versus zoo animals, things found in a kitchen versus things found in a living room, or the like. This can be an opportunity to introduce words that refine existing knowledge, such as *sofa*, *couch*, *stool*, or *spatula*. To take this one step further, children can sort by more than two categories.

Venn diagrams can be used to show children that some items can be part of more than one class. A Venn diagram consists of two intersecting circles. For example, one circle might be labeled "Things with fur" and the other "Things that fly." On the "fur" side, a *cat*, *dog*, *lion*, *ocelot*, *leopard*, and so on might be included, taking care to include animals that might not be known to children (i.e., Tier 2 words). The other side might include a *bird*, *butterfly*, *bee*, *owl*, *hornet*, and so on. A *bat* might be in the middle because it fits both categories.

Although we have used a fairly simple set of categories in this example, Venn diagrams can be used with many sets of concepts. We have used them with the terms *rebellion* and *protest* to discuss concepts surrounding the American Revolution. (In the years preceding the American Revolution, the colonists protested various taxes and laws. King George viewed these protests as rebellion, and acted to suppress them. This difference in perception may be one of the causes of the revolution.) We used the Venn diagram to compare and contrast the features of these words. Venn diagrams can be a fast and easy way to talk about many different concepts.

Semantic Maps

Another activity that extends the child's ability to classify are semantic maps. These have been used in vocabulary instruction for a long time (Heimlich & Pittelman, 1986; Johnson, Toms-Bronowski, & Pittelman, 1982; Stahl & Vancil, 1986), especially in content area instruction. However, they adapt very easily to young children, even prereaders. A semantic mapping lesson has four parts.

1. *Brainstorming*. The teacher and the class brainstorm ideas that relate to a topic. For example, for the topic *weather*, a class might come up with *rain*, *snow*, *wind*, *hot*, *thermometer*, *hurricane*, *blizzard*, and so on. The teacher might stop and explain some of the terms that the students come up with. The teacher might also add some other terms, again explaining what they mean. These terms can be written on the board or pictured for young children.

2. *Mapping*. These terms can be drawn into a map. To draw the map, children (with the aid of the teacher) would come up with three or four categories that describe the terms on the board. These are arranged into a map. A possible map for *weather* is shown in Figure 5.1. A map made of pictures for prereaders on the topic of *animals* is shown in Figure 5.2. The *animals* map might be used to introduce terms such as *insects* or *mammals* or particular types of each.

3. *Reading*. After the map is complete, the students and teacher read a book or selection about that topic. For younger children, the teacher can read the text aloud; for children who can read, they might read in partners or by themselves. An alternative might be an observation.

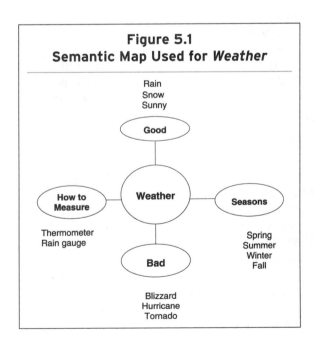

Figure 5.1
Semantic Map Used for *Weather*

Rain
Snow
Sunny

Good

How to Measure

Weather

Seasons

Thermometer
Rain gauge

Spring
Summer
Winter
Fall

Bad

Blizzard
Hurricane
Tornado

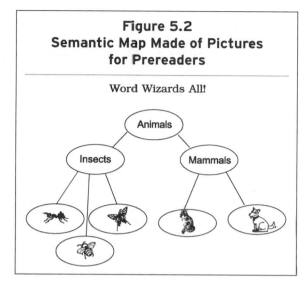

Figure 5.2
Semantic Map Made of Pictures for Prereaders

Word Wizards All!

Animals

Insects   Mammals

For a lesson on weather, this might involve going outside to see the current weather. For a lesson on plants, this might involve growing a plant.

4. *Completing the map.* After the reading, teachers and children as a group discuss what they have learned from the book. At this time, they might change categories or add another category to reflect what they have learned.

It is important that semantic maps not be used as an end in themselves. Instead, they should be connected to a book, an observation, or an ongoing part of the curriculum.

Teaching Word Meanings in Preschool and Early Elementary Classrooms

Although we have given some techniques that can be useful for teaching word meanings in early education, what is more important is maintaining a dialogue about words. This dialogue should be cognitively challenging, pushing students to expand their knowledge about the world by expanding the words they use to describe that knowledge. There should be an interplay between what the student knows and this ongoing dialogue. Words should not be too difficult—or they will be beyond the child's ability to learn—nor should they be too easy. Instead, they should be Goldilocks words—just right. Finding the right level is not hard. It comes from the kinds of interactions we have illustrated in this chapter.

Further, effective vocabulary teaching in the early years should make children curious about words. To be a good word learner, one must be hungry for words. Learning (and using) new words can be exciting because a new word not only is a sign of growing up, but it also is a sign of greater control and understanding about one's world. Effective instruction should make children seek out words, be sensitive about hearing and learning more about new words. It is not enough to fill children up with words as if they were an empty vessel. Instead, teachers and parents should create an environment where children go out and seek new words as well. Good vocabulary teaching in the primary grades is talking about words, when found in books, on trips, in the classroom, bringing them in and sending children out to find more.

Notes

[1]*Text*, when capitalized, refers to Olson's usage of that term. When used in lowercase letters, *text* refers to the conventional meaning.

References

Adams, M.J. (1990). *Beginning to read: Thinking and learning about print.* Cambridge, MA: MIT Press.

Anderson, R.C., & Pearson, P.D. (1984). A schema-theoretic view of basic processes in reading. In P.D. Pearson (Ed.), *Handbook of reading research* (pp. 255–292). White Plains, NY: Longman.

Beck, I.L., & McKeown, M.G. (2001). Text talk: Capturing the benefits of read aloud experiences for young children. *The Reading Teacher, 55*, 10–20.

Beck, I.L., & McKeown, M.G. (2003). Text Talk: An approach to storybook reading in kindergarten. In A.V. Kleeck, S.A. Stahl, & E.B. Bauer (Eds.), *On reading books to children: Parents and teachers* (pp. 10–35). Mahwah, NJ: Erlbaum.

Beck, I.L., Perfetti, C.A., & McKeown, M.G. (1982). Effects of long-term vocabulary instruction on lexical access and reading comprehension. *Journal of Educational Psychology, 74*, 506–521.

Berlin, B., & Kay, P. (1969). *Basic color terms: Their universality and evolution.* Berkeley, CA: University of California Press.

Biemiller, A., & Slonim, N. (2001). Estimating root vocabulary growth in normative and advantaged populations. *Journal of Educational Psychology, 93,* 498–510.

Bloom, L. (2000). The intentionality model of word learning: How to learn a word, any word. In *Becoming a word learner: A debate on lexical acquisition* (pp. 19–50). Oxford, UK: Oxford University Press.

Clay, M.M. (1991). Introducing a new storybook to young readers. *The Reading Teacher, 45,* 264–273.

Clay, M.M. (1993). *Reading recovery: A guidebook for teachers in training.* Portsmouth, NH: Heinemann.

Cunningham, A.E., & Stanovich, K.E. (1991). Tracking the unique effects of print exposure in children: Associations with vocabulary, general knowledge, and spelling. *Journal of Educational Psychology, 83,* 264–274.

deTemple, J. (1994). *Book reading styles of low-income mothers with preschoolers and children's later literacy skills.* Unpublished doctoral dissertation, Harvard Graduate School of Education, Cambridge, MA.

deTemple, J., & Snow, C. (2003). Learning words from books. In A.V. Kleeck, S.A. Stahl, & E.B. Bauer (Eds.), *On reading storybooks to children: Parents and teachers* (pp. 16–36). Mahwah, NJ: Erlbaum.

Dickinson, D.K., & Tabors, P.O. (2001). *Beginning literacy with language: Young children learning at home and school.* Baltimore: Brookes.

Elley, W.B. (1989). Vocabulary acquisition from listening to stories. *Reading Research Quarterly, 24,* 174–187.

Fountas, I.C., & Pinnell, G.S. (1996). *Guided reading: Good first teaching for all children.* Portsmouth, NH: Heinemann.

Hart, B., & Risley, T.R. (1995). *Meaningful differences in the everyday expressions of young American children: The everyday experience of one and two year old American children.* Baltimore: Brookes.

Hart, B., & Risley, T. (1999). *The social world of the child learning to talk.* Baltimore: Brookes.

Hayes, D.P., & Ahrens, M.G. (1988). Vocabulary simplification for children: A special case of "motherese." *Journal of Child Language, 15,* 395–410.

Heimlich, J.E., & Pittelman, S.D. (1986). *Semantic mapping: Classroom applications.* Newark, DE: International Reading Associations.

Huttenlocher, J., Haight, W., Bryk, A., Seltzer, M., & Lyons, T. (1991). Early vocabulary growth: Relation to language input and gender. *Developmental Psychology, 27,* 236–248.

Johnson, D.D., Toms-Bronowski, S., & Pittelman, S.D. (1982). *An investigation of the effectiveness of semantic mapping and semantic feature analysis with intermediate grade children* (Program Report 83-3). Madison, WI: Wisconsin Center for Educational Research, University of Wisconsin.

Juel, C. (2002, May). *Presentation at the Reading Hall of Fame meeting.* Annual convention of the International Reading Association, San Francisco, CA.

Kintsch, W., & van Dijk, T.A. (1978). Toward a model of text comprehension and production. *Psychological Review, 85,* 363–394.

Kuhn, M.R., & Stahl, S.A. (1998). Teaching children to learn word meanings from context: A synthesis and some questions. *Journal of Literacy Research, 30,* 119–138.

Nagy, W.E., Anderson, R.C., & Herman, P.A. (1987). Learning word meanings from context during normal reading. *American Educational Research Journal, 24,* 237–270.

Nelson, K. (1996). *Language in cognitive development: Emergence of the mediated mind.* Cambridge, UK: Cambridge University Press.

Neuman, S.B., & Celano, D. (2001). Access to print in low-income and middle-income communities: An ecological study of four neighborhoods. *Reading Research Quarterly, 36,* 8–27.

Nunberg, G. (2002, Sept. 3). *A loss for words.* Fresh Air Commentary, National Public Radio.

Olson, D.R. (1977). From utterance to text: The bias of language in speech and writing. *Harvard Educational Review, 47,* 257–281.

Piaget, J. (1990). *The child's conception of the world.* New York: Littlefield Adams.

Rey, H. (1947). *Curious George gets a job.* New York: Houghton Mifflin.

Schwanenflugel, P.J., Stahl, S.A., & McFalls, E.L. (1997). *Partial word knowledge and vocabulary growth during reading comprehension* (Research Report No. 76). Athens, GA: University of Georgia, National Reading Research Center.

Smith, L.B. (2000). Learning how to learn words: An associative crane. In *Becoming a word learner: A debate on lexical acquisition* (pp. 51–80). Oxford, UK: Oxford University Press.

Stahl, S.A. (1991). Beyond the instrumentalist hypothesis: Some relationships between word meanings and comprehension. In P.J. Schwanenflugel (Ed.), The *psychology of word meanings* (pp. 157–186). Hillsdale, NJ: Erlbaum.

Stahl, S.A., & Fairbanks, M.M. (1986). The effects of vocabulary instruction: A model-based meta-analysis. *Review of Educational Research, 56*(1), 72–110.

Stahl, S.A., & Vancil, S.J. (1986). Discussion is what makes semantic maps work. *The Reading Teacher, 40,* 62–67.

Stanovich, K.E. (1986). Matthew effects in reading: Some consequences of individual differences in the acquisition of literacy. *Reading Research Quarterly, 21,* 360–407.

Stanovich, K.E. (2000). *Progress in understanding reading: Scientific foundations and new frontiers.* New York: Guilford Press.

Teale, W.H. (1984). Reading to young children: Its significance for literacy development. In H. Goelman, A. Boerg, & F. Smith (Eds.), *Awakening to literacy* (pp. 110–121). Portsmouth, NH: Heinemann.

Trabasso, T. (1981). On the making of inferences during reading and their assessment. In J.T. Guthrie (Ed.), *Comprehension and reading: Research reviews* (pp. 56–76). Newark, DE: International Reading Association.

White, T.G., Graves, M.F., & Slater, W.H. (1990). Growth of reading vocabulary in diverse elementary schools:

Decoding and word meaning. *Journal of Educational Psychology, 82,* 281–290.

Woodward, A.L. (2000). Constraining the problem in early word learning. In *Becoming a word learner: A debate on lexical acquisition* (pp. 81–114). Oxford, UK: Oxford University Press.

Questions for Reflection

• This article points out the importance of word-rich conversation in supporting young children's vocabulary growth and describes research that has shown repeatedly that children from lower SES communities may be lacking opportunities for these conversations. What do you know about the home and neighborhood lives of the children in your classes? What can you do to communicate to parents and caregivers about the importance of language use for young children's later success in school?

• How actively do you encourage classroom conversation? How do you strike a balance between encouraging lively discussion and ensuring that children know when it's time to listen to you or to others?

Teaching Vocabulary:
Early, Direct, and Sequential

Andrew Biemiller

During the past 10 years, Jeanne Chall encouraged me to focus on the study of vocabulary and how vocabulary growth might be encouraged. Both of us had come to the conclusion that vocabulary growth was inadequately addressed in current educational curricula, especially in the elementary and preschool years and that more teacher-centered and planned curricula were needed, just as had been the case with phonics. Jeanne had come to this conclusion through her work on the stages of reading development (Chall, 1983/1996), her work on textbook difficulty (Chall & Conard, 1991), and especially through the findings of her joint research project with Catherine Snow on families and literacy (Chall, Snow et al., 1982), as summarized in *The Reading Crisis* (Chall, Jacobs, & Baldwin, 1990). In this book, Chall and her colleagues traced the relative decline in reading achievements experienced by working-class children who had become competent readers by third grade but whose vocabulary limitations increasingly had a negative effect on their reading comprehension as they advanced to seventh grade. (Jeanne mentioned to me several times her disappointment that *The Reading Crisis* was not more widely discussed.)

I had been particularly influenced by Wesley Becker's famous *Harvard Educational Review* article (1977) noting that the impact of early DISTAR success with decoding was muted for reading comprehension in later elementary grades by vocabulary limitations. Becker argued that this was a matter of experience rather than general intelligence by observing that while his DISTAR students' reading comprehension fell relative to more advantaged students by grade 4, their mathematics performance remained high. He suggested that the difference was that all the knowledge that is needed for math achievement is taught in school, whereas the vocabulary growth needed for successful reading comprehension is essentially left to the home. Disadvantaged homes provide little support for vocabulary growth, as recently documented by Hart and Risley (1995). I was further influenced by the finding of my doctoral student, Maria Cantalini (1987), that school instruction in kindergarten and grade 1 apparently had no impact on vocabulary development as assessed by the Peabody vocabulary test. Morrison, Williams, and Massetti (1998) have since replicated this finding. This finding is particularly significant in view of Cunningham and Stanovich's (1997) recently reported finding that vocabulary as assessed in grade 1 predicts more than 30% of grade 11 reading comprehension, much more than reading mechanics as assessed in grade 1 do. Finally, I have been influenced by the consistent finding in the oral reading miscue literature that when overall error rates reach 5% of running words (tokens), that "contextual" errors (those that make sense in context) virtually disappear. I infer from this that when readers (or listeners?) understand less than 95% of the words in a text, they are likely to lose the meaning of

From Biemiller, A. (2001). Teaching vocabulary: Early, direct, and sequential. *American Educator, 25*(1), 24-28, 47. (Adapted from *Perspectives*, Fall 2000, Vol. 26, No. 4) Reprinted with permission from the Spring 2001 issue of the *American Educator*, the quarterly journal of the American Federation of Teachers, AFL-CIO, and from the International Dyslexia Association.

that text (and be especially unlikely to infer meanings of unfamiliar words).

In short, as Gough and Tunmer (1986) have pointed out, vocabulary development is both important and ignored. Can we—educators—do better, or are we simply bumping into constitutional limitations that are beyond the power of schools to affect? In the remainder of this article, I am going to summarize a few points that support the argument for an increased emphasis on vocabulary and suggest the need for a more teacher-centered and curriculum-structured approach to ensure adequate vocabulary development.

The consequences of an increased emphasis on phonics. In recent years, we have seen a tremendous emphasis on the importance of phonics instruction to ensure educational progress. We also have seen that while more children learn to "read" with increased phonics instruction, there have not been commensurate gains in reading comprehension (e.g., Gregory, Earl, & O'Donoghue, 1993; Madden et al., 1993; Pinnell et al., 1994). What is missing for many children who master phonics but don't comprehend well is vocabulary, the words they need to know in order to understand what they're reading. Thus vocabulary is the "missing link" in reading/language instruction in our school system. Because vocabulary deficits particularly affect less advantaged and second-language children, I will be arguing that such "deficits" are fundamentally more remediable than many other school learning problems.

Schools now do little to promote vocabulary development, particularly in the critical years before grade 3. The role of schooling in vocabulary acquisition has been the subject of much debate. Early (pre-literacy) differences in vocabulary growth are associated with social class (Duncan, Brooks-Gunn, & Klebanov, 1994; Hart & Risley, 1995; McLloyd, 1998). Nagy and Herman (1987) and Sternberg (1987) argue that much vocabulary acquisition results from literacy and wide reading rather than from direct instruction. However, it is obvious that a great deal of vocabulary acquisition occurs before children become literate, and before they are reading books that introduce unfamiliar vocabulary (Becker,

1977). Cantalini (1987) and Morrison, Williams, and Massetti (1998) both report that vocabulary acquisition in kindergarten and grade 1 is little influenced by school experience, based on finding that young first-graders have about the same vocabulary (Peabody Picture Vocabulary Test) as older kindergarten children. Cantalini reported the same result for second grade.

The relatively small number of words that need to be learned. It is sometimes argued that the number of words children need to learn is so great that this can only happen incidentally through wide reading (Anderson, 1996; Nagy & Herman, 1987; Sternberg, 1987). This argument is quite reminiscent of the argument that the spelling-to-sound structure of English is so difficult that it can't be taught but only learned through experience. In both cases, the complexity of what needs to be learned has been somewhat exaggerated. Many years ago, Lorge and Chall (1963) argued that traditional dictionary sampling methods for assessing vocabulary had greatly overestimated the volume of vocabulary children needed to acquire. As Lorge and Chall, Beck and McKeown (1990), and others have noted, we need to focus on root word growth rather than the acquisition of all inflected and derived forms of words. Jeremy Anglin's (1993) monograph suggests that children acquire about 1,200 root words a year during the elementary years with perhaps half that many root words learned per year prior to grade 1. (He also argues that perhaps twice that many words need to be learned, particularly including idiomatic forms.) My own research (Biemiller & Slonim, in press) suggests that the average number of root word meanings acquired per year may be somewhat smaller, more like 600 root word meanings a year from infancy to the end of elementary school. This conclusion, based on root word meanings sampled from Dale & O'Rourke's *Living Word Vocabulary* (1981), is partly based on the observation that many similar meanings are acquired at about the same age and probably do not require separate instruction.

Evidence that vocabulary differences present by grade 2 may account for most vocabulary differences in elementary school.

There has been relatively little discussion or examination of individual differences in vocabulary growth. Hart and Risley (1995) observed large differences associated with word learning opportunities in the preschool years. In our current research, Naomi Slonim and I are finding that large vocabulary differences are present by the end of grade 2—amounting to more than 3,000 root words between high and low quartiles in a normative population (Biemiller & Slonim, in press). After grade 2, cross-sectional data indicate that the lowest-quartile children may actually add root word vocabulary faster than the higher-quartile children. However, by grade 5, they have only reached the median for grade 2 children. Thus, if we could find ways of supporting more rapid vocabulary growth in the early years, more children would be able to comprehend "grade level" texts in the upper elementary grades. (Note that the "reading grade level" of texts is in fact almost entirely determined by the vocabulary load of those texts [Chall & Conard, 1991; Chall & Dale, 1995].) Thus early vocabulary limitations make "catching up" difficult even though once in school, children appear to acquire new vocabulary at similar rates. To "catch up," vocabulary-disadvantaged children have to acquire vocabulary at above-average rates.

The sequential nature of vocabulary acquisition. Much evidence clearly indicates that vocabulary is acquired in largely the same order by most children. The existence of empirical vocabulary norms (as in the Peabody and *Living Word* Vocabulary) indicate that some words are acquired later than others. Slonim and I have found very high correlations (mostly over .90) between mean scores for words obtained from different grades (Biemiller & Slonim, in press). We also found that when data is ordered by children's vocabulary levels rather than their grade level, we can clearly identify a range of words known well (above 75%), words being acquired (74%–25%), and those little known. Furthermore, these ranges are sequential. At any given point in vocabulary acquisition, a preliminary conclusion from this work is that there are about 2,000–3,000 root words that a child is likely to

be learning. This makes the construction of a "vocabulary curriculum" plausible.

Defining an essential vocabulary for high school graduates. A corollary of the sequential nature of vocabulary acquisition is the possibility of defining a common vocabulary needed by most high school graduates. Several studies have shown that college entrants need 11,000 to 14,000 root words, while college graduates typically have about 17,000 root words (D'Anna, Zechmeister, & Hall, 1991; Goulden, Nation, & Read, 1990; Hazenberg & Hulstijn, 1996). We need further research on the degree to which we can identify these words. (It is clear that all do not know the same exact words. It is equally clear that there is a substantial common vocabulary plus a further more discipline-specific vocabulary.)

The hypothesis that most root word and idiomatic vocabulary learned before and during elementary school results from direct explanation of words. We know relatively little about the processes by which children add words to their vocabularies. Some of the data are negative—evidence that children do not easily acquire words by inference, especially children younger than age 10 (Robbins & Ehri, 1994; Werner & Kaplan, 1952). In Bus, van IJzendoorn, and Pellegrini's (1995) summary of the effects of reading to children, there is evidence that younger children profit less from simply being "read to." There is also positive evidence that children do readily acquire vocabulary when provided with a little explanation as novel words are encountered in context (Beck, Perfetti, & McKeown, 1982; Elley, 1989; Feitelson et al., 1986; Feitelson et al., 1991; Whitehurst et al., 1998). Preliminary evidence from directly interviewing children about word acquisition suggests that as late as grade 5, about 80% of words are learned as a result of direct explanation, either as a result of the child's request or instruction, usually by a teacher (Biemiller, 1999b). Overall, I believe that before age 10, the evidence supports the conclusion that a substantial majority of new root words are acquired through explanation by others (including explanations in texts) rather than by inference while reading, as has often been argued by Anderson, Nagy and Herman, and by Sternberg.

For practical purposes, we should be prepared to ensure the availability and use of explanations of word meanings throughout at least the elementary school years.

Although children differ in their opportunities to learn words and the ease with which they learn words, evidence suggests that most can learn vocabulary at normal rates. There is clear evidence that vocabulary is associated with socioeconomic status—presumably reflecting differences in opportunity (as documented by Hart & Risley, 1995; and Snow, Burns, & Griffin, 1998). There is also clear evidence relating vocabulary development to various phonological skills or capacities (e.g., Gathercole et al., 1997). It is likely that environment and "capacity" interact—that constitutionally more-advantaged children also may be environmentally more advantaged. However, a number of studies summarized in Biemiller (1999a), Stahl (1999), and elsewhere clearly indicate that children can acquire and retain two or three words a day through instruction involving contextualized introduction and explanation of new words. Furthermore, while less verbally fluent or lower vocabulary children and adolescents have been found to benefit little from inferring word meanings (Cain & Oakhill, in preparation; Elshout-Mohr & van Daalen-Kapteijns, 1987), more-direct approaches have been reported to work well with these children (see Elley, Feitelson, & Whitehurst references cited previously). Overall, I hypothesize that most children (90% plus) can acquire new vocabulary at rates necessary to reach "grade level" or near grade level vocabulary in middle elementary school, if given adequate opportunity to use new words and adequate instruction in word meanings.

The need for planned introduction and explanation of vocabulary plus various tools to help children become more independent in dealing with new vocabulary. I have suggested above the hypothesis that 80% or more of the root words learned by grade 6 are learned as a result of direct explanation by parents, peers, teachers, and texts. Those who learn more words almost undoubtedly encounter more words and receive more explanations of word meanings.

This suggests that we could do considerably more than we now do to ensure the development of adequate vocabulary through systematic exposure to two to three new words a day combined with adequate explanation of these words and opportunities to use them. (I am referring to new meanings not simply words that are unfamiliar in print.) Present school practices fall far short of this objective in the primary grades. (Schools may do better in the upper elementary grades.) Other types of vocabulary instruction (e.g., using affixes, word family approaches, and direct instruction in inferencing) will also be useful, especially in grades 3 and above.

This particular objective raises the possibility of returning to a more basal approach, at least as one component of classroom language and reading instruction. If vocabulary acquisition is largely sequential in nature, it would appear possible to identify that sequence and to ensure that children at a given vocabulary level have an opportunity to encounter words they are likely to be learning next, within a context that uses the majority of the words that they have already learned. Some researchers are already beginning to work on this objective (e.g., David Francis and Barbara Foorman in Texas, Jan Hulstijn in the Netherlands, Margaret McKeown and Isabel Beck in Pittsburgh, William Nagy in Seattle, and John Morgan and myself in Toronto). Many problems need to be solved. Existing lists of words (e.g., *Living Word Vocabulary*) do not correspond closely enough to observed sequences of word acquisition to be great guides (although they are better than nothing). Word frequency in print data (e.g., Carroll, Davies, & Richmond, 1971) bears relatively little relationship to observed word knowledge. (In my studies, Carroll's SFI index accounted for 7% of observed root word knowledge. In contrast, *Living Word Vocabulary* levels accounted for more than 50% of our data.) William Nagy (personal communication) has proposed combining Dale and O'Rourke's data with expert ratings—a very plausible suggestion.

Given the establishment of plausible vocabulary lists, teachers could relate these lists to vocabulary being introduced in books (short stories, novels, texts) being studied, be aware of words to introduce or explain (or to query children about if they don't ask!), and be aware of some important words that aren't going to be covered in the established curriculum. These words could be taught directly, or other materials (e.g., stories to be read to class) could be introduced that include them.

Conclusion: A substantially greater teacher-centered effort is needed to promote vocabulary development, especially in the kindergarten and early primary years. In her last book, *The Academic Achievement Challenge*, Jeanne Chall (2000) presented a summary of research supporting the effectiveness of "teacher centered" approaches to education. The information reviewed here similarly points to the need for more planned (but contextualized) introduction of vocabulary. This is especially true in the pre-reading years (before grades 3 or 4 when children begin to read books that are likely to introduce new vocabulary). Specifically, increased teacher-centered vocabulary work should include the deliberate introduction of a wider range of vocabulary in the early primary years through oral sources (most children are limited in what they can read at this age level), ensuring coverage of about 4,000 root words by the end of grade 2. In the later elementary years, continued development will include adding another 500 to 750 root words per year, additional idioms, and increased fluency in using derived words. In addition, in the upper elementary grades, instruction is needed in deriving word meanings from affixes, word families, etc., as well as in ways of inferring word meanings. If we are serious about "increasing standards" and bringing a greater proportion of schoolchildren to high levels of academic accomplishment, we cannot continue to leave vocabulary development to parents, chance, and highly motivated reading.

Thus, I strongly recommend a more teacher-directed and curriculum-directed approach to fostering vocabulary and language growth. If education is going to have a serious "compensatory" function, we must do more to promote vocabulary. Our current data show large "environmental" effects in kindergarten to grade 2.

Large differences remain by grade 5 (e.g., children in the lowest grade 5 quartile have vocabularies similar to median second-grade children). Is this simply the product of "intelligence"? I believe it is in considerable part the result of different learning opportunities. After grade 2, vocabulary growth rates look similar or faster for "low quartile" children. If we could keep them from being so far behind by grade 2, they apparently wouldn't be so far behind in grade 5!

I don't believe we can make all kids alike. But I think we could do more to give them similar tools to start with. Some kids may have to work harder to add vocabulary. Educators may have to work harder with some kids. So what's new? But now, educators do virtually nothing before grade 3 or 4 to facilitate real vocabulary growth. By then, it's too late for many children.

References

Anderson, R.C. (1996). Research foundations to support wide reading. In V. Greaney (Ed.), *Promoting reading in developing countries*. Newark, Del.: International Reading Association.

Anglin, J.M. (1993). Vocabulary development: A morphological analysis. *Monographs of the Society for Research in Child Development*, Serial No. 238, 58.

Beck, I., & McKeown, M. (1990). Conditions of vocabulary acquisition. In R. Barr, M.L. Kamil, P.B. Mosenthal, & P.D. Pearson, (Eds.) *Handbook of reading research*, (Vol. 2, pp. 789–814). New York, N.Y.: Longman.

Beck, I.L., Perfetti, C., & McKeown, M.G. (1982). Effects of long-term vocabulary instruction on lexical access and reading comprehension. *Journal of Educational Psychology*, 74, 506–521.

Becker, W.C. (1977). Teaching reading and language to the disadvantaged: What we have learned from field research. *Harvard Educational Review*, 47, 518–543.

Biemiller, A. (1998, April). *Oral vocabulary, word identification, and reading comprehension in English second language and English first language elementary school children*. Paper presented at the annual meeting of the Society for the Scientific Study of Reading, San Diego.

Biemiller, A. (1999a). *Language and reading success*. Cambridge, Mass.: Brookline Books.

Biemiller, A. (1999b). *Estimating vocabulary growth for ESL children with and without listening comprehension instruction*. Paper presented at the annual conference of the American Educational Research Association, Montreal, Quebec.

Biemiller, A., & Slonim, N. (in press). Estimating root word vocabulary growth in normative and advantaged populations: Evidence for a common sequence of vocabulary acquisition. *Journal of Educational Psychology*, Fall 2001.

Cain, K., & Oakhill, J. (in preparation). *Reading comprehension and the ability to learn new vocabulary items from context.*

Cantalini, M. (1987). *The effects of age and gender on school readiness and school success.* Unpublished doctoral dissertation. Ontario Institute for Studies in Education. Toronto, Ontario.

Carroll, J.B., Davies, P., & Richmond, B. (1971). *The American Heritage word frequency book.* Boston: Houghton Mifflin.

Chall, J.S. (1983/1996). *Stages of reading development* (2nd ed.). New York, N.Y.: Harcourt Brace.

Chall, J.S. (2000). *The academic achievement challenge: What really works in the classroom?* New York, N.Y.: Guilford.

Chall, J.S., & Conard, S.S. (1991). *Should textbooks challenge students?* New York, N.Y.: Teachers College Press.

Chall, J.S., & Dale, E. (1995). *Readability revisited: The new Dale–Chall readability formula.* Cambridge, Mass.: Brookline Books.

Chall, J.S., Jacobs, V.A., & Baldwin, L.E. (1990). *The reading crisis: Why poor children fall behind.* Cambridge, Mass.: Harvard University Press.

Chall, J.S., Snow, C., Barnes, W.S., Chandler, J., Goodman, I.F., Hemphill, L., & Jacobs, V. (1982). *Families and literacy: The contribution of out-of-school experiences to children's acquisition of literacy.* Final report to the National Institute of Education, Dec. 22, 1982. ERIC Document Reproduction Service No. ED 234 345.

Cunningham, A.E., & Stanovich, K.E. (1997). Early reading acquisition and its relation to reading experience and ability 10 years later. *Developmental Psychology, 33,* 934–945.

D'Anna, C.A., Zechmeister, E.B., & Hall, J.W. (1991). Toward a meaningful definition of vocabulary size. *Journal of Reading Behavior, 23*(1), 109–122.

Dale, E., & O'Rourke, J. (1981). *The living word vocabulary.* Chicago: World Book/Childcraft International.

Duncan, G., Brooks-Gunn, J., & Klebanov, P. (1994). Economic deprivation and early childhood development. *Child Development, 65,* 296–318.

Elley, W.B. (1989). Vocabulary acquisition from listening to stories. *Reading Research Quarterly, 24,* 174–186.

Elshout-Mohr, M., & van Daalen-Kapteijns, M.M. (1987). Cognitive processes in learning word meanings. In M.G. McKeown & M.E. Curtis (Eds.), *The nature of vocabulary acquisition* (pp. 53–72). Hillsdale, N.J.: Erlbaum.

Feitelson, D., Goldstein, Z., Iraqi, J., & Share, D.I. (1991). Effects of listening to story reading on aspects of literacy acquisition in a diglossic situation. *Reading Research Quarterly, 28,* 70–79.

Feitelson, D., Kita, B., & Goldstein, Z. (1986). Effects of listening to series stories on first-graders' comprehension

and use of language. *Research in the Teaching of English, 20,* 339–356.

Gathercole, S.E., Hitch, G.J., Service, E., & Martin, A.J. (1997). Phonological short-term memory and new word learning in children. *Developmental Psychology, 33,* 966–979.

Gough, P.B., & Tunmer, W.E. (1986). Decoding, reading and reading disability. *Remedial and Special Education, 7,* 6–10.

Goulden, R., Nation, P., & Read, J. (1990). How large can a receptive vocabulary be? *Applied Linguistics, 11*(4), 341–363.

Graves, M.F., Juel, C., & Graves, B. (1998). *Teaching reading in the 21st century.* Boston: Allyn and Bacon.

Gregory, D., Earl, L., & O'Donoghue, B. (1993). *A study of Reading Recovery in Scarborough: 1990–1992.* Publication #92/93-15. Scarborough, Ontario: Scarborough Board of Education.

Hart, B., and Risley, T.R. (1995). *Meaningful differences in the everyday experience of young American children.* Baltimore, MD.: Paul H. Brookes Publishing Co.

Hazenberg, S., & Hulstijn, J.H. (1996). Defining a minimal receptive second-language vocabulary for non-native university students: An empirical investigation. *Applied Linguistics, 17*(2), 145–163.

Lorge, I., & Chall, J.S. (1963). Estimating the size of vocabularies of children and adults: An analysis of methodological issues. *Journal of Experimental Education, 32,* 147–157.

Madden, N.A., Slavin, R.E., Karweit, J.L., Dolan L.J., & Wasik, B.A. (1993). Success for All: Longitudinal effects of a restructuring program for inner-city schools. *American Educational Research Journal, 30,* 123–148.

McLloyd, V.C. (1998). Socioeconomic disadvantage and child development. *American Psychologist, 53,* 185–204.

Morrison, F.J., Williams, M.A., & Massetti, G.M. (1998, April). *The contributions of IQ and schooling to academic achievement.* Paper presented at the annual meeting of the Society for the Scientific Study of Reading, San Diego.

Nagy, W.E., & Herman, P.A. (1987). Breadth and depth of vocabulary knowledge: Implications for acquisition and instruction. In M.G. McKeown & M.E. Curtis (Eds.), *The nature of vocabulary acquisition* (pp. 19–36). Hillsdale, N.J.: Erlbaum.

Pinnell, G.S., Lyons, C.A., Deford, D.E., Bryk, A.S., & Seltzer, M. (1994). Comparing instructional models for the literacy education of high-risk first-graders. *Reading Research Quarterly, 29,* 9–38.

Robbins, C., and Ehri, L.C. (1994). Reading storybooks to kindergartners helps them learn new vocabulary words. *Journal of Educational Psychology, 86,* 54–64.

Snow, C., Burns, M.S., & Griffin, P. (Eds.) (1998). *Preventing reading difficulties in young children.* Washington, D.C.: National Academy Press.

Stahl, S.A. (1999). *Vocabulary development*. Cambridge, Mass.: Brookline Press.

Sternberg, R.J. (1987). Most vocabulary is learned from context. In M.G. McKeown and M.E. Curtis (Eds.), *The nature of vocabulary acquisition* (pp. 89–106). Hillsdale, N.J.: Erlbaum.

Werner, H., & Kaplan, B. (1952). The acquisition of word meanings: A developmental study. *Monographs of the Society for Research in Child Development*, *15* (Serial No. 51, No. 1).

Whitehurst, G.J., Falco, F.L., Lonigan, C., Fischel, J.E., DeBaryshe, B.D., Valdez-Menchaca, M.C., & Caulfield, M. (1988). Accelerating language development through picture book reading. *Developmental Psychology*, *24*, 552–588.

Questions for Reflection

- Think about your explicit teaching of vocabulary. Do you ensure that children in your classes have "systematic exposure to two to three new words a day combined with adequate explanation of these words and opportunities to use them"? If not, how can you meet this goal?

- If you work in an elementary school, what can you do to ensure that teachers at *all* grade levels are working together to ensure strong vocabulary instruction beginning in the early grades and continued support as children move into the upper elementary years?

Text Talk: Capturing the Benefits of Read-Aloud Experiences for Young Children

Isabel L. Beck and Margaret G. McKeown

Concern about young children's language development has recently centered on the large individual differences among children in vocabulary and comprehension abilities as they begin school (Biemiller, 1999; Hart & Risley, 1995). The goal of the project we describe here is to enhance young children's language and comprehension abilities through in-depth and extensive experiences listening to and talking about stories read to them.

Of course reading aloud to children has been pursued at home and in schools for centuries, and indeed is probably the most highly recommended activity for encouraging language and literacy (Adams, 1990; Anderson, Hiebert, Scott, & Wilkinson, 1985; Goldfield & Snow, 1984). Yet studies do not always show strong effects from reading aloud (Scarborough & Dobrich, 1994; Whitehurst et al., 1994). The issue at hand is to discern what makes read-aloud experiences effective for enhancing children's language development.

This article starts with consideration of what the research literature suggests about the kinds of texts and kinds of talk that are most beneficial for read-aloud experiences. We then discuss what we learned from observations of kindergarten and first-grade teachers reading to students. Next we provide an overview of Text Talk, an approach to read-alouds directed toward enhancing young children's ability to construct meaning. This section includes examples of teacher/ student interactions and suggests aspects of reading aloud that need attention in order to make these experiences more effective for children's literacy development.

What Kind of Texts?

Texts that are effective for developing language and comprehension ability need to be conceptually challenging enough to require grappling with ideas and taking an active stance toward constructing meaning. The point is that young children can handle challenging content. Yet the limits of young children's developing word recognition ability make it difficult to provide challenging content in the books they read on their own. However, because young children's aural comprehension ability outstrips their word recognition competence, challenging content can be presented to young children from book selections that are read aloud.

What Kind of Talk?

Researchers suggest that the most valuable aspect of the read-aloud activity is that it gives children experience with decontextualized language, requiring them to make sense of ideas that are about something beyond the here and now (Cochran-Smith, 1984; Heath, 1983; Snow, 1993; Snow & Dickinson, 1991; Snow, Tabors,

Reprinted from Beck, I.L., & McKeown, M.G. (2001). Text Talk: Capturing the benefits of read-aloud experiences for young children. *The Reading Teacher*, 55(1), 10–20.

Nicholson, & Kurland, 1995). As Donaldson (1978) pointed out,

> children come to school well able to think and reason about the world in situations that make human sense to them. What they have to learn to do in school is to think and reason in "disembedded contexts"...to use symbol systems and deal with representations of the world. (pp. 88–89)

The key to experiences with decontextualized language that make them valuable for future literacy seems to lie in not merely listening to book language, but in talking about the ideas. Cochran-Smith (1984), Heath (1983), and Snow and her colleagues (Snow, 1993; Snow & Dickinson, 1991; Snow et al., 1995) all highlight the role of the talk that surrounds book reading in becoming literate. According to Snow, quality talk around books can promote familiarity with

> relatively rare vocabulary, understanding the lexical and grammatical strategies for adjusting to a nonpresent audience, identifying the perspective of the listener so as to provide sufficient background information, and knowing the genre-specific rules for various forms of talk such as narrative and explanation. (1993, p. 15)

Evidence for the role of talking about books in enhancing children's language development comes from studies by Dickinson and Tabors (1991), Freppon (1991), Morrow (1992), and Snow et al. (1995) who concluded, for example, that "talk surrounding the text" (Morrow, p. 253) or "getting children to think about what was going on in the story" (Freppon, p. 144) were keys to literacy growth.

More specifically, Teale and Martinez (1996) concluded that the most effective talk involved encouraging children to focus on important story ideas and giving them opportunities to reflect rather than expecting a quickly retrieved answer. Relatedly, Dickinson and Smith (1994) found that talk that was "analytic in nature," requiring children to reflect on story content or language, was most beneficial.

Dickinson and Smith's (1994) and Teale and Martinez's (1996) ideas about the most effective read-aloud strategies are quite consistent. The most effective features include focusing the discussion on major story ideas, dealing with ideas as they are encountered in contrast to after the entire story has been read, and involving children in the discussion with opportunities to be reflective. However, it is clear from these investigations that the most effective read-aloud strategies are far from the most common ones.

Our observations are consistent with those of Dickinson and Smith (1994) and Teale and Martinez (1996). At the start of the project we describe here, we observed kindergarten and first-grade teachers reading to their classrooms and found that they tended not to involve children in focusing on and discussing major story ideas. Among the reasons this is the case is that in reading to young children, creating a focus on major story ideas is not as simple as it may first appear. This is because young children tend to respond to stories by using what is easily accessible to them in contrast to the linguistic content (Neuman, 1990). Specifically, we observed how children frequently ignored text information and responded to questions on the basis of the pictures and their background knowledge. The problem is that this reduces the opportunities for children to construct meaning from decontextualized language which, as we have noted earlier, is essential for building mature literacy skills.

What We Learned From Observations

Prevalence of Responding on the Basis of Pictures

Vivid, delightful pictures are a hallmark of children's trade books, and children are naturally drawn to them. However, if children rely on pictures to construct their understanding of a story, they may focus on characteristics of the pictures that interfere with constructing meaning of the story. As an example, consider our observation of a teacher reading a book called *Socrates* (Bogaerts & Bogaerts, 1992) to a class of kindergartners. The book's cover shows a sweet-faced dog wearing a pair of large red glasses. The teacher indicated that the little dog was Socrates and that they would learn about him in the story, and began reading.

The story opens with a heart-wrenching description of Socrates's parents being taken away by the dog catcher and Socrates being left an orphan with no friends and no one to care for him. After this opening, the teacher stopped and asked, "What do we know about Socrates so far?" The first response was, "He needs glasses." Clearly the child ignored the linguistic content about Socrates's situation and answered on the basis of the picture. Thus this child constructed a completely different problem as the central focus of the story.

In this case, the picture was not congruent with the text content at that point. But even when pictures and text are congruent, it was our observation that children often rely on the pictures for constructing meaning and thus miss opportunities to engage in constructing meaning from the linguistic content.

Children's reliance on pictures is easy to explain, as pictures closely represent what children are accustomed to encountering in the world around them. They can more readily derive information from pictures in comparison to text language. As Snow and Dickinson (1991) pointed out, comprehending and finding language to express ideas that go beyond the here and now is a new and challenging experience for young children.

Prevalence of Responding on the Basis of Background Knowledge

Research has shown that background knowledge is a very important aspect of understanding text (Anderson et al., 1985; Beck, Omanson, & McKeown, 1982; McKeown, Beck, Sinatra, & Loxterman, 1992; Pearson, Hansen, & Gordon, 1979). Attention to background knowledge has certainly found its way into instruction, to the extent that teachers customarily invite children to share background knowledge related to the story being read. The goal of invoking background knowledge is to integrate it with text content in order to assist comprehension. But in our observations we found that this is not necessarily the way background knowledge is used by young children. Rather, we observed a tendency for children to respond to questions from background knowledge alone and ignore what had just been read to them from the story.

For example, the story *Curious George Takes a Job* (Rey, 1975) begins as follows, "This is George. He lived in the zoo. He was a good little monkey and always very curious. He wanted to find out what was going on outside the zoo." At this point the teacher asked, "What do we know so far about George?" and the first response was "He likes bananas." Of course, because George is a monkey he probably does like bananas. But his fondness for bananas was not stated in the story, and more importantly it does not help establish the major story concept of George as a zoo-bound monkey who wants to know what life is like in the world.

In some situations children simply took a notion from the text and drew an association to something in memory that was irrelevant or, at best, tangential to the text situation. For example, in the story *The Wolf's Chicken Stew* (Kasza, 1987) a wolf leaves food for a chicken because he's trying to fatten her up for his dinner. Unbeknownst to the wolf, the chicken is feeding her large family with the food. As the story moved to its climax the teacher began to probe the children as to whether the chicken knows the source of the food. The teacher asked, "What did she think the food was for?" and a student replied "Poison." The teacher pressed, seeming to probe the student for reconsideration, "Did she think it was poisoned?" Several students replied "Yes," and began to discuss incidents they had heard about involving poisoned Halloween candy. This discussion took the class a considerable distance from the story ideas.

Children tend to report on their own experiences because they can more readily derive information from them in comparison to text language. However, when what they report goes too far afield, children can be distracted from the story or the inappropriate associations that they bring in may be remembered as part of the story (Neuman, 1990; Nicholson & Imlach, 1981).

Teachers' Interactions in Read-Alouds

Thus far a major point has been that several things children "naturally" do in talking about a story—rely on the pictures and report their knowledge of things associated with the story—may stand in the way of their constructing meaning from story information. Now let us turn to the teacher's role in prompting children's interactions with text and the extent to which it supports constructing meaning.

In our observations of teachers reading to children, two types of interactions seemed to dominate. One was directed toward clarifying some content or unfamiliar vocabulary by asking, for example, "Does anybody know what a ukulele is?" The other appeared to be attempts to involve children in the ongoing story by asking a question about what was just read. However, these questions were virtually always phrased in ways that produced only brief answers about a detail. For example, "Harry likes everything except taking a what?" "What kind of place were Mr. and Mrs. Mallard looking for to hatch their ducklings?" The problem with such questions is that they constrain children's responses to a fact here and a detail there. Table 1 presents examples of questions we observed teachers ask while reading *Harry the Dirty Dog* (Zion, 1984), *The Mitten* (Brett, 1989), and *Brave Irene* (Steig, 1986) and the children's responses to those questions.

As can be seen, all the responses are correct, and thus it is easy for a teacher to assume that understanding is in place. But dealing with these local issues does not add up to developing understanding of a story.

Text Talk Overview

Our review of the research literature and our observations in classrooms motivated the development of Text Talk, which is an approach to read-alouds that is designed to enhance young children's ability to construct meaning from decontexualized language. This goal includes not only promoting comprehension, but also furthering children's language development.

The project began with the selection of stories for kindergarten and first grade, the development of questions for each story, and tryouts of these materials. In the second phase we implemented Text Talk in kindergarten and first-grade classrooms and worked closely with the teachers to modify and augment the interactions among the teacher, students, and text as issues arose. The school was located in an urban public school district in a high-poverty a rea. Seventy-five percent of the students received free or reduced-cost lunch. All the students were African American.

Text Talk interactions are based on open questions that the teacher poses during reading that ask children to consider the ideas in the story

---

Table 1
Examples of Children's Responses to Constrained Questions

Questions	Responses
As they started scrubbing, what came off?	Dirt
What does George want to do with his friend?	Find him
How have things turned out for George, good or bad?	Good
How is George doing at his job right now?	Fine
George looks like he's in a lot of what?	Trouble
The mole found a new _____	Home
The mitten will be colored like snow, so it would be hard to what?	Find
Who needs the dress?	The duchess

and talk about and connect them as the story moves along. Our development of Text Talk was informed by our Questioning the Author work (Beck, McKeown, Hamilton, & Kucan, 1997). Questioning the Author is an approach to text-based instruction that was developed around the principle of "teaching for understanding." Features of Questioning the Author align very closely with the features that Dickinson and Smith (1994) and Teale and Martinez (1996) identified as making read-aloud interactions most effective. That is, Questioning the Author focuses on text ideas and encourages students' participation in building meaning from those ideas as they read the text. Among the major differences between Text Talk and Questioning the Author is that the latter is directed to intermediate-grade students who are reading their own texts in contrast to the focus of the current project, which is reading aloud to kindergarten and first-grade children.

The treatment of pictures and background knowledge in Text Talk was influenced by our observations, discussed earlier. In Text Talk the pictures are for the most part shown after children have constructed meaning from what has been read. When background knowledge is elicited, the teacher scaffolds children's responses to make clear the relationship of background knowledge to text ideas.

Beyond building comprehension of the specific story, Text Talk attends to children's language development in two ways. One is that the kind of questions asked elicit greater language production. The other is that Text Talk takes advantage of some of the sophisticated vocabulary found in young children's trade books by explicitly teaching and encouraging use of several words from a story after the story has been read. Table 2 provides an overview of components involved in read-aloud experiences and a description of how those components are handled in Text Talk.

Texts

Our criteria for selecting texts were that they be intellectually challenging and provide the grist for children to explore ideas and to use language to explain ideas. In particular, in choosing stories we looked for some complexity of events,

Table 2
How Components of Reading Aloud Are Handled in Text Talk

Components	Text Talk approach
Selection of texts	Stories that exhibit an event structure and some complexities of events to provide grist for children to build meaning.
Initial questions	Interspersed open questions require children to describe and explain text ideas, rather than recall and retrieve words from text.
Follow-up questions	Questions scaffold students' thinking by using their initial responses to form questions that encourage elaboration and development of initial ideas.
Pictures	In general, pictures are presented after children have heard and responded to a section of text.
Background knowledge	Invitations for background knowledge are issued judiciously to support meaning building rather than encouraging students to tap into tangential experiences.
Vocabulary	Some sophisticated words are selected for direct attention after reading and discussion of the story is completed.

subtleties in expressing ideas, or presentation of unfamiliar ideas and topics.

Given our goal of promoting the construction of meaning from linguistic content, we sought books in which the linguistic content was primary—that is, the book did not rely too heavily on the pictures for communicating the story. A final criterion in consideration of constructing meaning was stories that exhibited an event structure rather than a series of situations, a format that is sometimes used in books for young children. Examples of this format include Seymour Simon's *Animal Fact/Animal Fable* (1979), which presents one-page essays about different animals in response to a question (e.g., Do porcupines shoot their quills when they're angry? Do goats eat tin cans?) and *Family Pictures: Cuadros de Familia* (Garza, 1990), which presents a series of pictures with extended captions explaining "what's going on" (e.g., celebrating a feast day, harvesting oranges). Although these are very attractive and interesting books for children to explore, they do not provide the extended, connected content for building meaning that is the focus of Text Talk.

Initial Questions

As noted above, we developed questions that teachers could use to initiate discussion at important points in a story. In contrast to the questions shown in Table 1, which constrain responses, questions developed for Text Talk prompt students to talk about ideas. Table 3

Table 3
Examples of Children's Responses to Open Questions

Questions	Responses
How does what Harry did fit in with what we already know about him?	He doesn't really want to get clean, he just wants to stay dirty.
When the family looked out and said, "There's a strange dog in the backyard," why did they call Harry a strange dog?	Because when he got all dirty, his family didn't know who he was.
What's Harry up to now?	He decided to dig a hole and get the brush so he could wash, and then they would recognize him.
They called Harry "this little doggie." What does that tell us?	That means that they don't know that it's their doggie. They don't know its name, so they just call him little doggie.
Why do you think the children shouted, "Come quick"?	Because the kids knowed that that's the dog they had.
It says that "the mitten swelled and bulged, but Baba's good knitting held fast." What does that mean?	That it was strong, and she's a good knitter.
What do you think Baba meant when she said, "If you drop one in the snow you'll never find it"?	The gloves are the same color as the snow. That if you drop it in the snow it's colored like snow.
It says, "Mrs. Bobbin...was tired and had a bad headache, but she still managed to sew the last stitches in the gown she was making." What's going on?	She's sick, but she is still going to try and finish her dress.

---

shows examples of Text Talk questions and the language they elicited from children collected from pilot work in kindergarten and first-grade classes. As with Table 1, the examples are drawn from read-alouds of *Harry the Dirty Dog* (Zion, 1984), *The Mitten* (Brett, 1989), and *Brave Irene* (Steig, 1986), albeit from different classrooms.

Follow-Up Questions

It is important to emphasize that the kind of elaborated responses shown in Table 3 do not arise automatically from asking open-ended questions. Indeed, in our Text Talk work, we found that children initially have difficulty constructing these kinds of responses in contrast to the customary responses of a word or two. Helping students to construct meaning requires teachers to take cues from a student's initial response, which for young children is often very limited, and proceed from there. This territory between a first, likely sparse response, and an elaborated constructed response is the territory that requires teacher effort in creating thoughtful follow-up questions to support students' construction of meaning.

For example, consider a kindergarten classroom in which the teacher was reading the story *Abiyoyo* (Seeger, 1986). After the part of the story in which Abiyoyo is introduced as "a giant called Abiyoyo...as tall as a tree and he could eat people up," the teacher asked, "Who is Abiyoyo?" Her intent was that the children describe Abiyoyo, and understand why people fear him—because he eats people. However, in the excerpt below it is clear that children do not get very far into these ideas. The discussion that ensued after the teacher's initial question "Who is Abiyoyo?" follows:

S: A monster.

T: Did the story say he was a monster?

S: It's a big green man.

T: A big green man. But does the story say what the big green man was?

S: He's tall.

S: A giant.

T: He's a giant, and he's tall as a _____

Class: Tree.

T: Tree, OK. So what's this all about?

S: Monsters.

T: What's this story all about?

S: Giant.

As the excerpt shows, the teacher made several attempts to get the children to expand their responses, but they did little beyond providing a word or two. Even when the teacher's questioning moved beyond focusing on Abiyoyo himself by asking "What's this story all about?" children stayed with simple one-word responses: "Monsters," "Giant."

Another kind of student response that requires consideration and careful follow up is related to a major theme of this article—children's difficulty interacting with decontextualized language. Consider, for example, a kindergarten class read-aloud of *The Giant Jam Sandwich* (Lord, 1972), a story about a town beset by a swarm of four million wasps. As the problem develops, the villagers hold a meeting to discuss how to solve their problem, but no one can come up with a solution. At this point in the story, the teacher asks, "What happened at the meeting?" but the children seemed unable to deal with the just-read linguistic event that the villagers could not come up with a solution to the wasp problem. The teacher calls on three different children to answer the question, "What happened at the meeting?" but each child talks only about the general situation of the wasps in town:

S1: There was the bees.

S2: Everyone was running around the town.

S3: They were stinging them.

The asked the same question again, but got a s teacher imilar response:

S: Trying to sting them.

The teacher then reread the story portion about the meeting, with exaggerated expression, and repeated, "What happened at the meeting?" The next child's response was more related to the events of the meeting:

S: He's trying to get those things out of there so they don't sting.

Children's difficulty in responding to the question likely occurred because it was much easier for the children to respond to the general situation of wasps in town. That concept had already been discussed, and is more vividly imaginable than a meeting of indecisive villagers. Thus it was difficult for children to focus on and respond to the meeting and its consequence. As such examples arose, we and the teachers began to understand in a deeper way the difficulties children faced when asked to respond to decontextualized language, as much as the language may have seemed explicit and clear to us as adult readers.

As these examples illustrate, initial questions may not bring forth meaningful responses from young children. Yet simply asking more questions will not necessarily prompt richer comments. Thus a great deal of our emphasis in working with teachers as they implemented Text Talk was focused on how to follow up children's initial responses in productive ways. Several concepts were developed that seemed useful. One that was used frequently was to repeat and rephrase what children were saying. This both encouraged more elaborated language and invited other children to connect to the ideas that were being discussed. This approach to following up children's responses confirms findings from several studies. Orsolini and Pontecorvo (1992) found that 5-year-old children's talk was more likely extended when preceded by teacher repetition and rephrasing of what students had said. Nystrand and Gamoran (1991) found that teachers who employed uptake—incorporating previous student responses into subsequent questions—had a strong positive effect on students' understanding of literature.

Another approach to following up children's initial responses included generic probes that prompted them to explain: "What's that all about?" "What's that mean?" We also found that when children had difficulty responding to a probe it was useful to reread the relevant portion of the text and repeat the initial question. This helped students to focus on the text language as the source for their responses. And even with all this, it takes time for students to expand their abilities to construct meaning from decontextualized language.

Pictures

As noted earlier, during our observations we became very aware of how children often ignored the linguistic content and relied on pictures to respond to questions about a story. Thus, as we developed initial questions for Text Talk stories, we were alert to how children might use the content of pictures. There were two situations in which we deliberately decided to wait to show pictures until after reading and discussion of a story portion.

One situation was when pictures mirrored the linguistic content of a text. For example, in the story *The Wolf's Chicken Stew* (Kasza, 1987), after a wolf has been following a chicken, the text reads: "The wolf crept closer. But just as he was about to grab his prey...." The picture on this page shows the wolf on his hind feet about to pounce on the chicken. We wanted children to talk about what was happening in the story at that point, so we posed the question "What's happening?" If the children saw the picture as they were being asked that question, they certainly could ignore the linguistic content and respond just from the visual. Because we wanted them to construct their idea from the text language, we did not show the picture until students had responded.

Another potential problematic situation with pictures was when the content of pictures was in conflict with what was going on in the text. For example, in *The Bremen-Town Musicians* (Plume, 1980) there is a section in which a dog is explaining to a donkey that he has run away because his master planned to shoot him. The donkey then suggests that the dog join him, and they leave for Bremen Town. The picture, however, shows the dog hiding behind a tree and a man with a rifle in his hand looking for him. This illustration represents part of the story that the dog was relaying to the donkey. But the idea that builds the plot of the story is that the dog and the donkey have joined forces and are on their way to Bremen Town. The vividness of the picture could well lead children to misunderstand what was happening in the story at that point. Thus, we posed the question of "What's going on?" and elicited responses before showing the picture.

Our observations of Text Talk showed us that, for the children, the format of seeing the pictures later took some getting used to, but they soon came to understand the expectations of Text Talk and became more attentive to the linguistic content as it was read. Several times when we observed teachers presenting Text Talk read-alouds early in the year, we noticed children being caught off guard, unable to answer the questions and asking to see the pictures. It struck us that they had paid little or no attention to the words and were awaiting the pictures to fill them in on the story. When children were unable to respond, the teachers would reread the portion of text and explicitly remind children to listen to the words of the story to answer the question. With this support, children were able to respond. As the implementation progressed, we noticed that the teachers became alert to the importance of timing for presenting pictures in order to keep the linguistic content primary. With this new awareness, they were surprised at the extent to which pictures were often the primary source from which children answered questions.

The use of pictures needs to be considered from the perspective that constructing meaning from text content is a major feature of what prepares one for becoming a successful reader. Thus care needs to be taken that pictures do not cause students to skip attending to the language component of stories. That is, in the course of reading to children, teachers should use pictures judiciously. Often this means after some event or idea has been explained linguistically.

Background Knowledge

As noted earlier, during our initial observations we became aware of how often children responded to questions about the story based on their background knowledge alone. As we worked with teachers in Text Talk, they too became cognizant of when children were using just background knowledge rather than story information. From these experiences teachers developed ways of acknowledging a student's comment while pointing out the distinctions between their own experiences and the story. For example, following the exchange about Curious George presented earlier, the teacher responded to the child by saying, "Monkeys do like bananas, but let's think about what the story told us about George."

Additionally, consider the exchange from our earlier observation of *The Wolf's Chicken Stew* read-aloud, when children focused on the idea that the food left for the chicken might have been poisoned. When we brought this example to the teachers during a meeting about Text Talk, they had some suggestions for dealing with this type of situation. The tack they decided they would take was as follows: "We sometimes do hear about food being poisoned, especially bad people doing that at Halloween, but let's think about what's happening in the story. Why did this food get left for the chicken? Who can remind us?" Presumably children would recall that the food was left to fatten up the chicken. From here the teacher could lead children to see that the food therefore would have been good food, not poisoned.

Using the kind of exchanges noted above, teachers helped children sort out the difference between simply responding from background knowledge and responding from story information. Children need help in bringing background knowledge to bear in appropriate ways, rather than simply tapping into tangential experiences. There is evidence that readers' elaborations of knowledge and experiences that are not integrally related to text information can disrupt the process of comprehension rather than enhance it (Strang, 1967; Trabasso & Suh, 1993).

Vocabulary

The acquisition of vocabulary is an obvious focus for any program aiming to enhance children's literacy, because of the strong, well-documented relationship that vocabulary has to reading proficiency in particular and school achievement in general (Anderson & Freebody, 1981; Sternberg, 1987). Additionally, an important motivation for providing vocabulary experiences stems from the huge individual differences that exist in vocabulary size. In particular there is an enormous discrepancy between high- and low-achieving learners (Graves & Slater, 1987; Seashore & Eckerson, 1940).

Trade books are superb sources of vocabulary, and our Text Talk project takes advantage of this by explicitly emphasizing vocabulary. From 80 books (40 targeted to kindergarten and another set of 40 targeted to first grade) we identified about 1,500 words that could be taught to children. A word was considered a good candidate if it seemed likely to be unfamiliar to young children but was a concept they could identify with and use in normal conversation. We selected two to four words per story for direct teaching following the story, and thus kindergarten and first-grade children are provided instruction for approximately 100 fairly sophisticated words per grade. To illustrate the kind of words we included, Table 4 presents the words from three of the stories used in Text Talk.

The instructional activities for each word began by bringing to mind the use of the word from the story and explaining its meaning. Then students were involved with using or responding to use of the word. Each activity also included having children repeat the word so they had a phonological representation of what they were learning. The following are teachers' notes for the activity for the word *reluctant* from *A Pocket for Corduroy* (Freeman, 1978).

> In the story, Lisa was *reluctant* to leave the laundromat without Corduroy. *Reluctant* means you are not sure you want to do something. Say the word with me: *reluctant*.
>
> Someone might be reluctant to eat a food that they never had before, or someone might be reluctant to ride a roller coaster because it looks scary.
>
> Think about something you might be reluctant to do. Start your sentence with "I might be reluctant to _____." After each child responds call on another child to explain the response. For example, if a child says, "I might be reluctant to eat spinach" ask another child "What does it mean that [child's name] is reluctant to eat spinach?"

Our previous program of work in vocabulary (see for example, Beck, Perfetti, & McKeown, 1982; McKeown, Beck, Omanson, & Perfetti, 1983) demonstrated the importance of maintaining words after initial instruction. That is, if children do not think about and use a word after initial instruction it is unlikely to become part of their vocabulary repertoire. Borrowing from our previous work, especially the "Word Wizard" device (where students earned points for seeing, hearing, or using words they had been introduced to), we developed a simple way for teachers to encourage and keep track of children's awareness of instructed words. Specifically, we created charts of the words from each story, which enabled teachers to tally each use or citing of a word. This appeared to be quite successful, as each time we visited classrooms we noticed the continuing accumulation of tallies next to words. Attention differed a great deal according to individual words. For example, the words *nuisance* and *commotion* were favorites among kindergartners, who often identified which of their classmates were being a nuisance and pointed out commotions in the classroom or hallway.

Table 4
Examples of Instructed Vocabulary From Three Stories

Story	Vocabulary
Abiyoyo (Seeger, 1986)	disappear precious foolish
Alexander and the Wind-Up Mouse (Lionni, 1969)	adventure searched envy
Amos & Boris (Steig, 1971)	miserable immense leisurely

Additionally, we observed and the teachers reported that often in story reading children recognized and remarked on the use of a word they had learned from an earlier story.

Focus, Monitor, and Scaffold

Enhancing young children's comprehension and language capabilities is essential for promoting literacy growth. Reading aloud and discussing what is read is an important avenue for helping children deal with decontextualized language. But there are discrepancies between common classroom practices in reading aloud and those practices that have been found most effective for laying the foundation for children's future literacy capabilities. Thus, in an effort to make reading aloud more beneficial for young children, we developed Text Talk, an approach to enhancing young children's ability to build meaning from text in which the teacher intersperses reading with open questions and discussion, and follows each story with explicit attention to vocabulary.

From working with teachers as they implemented Text Talk, we can point to several concepts that can guide the development of more effective read-aloud experiences. They include the following:

- awareness of the distinction between constructing meaning of ideas in a text and simply retrieving information from the text;
- understanding the difficulty of the task young children face in gaining meaning from decontextualized language;
- designing questions that encourage children to talk about and connect ideas and developing follow-up questions that scaffold, building meaning from those ideas;
- helping students to meaningfully incorporate their background knowledge and reduce the kind of surface association of knowledge that brings forth a hodgepodge of personal anecdotes;

- awareness of how pictures can draw attention away from processing the linguistic content in a text, and thus attention to the timing of the use of pictures; and
- taking advantage of the sophisticated words found in trade books by using them as a source of explicit vocabulary activities.

Although reading a story to children is not a difficult task for a literate adult, taking advantage of the read-aloud experience to develop children's literacy is complex and demanding. Even with awareness of what makes reading aloud most effective, it is difficult to keep discussions consistently focused on the most productive features. Especially for young children, there is much to manage in conducting a good read-aloud discussion. Key to the task is keeping important text ideas in focus while monitoring children's often limited responses and scaffolding their ideas toward constructing meaning.

References

Adams, M.J. (1990). *Beginning to read*. Cambridge: MIT Press.

Anderson, R.C., & Freebody, P. (1981). Vocabulary knowledge. In J.T. Guthrie (Ed.), *Comprehension and teaching: Research reviews* (pp. 77–117). Newark, DE: International Reading Association.

Anderson, R.C., Hiebert, E.F., Scott, J.A., & Wilkinson, I.A. (1985). *Becoming a nation of readers: The report of the Commission on Reading*. Washington, DC: The National Institute of Education.

Beck, I.L., McKeown, M.G., Hamilton, R., & Kucan, L. (1997). *Questioning the Author: An approach for enhancing student engagement with text*. Newark, DE: International Reading Association.

Beck, I.L., Omanson, R.C., & McKeown, M.G. (1982). An instructional redesign of reading lessons: Effects on comprehension. *Reading Research Quarterly, 17*, 462–481.

Beck, I.L., Perfetti, C.A., & McKeown, M.G. (1982). Effects of long-term vocabulary instruction on lexical access and reading comprehension. *Journal of Educational Psychology, 74*, 506–521.

Biemiller, A. (1999). *Language and reading success: From reading research to practice* (Vol. 5). Cambridge, MA: Brookline.

Cochran-Smith, M. (1984). *The making of a reader*. Norwood, NJ: Ablex.

Dickinson, D.K., & Smith, M.W. (1994). Long-term effects of preschool teachers' book readings on low-income children's vocabulary and story comprehension. *Reading Research Quarterly, 29*, 104–122.

Dickinson, D.K., & Tabors, P.O. (1991). Early literacy: Linkages between home, school, and literacy achievement at age five. *Journal of Research in Childhood Education, 6*, 30–46.

Donaldson, M. (1978). *Children's minds*. Glasgow, Scotland: Fontana/Collins.

Freppon, P.A. (1991). Children's concepts of the nature and purpose of reading and writing in different instructional settings. *Journal of Reading Behavior: A Journal of Literacy, 23*, 139–163.

Goldfield, B.A., & Snow, C.E. (1984). Reading books with children: The mechanics of potential influence on children's reading achievement. In J. Flood (Ed.), *Promoting reading comprehension* (pp. 204–215). Newark, DE: International Reading Association.

Graves, M.F., & Slater, W.H. (1987, April). *The development of reading vocabularies in rural disadvantaged students, inner-city disadvantaged students, and middle-class suburban students*. Paper presented at the meeting of the American Educational Research Association, Washington, DC.

Hart, B., & Risley, T. (1995). *Meaningful differences*. Baltimore: Paul H. Brookes.

Heath, S.B. (1983). *Ways with words*. Cambridge, England: Cambridge University Press.

McKeown, M.G., Beck, I.L., Omanson, R.C., & Perfetti, C.A. (1983). The effects of long-term instruction on reading comprehension: A replication. *Journal of Reading Behavior, 15*(1), 3–18.

McKeown, M.G., Beck, I.L., Sinatra, G.M., & Loxterman, J.A. (1992). The contribution of prior knowledge and coherent text to comprehension. *Reading Research Quarterly, 27*, 79–93.

Morrow, L.M. (1992). The impact of a literature-based program on literacy achievement, use of literature, and attitudes of children from minority backgrounds. *Reading Research Quarterly, 27*, 250–275.

Neuman, S.B. (1990). Assessing inferencing strategies. In J. Zutell & S. McCormick (Eds.), *Literacy theory and research* (pp. 267–274). Chicago: National Reading Conference.

Nicholson, T., & Imlach, K. (1981). Where do their answers come from? A study of the inferences which children make when answering questions about narrative stories. *Journal of Reading Behavior, 13*, 111–129.

Nystrand, M., & Gamoran, A. (1991). Instructional discourse, students' engagement, and literature achievement. *Research in the Teaching of English, 25*, 261–290.

Orsolini, M., & Pontecorvo, C. (1992). Children's talk in classroom discussions. *Cognition and Instruction, 9*, 113–136.

Pearson, P.D., Hansen, J., & Gordon, C. (1979). The effect of background knowledge on young children's comprehension of explicit and implicit information. *Journal of Reading Behavior, 11*, 201–209.

Scarborough, H.S., & Dobrich, W. (1994). On the efficacy of reading to preschoolers. *Developmental Review, 14*, 245–302.

Seashore, R.H., & Eckerson, L.D. (1940). The measurement of individual differences in general English vocabularies. *Journal of Educational Psychology, 31*, 14–38.

Snow, C.E. (1993). Families as social contexts for literacy development. In C. Daiute (Ed.), *The development of literacy through social interaction* (No. 61, pp. 11–24). San Francisco: Jossey-Bass.

Snow, C.E., & Dickinson, D.K. (1991). Some skills that aren't basic in a new conception of literacy. In A. Purves & T. Jennings (Eds.), *Literate systems and individual lives: Perspectives on literacy and schooling* (pp. 175–213). Albany, NY: State University of New York Press.

Snow, C.E., Tabors, P.O., Nicholson, P.A., & Kurland, B.F. (1995). SHELL: Oral language and early literacy skills in kindergarten and first-grade children. *Journal of Research in Childhood Education, 10*, 37–47.

Sternberg, R.J. (1987). Most vocabulary is learned from context. In M.G. McKeown & M.E. Curtis (Eds.), *The nature of vocabulary acquisition* (pp. 89–105). Hillsdale, NJ: Erlbaum.

Strang, R. (1967). Exploration of the reading process. *Reading Research Quarterly, 2*, 33–45.

Teale, W.H., & Martinez, M.G. (1996). Reading aloud to young children: Teachers' reading styles and kindergartners' text comprehension. In C. Pontecorvo, M. Orsolini, B. Burge, & L.B. Resnick (Eds.), *Children's early text construction* (pp. 321–344). Mahwah, NJ: Erlbaum.

Trabasso, T., & Suh, S. (1993). Understanding text: Achieving explanatory coherence through on-line inferences and mental operations in working memory. *Discourse Processes, 16*, 3–34.

Whitehurst, G.J., Arnold, D.S., Epstein, J.N., Angell, A.L., Smith, M., & Fischel, J. E. (1994). A picture book reading intervention in day care and home for children from low-income families. *Developmental Psychology, 30*, 679–689.

Children's Books Cited

Bogaerts, Rascal, & Bogaerts, Gert. (1992). *Socrates*. San Francisco: Chronicle Books.

Brett, Jan. (1989). *The mitten*. New York: G.P. Putnam's Sons.

Freeman, Don. (1978). *A pocket for Corduroy*. New York: Puffin.

Garza, Carmen Lomas. (1990). *Family pictures: Cuadros de familia*. San Francisco: Children's Book Press.

Kasza, Keiko. (1987). *The wolf's chicken stew*. New York: Putnam & Grosset.

Lionni, Leo. (1969). *Alexander and the wind-up mouse*. New York: Alfred A. Knopf.

Lord, John Vernon. (1972). *The giant jam sandwich*. New York: Houghton Mifflin.

Plume, Ilse. (1980). *The Bremen-town musicians*. New York: Bantam.

Rey, H.A. (1975). *Curious George takes a job*. Boston: Houghton Mifflin.

Seeger, Pete. (1986). *Abiyoyo*. New York: Aladdin.

Simon, Seymour. (1979). *Animal fact/animal fable*. New York: Crown.

Steig, William. (1971). *Amos and Boris*. New York: Farrar, Straus & Giroux.

Steig, William. (1986). *Brave Irene*. New York: Farrar, Straus & Giroux.

Zion, Gene. (1984). *Harry the dirty dog*. New York: HarperCollins.

Questions for Reflection

- The authors note that, in their classroom observations, "children frequently ignored text information and responded to questions on the basis of the pictures and their background knowledge." What do you observe in your own classroom or in the classrooms of your colleagues who teach young children? What does this tell you about how you could change your read-aloud practices?

- Think about the books you have in your classroom library or the ones you select to read aloud to your students. Do you have texts that offer opportunities for children to explore extended, connected content? What are the features of such texts? Do the books in your classroom include the sort of rich vocabulary noted in Table 4?

Vocabulary Visits: Virtual Field Trips for Content Vocabulary Development

Camille L.Z. Blachowicz and Connie Obrochta

At a meeting of a teacher study group on vocabulary learning, a group of primary teachers were sharing stories of surprises they encountered when reading with their students. "I had a whole group of kids who didn't know what an umbrella was," lamented one teacher. Another chimed in, "I took a wonderful running record of one child who was reading about the Olympics. He decoded everything perfectly, and when we discussed the selection, he didn't know the word *athlete*...and he had read it perfectly 11 times!" The grade team leader asserted, "Our students are smart, but they need more concept and vocabulary development. Every time we take a field trip they learn a lot. I wish we could take more field trips!" Many of the teachers in the room nodded affirmatively.

Discussions like this are echoed in schools around the United States. They reflect a significant body of research that suggests wide differences in concept and vocabulary knowledge exacerbate the achievement gap seen in so many schools, especially those with large numbers of children living in poverty (Hart & Risley, 1995). Educators sometimes attribute this difference to the Matthew effect—the sad reality that having a well-developed vocabulary allows you to learn new words more easily than classmates who have a smaller fund of word knowledge (Stanovich, 1986). This is especially significant in the content areas—not knowing what a circle is will make it a lot harder for students to understand and learn new terms like *diameter*, *radius*, and *circumference*. Students need "anchor" concepts and vocabulary to learn new words, which are then connected to the concepts they already know.

Similar experiences, knowledge, and thinking led a reading specialist and a group of teachers in a multiethnic urban school to develop Vocabulary Visits—virtual field trips using books to develop the content vocabulary of first-grade students.

Why a Vocabulary Field Trip?

Because school budgets are stretched to the limit, teachers are limited in the number of field trips they can take during the school year. The school in which this strategy was designed has 50% of its students receiving free lunch and a 13% mobility rate, leaving little discretionary family income to contribute extra funds. Yet the teachers all recognized that students came back from field outings with new ideas, new questions to pursue, and new vocabulary to use in talking and writing about their learning. The teachers wanted to capture some of the positive aspects of field-trip learning and integrate them with the instructional program. The specialist and teachers spent considerable time thinking about and discussing what made a good field trip and why their students seemed to come away from these experiences with such increased concept and vocabulary knowledge. After some discussion,

Reprinted from Blachowicz, C.L.Z., & Obrochta, C. (2005). Vocabulary Visits: Virtual field trips for content vocabulary development. *The Reading Teacher, 59*(3), 262-268. doi: 10.1598/RT.59.3.6

they decided that the following characteristics of field trips help students develop vocabulary:

- Field trips have a content focus. Good field trips connect to the curriculum and its content, which provide an integrated context for learning and a relational set of concepts and terms.
- Field trips engage the senses. Students are seeing, hearing, smelling, feeling, and sometimes tasting as they encounter new concepts and vocabulary.
- Field trips are preceded by preparation that helps "plow the soil" for planting the seeds of new learning. Students know what they are going to encounter and often teachers do a read-aloud to get them ready.
- Field trips involve the mediation of an adult. A docent, teacher, parent, or other chaperone is there to help explain, clarify, focus, or point out interesting things.
- Field trips involve exploration, talk, reading, and writing by the students.
- Field trips often involve a follow-up of new concepts and terms.

The teachers decided to structure read-aloud book experiences as virtual field trips for the classroom using scaffolded book read-alouds, active learning with visuals, and other activities that appeal to the senses while developing new concepts and vocabulary.

Grounding Vocabulary Visits in Theory and Research

Two areas of theory and research ground the Vocabulary Visit instructional process: vocabulary development through read-alouds and active learning.

Read-alouds

Reading aloud to children, sometimes also referred to as shared storybook reading, gives students the opportunity to develop new vocabulary. Because children's books present more advanced, less familiar vocabulary than everyday speech (Cunningham & Stanovich, 1998), listening to books read helps students go beyond their existing oral vocabularies and presents them with new concepts and vocabulary. Discussion after shared storybook reading also gives students opportunities to use new vocabulary in the more decontextualized setting of a book discussion (Snow, 1991).

Numerous studies have documented that young students can learn word meanings incidentally from read-aloud experiences (Eller, Pappas, & Brown, 1988; Elley, 1988; Robbins & Ehri, 1994). Involving students in discussions during and after listening to a book has also produced significant word learning, especially when the teacher scaffolded this learning by asking questions, adding information, or prompting students to describe what they heard. Whitehurst and his associates (Whitehurst et al., 1994; Whitehurst et al., 1999) called this process "dialogic reading."

Research also suggests that scaffolding may be more essential to those students who are less likely to learn new vocabulary easily. Children with small vocabularies initially are less likely to learn new words incidentally and need a thoughtful, well-designed, scaffolded approach to maximize learning from shared storybook reading (Robbins & Ehri, 1994; Sénéchal, Thomas, & Monker, 1995). Research points to teacher read-alouds as a positive way to develop the oral vocabularies of young learners.

Active Learning

The role of active learning in vocabulary development has been well established. Students who engage with words by hearing them, using them, manipulating them semantically, and playing with them are more likely to learn and retain new vocabulary (Beck, McKeown, & Kucan, 2002; Blachowicz & Fisher, 2005; Stahl & Fairbanks, 1986). Furthermore, relating new words to what is already known creates elaborated schemata and links between concepts that provide for enduring learning (Anderson & Nagy, 1991).

A series of studies by Sénéchal and her colleagues (Hargrave & Sénéchal, 2000; Sénéchal & Cornell, 1993; Sénéchal et al., 1995) found that students' engagement and active participation in storybook reading was more productive for vocabulary learning in storybook read-alouds than passive listening, even to the most dramatic "performance" of book reading. This has been confirmed by a growing number of studies that scaffolded young students' learning by focusing their attention on target words and engaging them in interactive discussion about books using specific vocabulary before, during, and after reading (Brett, Rothlein, & Hurley, 1996; Penno, Wilkinson, & Moore, 2002; Wasik & Bond, 2001). So the activity of the learners is an important component of learning from read-alouds.

Use of the senses, particularly of visualization, is an important activity for engagement and for focusing attention in learning. Sensory representation helps learners connect with new information and provides alternative codes for understanding and retention (Paivio, 1971; Sadoski, Goetz, Kealy, & Paivio, 1997). Classic, seminal work on concept mapping (Johnson, Pittelman, Toms-Bronowski, & Levin, 1984) has been extended to current strategies such as concept muraling (Farris & Downey, 2004), which represents words and their relations to a topic in a semantically organized graphic. All of these studies attest to the enduring power of visualization in word learning.

When the teachers in this study decided to couple the power of field-trip learning with the research and theory on vocabulary learning, it was agreed that the process would share books and new vocabulary and concepts through teacher read-alouds, that the teacher's role would be to scaffold word learning by focusing attention on specific vocabulary, and that questioning and probing would be used to make students use the new vocabulary and relate it to what they already knew. Each lesson would also be linked to the senses that are stimulated in a real trip, and students would also be called on to use the words though semantic grouping, manipulation, speaking, and writing.

Planning a Vocabulary Visit

The first step in planning was to identify focal topics for the Visit. The teachers in this study decided to use content area books. Much new research on primary-age students and their learning suggests that the primary curriculum is ripe for content learning and that many more resources for content reading now exist (Duke, Bennett-Armistead, & Roberts, 2003). The Vocabulary Visit team decided to use the standards for social studies and science to help them pick topics. They looked at first-grade standards and also at later years to develop vocabulary that would bootstrap students in following years and provide an appropriate learning challenge (Biemiller, 2001). The topics they chose for the first trials were the human body (skeletons), weather and climate, animal habitats, and recycling. All of these topics were relevant to their curricula.

The next step was to assemble a set of at least five texts that could be used for the Visits. Read-alouds are an important part of the process and an important research-based strategy for increasing vocabulary knowledge. Such primary books are now easy to find online and through references on literature for school-age children. Consulting school and local librarians and just rummaging through various classroom libraries quickly produced a starter set. Choosing books in a range of difficulty allows for scaffolded learning and provides for individual differences.

The third step was reviewing the books and choosing a basic vocabulary set that the teacher wanted to use during the discussions. For example, for the set of skeleton books, some core words were *bone*, *skull*, *leg*, *arm*, *wrist*, *ankle*, *foot*, *ribs*, *brain*, *spine*, *backbone*, and some functional words such as *protect* (the skull *protects* the brain).

Last, after selecting the core vocabulary, one of the teachers made a poster with some interesting thematic pictures to stimulate discussion. This was the chart the class would "visit" (see Figure 1). Visuals must stimulate sensory response and lead to discussion of key concepts and vocabulary. Other materials needed are sticky notes, a large marker, and a piece of chart

Figure 1
Vocabulary Visits Chart—Skeletons

paper or poster board to make a poster. This chart forms a dynamic record of the visit.

The Vocabulary Visit

Jump-Start and First Write

Once the materials are prepared, the teacher gives the class a Jump-start to help them activate their prior knowledge. He or she introduces the topic and asks students to talk, briefly, about some things they know about it. Then each student takes a piece of paper and does a First Write, which is a simple list of words they can think of that connects to the topic (see Figure 2). These are archived in a folder and serve as a preassessment. First Write is also a good diagnostic tool for teachers and can provide surprising insights. Speaking about a very shy and quiet little first

grader, one teacher remarked, "I didn't know Keisha [pseudonym] knew so much about animals. It turns out she goes to the zoo almost every other week with her Daddy. I'll really have to draw on that in the discussions."

Group Talk

The next step is Group Talk. Students meet on the rug in the classroom, and the teacher brings out the poster and starts with the first question, "What do you see?" just as a teacher would on a regular field trip. As students contribute words related to what they see, the teacher records their contributions on sticky notes and puts them on the poster. For example, on the skeleton chart shown in Figure 1, the first word that came from the students was *skull*. The teacher recorded it on a sticky note and placed the word in a relevant

Figure 2
First Write

Name:_____

Here are some words I know about skeletons.

Ckincis | skins
Pitilas | patellas
hard
elbow
ribs

clarification and an example ("Where is your wrist?"), and to group them in some relational way. Other senses besides sight are used. For example, in the visit about weather, the teacher asked, "What do you hear in a storm? What are some words for how you feel in rain?" After 5–10 minutes, there are usually quite a number of words on the chart, which the students have now heard, seen, discussed, and sometimes acted out.

Reading and Thumbs Up

The next step is the reading of the first book. Reading aloud to students has been found to be a significant way to increase vocabulary. However, research suggests that this reading should have some mediation involved for new words and should not be a dramatic performance (Dickinson & Smith, 1994). It should be like the kind of reading a parent does with a child, sometimes stopping to clarify or ask about something, much as the highly popular Richard Scarry books call for labeling and finding. We use the Thumbs Up procedure to help students become active listeners. Students put their thumbs up when they hear one of the new words. Sometimes the teacher stops or rereads a sentence when no thumbs go up for a critical term, but the goal is to have a fairly normal reading experience.

After the reading, the students discuss what they learned and add a few new words to the chart. If time permits, the teacher sometimes does semantic sorting activities with the words and tries to involve more of the students' senses. For example, for a unit on weather, the teacher asked, after reading the first book, if there were sound words that they associated with thunderstorms. The students came up with *crash*, *boom*, *thunder*, *thunderclap*, and other words; some of them were from the book and some were from personal knowledge.

Finally, a short writing activity occurs in which the students write about something learned or something that particularly interested them. The books are also put in a central location for reading during independent reading time, and students are asked to read at least one of the

place on the chart. The second word to come up was *cranium*, which amazed the teacher. The children then informed her that Cranium was a game advertised for the holidays and was in the school game collection. This led to *head* and then *crown* followed by a chorus of the nursery rhyme "Jack and Jill."

As students make new suggestions, teachers must mediate as needed. They must make sure that supporting the students' learning with questions, explanations, and suggestions generates the targeted vocabulary. "Touch your skull. What is a skull for?" A student answered, "To protect your brain." The teacher added *brain* and *protect* to the chart and then asked, "How does it protect it?" This new question led to the word *hollow* for skull and then led to the teacher asking for an example of the word, which was supplied by a student who was surprised to find that his chocolate Easter bunny wasn't all chocolate. "Yeah, I hate that," agreed some of his classmates.

The words come fast, and it is the teacher's job to focus on the important ones, to ask for books each week and record it in their reading logs. One teacher noted,

> These books circulate four or five times more than they did last year. The read-alouds help my kids get interested in the topic and also make the other books accessible to them because they know some of the ideas and the vocabulary. It really works!

Follow-Up

The visit poster is kept on the classroom wall, and the activities are repeated for each book in the set. The students also start adding new words to the chart on their own and sometimes regroup the words. Over the course of the unit, students apply their new word knowledge through extension activities that include semantic sorting, word games, writing, reading new books on the same topic, and rereading the books the teacher has read. One participating teacher said,

> My students began making up some of their own activities. They would take the sticky notes and put them in new sets or make sentences with them. They got interested in the new words and were proud that they knew such grown-up ones.

Final Write

At the end of the entire five-book sequence, the students do two writing activities. One is a longer piece about their learning. In some classes, for example, students made their own books about the skeletal system, either to take home or to put in their classroom libraries. In others, students did a report on their favorite book. In first grade, this is often in the form of "The three most interesting things..." or "What the author could do to make this book better" (D. Gurvitz, personal communication, February 7, 2000) rather than a contrived book report form.

Students also do a Final Write, a list-writing activity of all the words they now can write that are associated with a certain topic. Their lists increased dramatically from First Write ($t = -8.453$, significance level $= .0001$). Those students who listed the fewest words at the beginning of the visit usually made the greatest gains, but even those starting with richer initial

Record of Word Growth		
Student	Words before Vocabulary Visit cycle	Words added after Vocabulary Visit
1	8	20
2	7	23
3	4	6
4	6	23
5	7	27
6	4	32
7	4	13
8	7	8
9	5	10
10	7	26
11	3	10
12	4	18
13	5	11
14	5	11
15	0	6
16	0	6
17	0	14
18	0	19

vocabularies made significant gains. Teachers can also evaluate word learning by students' uses of the words in all of these final activities. Another anecdotal bit of evaluation was provided by reports from parents of new word use and sharing and requests to get books on class topics from the library and bookstores.

A Last Word

We learned so many things from our first trial of this process that we are now trying to add a randomized sample study of Vocabulary Visits. We need to extend our list of topics to provide more text sets, and some students are still not active enough in the Thumbs Up part of the process. We are searching for other methods to help students focus on the words without losing the thread of the read-aloud. We also want to find more sensible, uncontrived, and motivating ways to revisit the newly learned words.

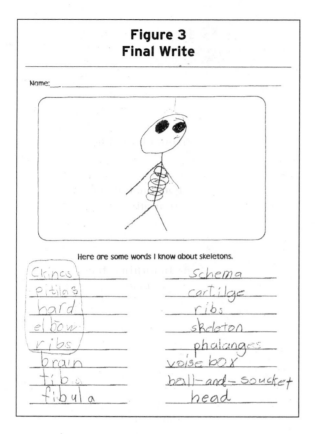

**Figure 3
Final Write**

Name:

Here are some words I know about skeletons.

Ckings	Schema
pitilas	cartilge
hard	ribs
elbow	skeleton
ribs	phalanges
brain	voise box
tiba	ball-and-soucket
fibula	head

Vocabulary Visits has proved to be an exciting and effective research-based strategy for teachers to add attention to vocabulary in thematic units. The pre- and postwriting activities provide evaluation information in a way that is positive for students and teachers alike; it is motivating to see how many topical words are added in the Final Write (see Figure 3). As students work their way through the books in the thematic text set, they become more knowledgeable and confident as they encounter repeated and related vocabulary. They are proud of learning big and technical words, and the spread of words can be infectious, especially with those that are long, funny, or interesting sounding. After playground duty on a day that was growing stormy, an incredulous fifth-grade science teacher popped into one classroom to ask, "How in the heck did all you kids get to know *cumulonimbus*?" They had been using the word in the playground. In explanation, the students pulled him over to the classroom wall and treated him to a tour of their word chart—a Vocabulary Visit all of his own!

References

Anderson, R.C., & Nagy, W.E. (1991). Word meanings. In R. Barr, M.L. Kamil, P.B. Mosenthal, & P.D. Pearson (Eds.), *Handbook of reading research* (Vol. 2, pp. 690–724). New York: Longman.

Beck, I.L., McKeown, M.G., & Kucan, L. (2002). *Bringing words to life: Robust vocabulary instruction.* New York: Guilford.

Biemiller, A. (2001). Teaching vocabulary: Early, direct, and sequential. *American Educator, 25*(1), 24–28, 47.

Blachowicz, C., & Fisher, P. (2005). *Teaching vocabulary in all classrooms* (3rd ed.). Columbus, OH: Merrill-Prentice Hall.

Brett, A., Rothlein, L., & Hurley, M. (1996). Vocabulary acquisition from listening to stories and explanations of target words. *The Elementary School Journal, 96,* 415–422.

Cunningham, A.E., & Stanovich, K.E. (1998, Spring/Summer). What reading does for the mind. *American Educator,* 8–17.

Dickinson, D.K., & Smith, M.W. (1994). Long-term effects of preschool teachers' book readings on low-income children's vocabulary and story comprehension. *Reading Research Quarterly, 29,* 104–122.

Duke, N.K., Bennett-Armistead, V.S., & Roberts, E.M. (2003). Bridging the gap between learning to read and reading to learn. In D.M. Barone & L.M. Morrow (Eds.), *Literacy and young children: Research-based practices* (pp. 226–242). New York: Guilford.

Eller, G., Pappas, C.C., & Brown, E. (1988). The lexical development of kindergartners: Learning from written context. *Journal of Reading Behavior, 20,* 5–24.

Elley, W.B. (1988). Vocabulary acquisition from listening to stories. *Reading Research Quarterly, 24 ,* 174–187.

Farris, P.J., & Downey, P. (2004). Concept muraling: Dropping visual crumbs along the instructional trail. *The Reading Teacher, 58,* 376–380.

Hargrave, A.C., & Sénéchal, M. (2000). A book reading intervention with pre-school children who have limited vocabularies: The benefits of regular reading and dialogic reading. *Early Childhood Research Quarterly, 15,* 75–95.

Hart, B., & Risley, T.R. (1995). *Meaningful differences in the everyday experience of young American children.* Baltimore: Paul H. Brookes.

Johnson, D.D., Pittelman, S.D., Toms-Bronowski, S., & Levin, K.M. (1984). *An investigation of the effects of prior knowledge and vocabulary acquisition on passage comprehension* (Program Rep. No. 84-5). Madison: Wisconsin Center for Education Research, University of Wisconsin.

Paivio, A. (1971). *Imagery and verbal processes.* New York: Holt, Rinehart & Winston.

Penno, J.F., Wilkinson, I.A.G, & Moore, D.W. (2002). Vocabulary acquisition from teacher explanation and repeated listening to stories: Do they overcome the Matthew effect? *Journal of Educational Psychology, 94,* 23–33.

Robbins, C., & Ehri, L.C. (1994). Reading storybooks to kindergarteners helps them learn new vocabulary words. *Journal of Educational Psychology, 86,* 54–64.

Sadoski, M., Goetz, E.T., Kealy, W.S., & Paivio, A. (1997). Concreteness and imagery effects in the written composition of definitions. *Journal of Educational Psychology, 89,* 518–526

Sénéchal, M., & Cornell, E.H. (1993). Vocabulary acquisition through shared reading experiences. *Reading Research Quarterly, 28,* 361–374.

Sénéchal, M., Thomas, E., & Monker, J. (1995). Individual differences in 5-year-olds acquisition of vocabulary during storybook reading. *Journal of Educational Psychology, 87,* 218–229.

Snow, C. (1991). The theoretical basis for relationships between language and literacy development. *Journal of Research in Childhood Education, 6,* 5–10.

Stahl, S., & Fairbanks, M. (1986). The effects of vocabulary instruction: A model-based meta-analysis. *Review of Educational Research, 56,* 72–110.

Stanovich, K.E. (1986). Matthew effects in reading: Some consequences of individual differences in the acquisition of literacy. *Reading Research Quarterly, 21,* 360–407.

Wasik, B.A., & Bond, M.A. (2001). Beyond the pages of a book: Interactive book reading and language development in preschool classrooms. *Journal of Experimental Psychology, 93,* 243–250.

Whitehurst, G.J., Epstein, J.N., Angell, A.L., Payne, A.C., Crone, D.A., & Fischel, J.E. (1994). Outcomes of an emergent literacy intervention in Head Start. *Journal of Educational Psychology, 86,* 542–555.

Whitehurst, G.J., Zevenberg, A.A., Crone, D.A., Schultz, M.D., Velting, O.N., & Fischel, J.E. (1999). Outcomes of an emergent literacy intervention from Head Start through second grade. *Journal of Educational Psychology, 91,* 261–272.

Questions for Reflection

• Examples in this article are drawn from experiences in a first-grade classroom, using focal topics drawn from content area texts. How might you adapt this activity for use in other grades? What other sources are there for deciding on focal topics, and what texts might be used to support Vocabulary Visits centered on these topics?

• The authors note that the Thumbs Up portion of the activity is not always successful. What ideas do you have for helping students attend to vocabulary words during read-alouds, without interfering with their overall attention to the text they are listening to?

"Extraordinary," "Tremendous," "Exhilarating," "Magnificent": Middle School At-Risk Students Become Avid Word Learners With the Vocabulary Self-Collection Strategy (VSS)

Martha Rapp Ruddell and Brenda A. Shearer

"I used to only think about vocabulary in school. The whole world is vocabulary."

"It bugs me if I don't know a word, and I or like, look it up."

"Mr. G used the word magnanimous today, and he didn't think anyone would know it; and I did!"

"Jason, would you please recapitulate what we just read?"

"I hear words hate that, because I just have to find out, everywhere that would be good to use."

These comments are the kind of insights about vocabulary that most teachers would attribute to the very best students, the ones who love to read, love to write, and have developed a repertoire of strategies for independent vocabulary acquisition. It would probably surprise

most to discover that these remarks were actually made by students who had been designated as at risk and referred for reading intervention; the kind of students who struggle with reading, seldom read for pleasure, and rarely pursue the meanings of unknown words either in or out of school. What kinds of classroom interactions contributed to the awareness and motivation of these students? What makes them so curious now when they encounter an unknown word that they simply have to find out what it means? What has opened their eyes, ears, and hearts to the world of words? To address these questions, we will describe what we learned about the effects of the Vocabulary Self-Collection Strategy (VSS) (Haggard [now Ruddell], 1982, 1986a, 1986b, 1989; Ruddell, 1992, 2001) on a population of middle school students in an intensive reading intervention program.

Project History

Martha: The setting was years ago in a junior high seventh-grade language arts class that was the low track in a two-tiered tracking system. As a young English teacher, I was following

Reprinted from Ruddell, M.R., & Shearer, B.A. (2002). "Extraordinary," "tremendous," "exhilarating," "magnificent": Middle School at-risk students become avid word learners with the Vocabulary Self-Collection Strategy (VSS). *Journal of Adolescent & Adult Literacy, 45*(5), 352-363.

ERRATA

Essential Readings on Vocabulary Instruction

The International Reading Association regrets typographical errors in the opening quotations on page 56 of the article "Extraordinary,' 'Tremendous,' 'Exhilarating,' 'Magnificent': Middle School At-Risk Students Become Avid Word Learners With the Vocabulary Self-Collection Strategy (VSS)." The quotations should read as follows:

"I used to only think about vocabulary in school. The whole *world* is vocabulary."

"It bugs me if I don't know a word, and I hate that, because I just *have* to find out, or like, look it up."

"Mr. G used the word *magnanimous* today, and he didn't think anyone would know it; and I did!"

"Jason, would you please *recapitulate* what we just read?"

"I hear words everywhere that would be good to use."

the normal Monday routine of introducing the week's spelling words. We were studying compound words that week, and my students were attending marginally, as usual. They had no real interest in any of the words, were rarely successful beyond the C level on the weekly spelling tests, and found nothing intrinsically—or extrinsically—interesting about the newest spelling list to be placed in front of them or in the lesson itself. I was busily explaining and reexplaining the meaning of the word *heretofore*. Everyone was having trouble, myself as well as the students. None of them had ever heard the word *heretofore*, I was tripping over my own words trying to find various new ways to define it, and *everyone* wondered why, in modern life, one wouldn't simply say, "before now." Finally, as we struggled, one student bravely asked, "Why do we have to learn these words anyway?"

Why, indeed. It brought me up short, and in a split-second assessment of the situation I had the presence of mind to say, "Okay. If you don't want to learn *these* words, here's the deal. Tomorrow when you walk into class I want each of you to write one word on the chalkboard that you've heard or seen and that you think would be a good word for our class to learn. You can find the words anywhere you want—here at school, at home, in something you're reading, on television. When you write your word on the board, spell it as best you can—you don't have to look it up—and tell us where you found the word, what you think it means, and why you think we should learn it. I get to bring a word too."

So was born the idea for the Vocabulary Self-Collection Strategy (VSS). Over the course of that school year I became convinced of the power of inviting students to choose their own spelling and vocabulary words. My students eagerly awaited each Monday for presentation and discussion of their new words; we pretty much abandoned the spelling book because the words students brought were so much more important than the lists created by unknown others. I taught spelling patterns as they occurred naturally in our weekly lists. Students routinely got A's and B's on weekly spelling tests and I had to work hard to confine the word presentation discussion to one

class period so as to keep "spelling" from taking over the seventh-grade language arts curriculum.

Brenda: Three years ago I took a leave of absence from the university to teach struggling seventh- and eighth-grade readers in a rural middle school. I knew that I would work with students very similar to the ones Martha just described. They would be middle school (and high school) struggling readers, unable to make sense of words they encountered in text. These students not only lack strategies for constructing useful meanings for these words, but also lack interest in and curiosity about unknown words encountered in or out of school. Indeed, they frequently appear unaware of the presence of *any* unknown words in the texts they read.

Equally discouraging was the fact that these students' lack of word analysis ability not only placed them at the bottom on tests of vocabulary and spelling in language arts programs, but was, in itself, a potent barrier to comprehension and to improvement of their reading and writing abilities. I knew that my teaching should aim to create lasting changes in the ability of these students to become independent, active word learners. I consulted with Martha to design a program for vocabulary study using the Vocabulary Self-Collection Strategy (VSS). We chose VSS because it focuses on words that students want to know, that are important to them, and about which they have expressed interest and curiosity. My goal was to give students immediate access to the vocabulary of their individual and collective worlds, a knowledge of strategic and powerful ways to learn new words, and the skills necessary for continued, independent vocabulary growth.

Theoretical Foundations

The Vocabulary Self-Collection Strategy is supported by social constructivist, transactional (Paratore & McCormack, 1997; Rosenblatt, 1978, 1994; Vygotsky, 1978, 1986; Windschitl, 1999) and activity theory (Engstrom, 1996; Tolman, 1999) in which learners create meaning through transactions with text and with one another. Vygotsky (1986) emphasized the link between concept development and word learning and the importance of ongoing, rich discussion between teacher and students and among student peers to develop new concepts as well as new word meanings. Indeed, social interaction was the basis of his theory of the Zone of Proximal Development whereby students, working with an adult or peer, at first do things with help that they are later able to do independently. From an activity theory perspective, language mediates the accumulation and transformation of social knowledge. As students negotiate meaning, the activity influences the nature of their external behavior as well as their mental functioning (Engstrom, 1996; Tolman, 1999).

Rosenblatt's transactional theory (1978, 1994) provided additional support for a social constructivist perspective. In her discussion of effective pedagogy for developing students' literacy abilities she stated,

> [T]he teaching of reading and writing at any developmental level should have as its first concern the creation of environments and activities in which students are motivated and encouraged to draw on their own resources to make "live" meanings....
>
> [S]peech is a vital ingredient of transactional pedagogy. Its importance in the individual's acquisition of a linguistic-experiential capital is clear. Dialogue between teacher and students and interchange among students can foster growth and cross-fertilization in both reading and writing processes. Such discussion can help students develop insights concerning transactions with texts as well as metalinguistic understanding of skills and conventions in meaningful contexts. (1994, pp. 1082–1083)

With regard specifically to word (and concept) learning, Vygotsky (1986) cited Tolstoy ("with his profound understanding of the nature of word and meaning," p. 150) to highlight the ineffectiveness of traditional, synonym-teaching vocabulary instruction practices and the importance of experience in word learning:

> When you explain any word...you put in its place another equally incomprehensible word, or a whole series of words, with the connection between them as incomprehensible as the word itself.
>
> [But]...when [a student] has heard or read an unknown word in an otherwise comprehensible sentence, and another time in another sentence, [she or] he begins to have a hazy idea of the new concept; sooner or later [she or] he will...feel the need to use that word—and once [she or] he has used it, the word and the concept is [hers or] his. (Tolstoy, 1903, cited in Vygotsky, 1986, pp. 150–151)

Thus, in a social constructivist model, students learn new words not by hearing them explained with other new words, but rather from ongoing and extended transactions with the words, their peers, and their teacher within the context of life and classroom experience.

Word Learning and Teaching in School

Estimates of the number of words encountered by children in their reading at school exceed 100,000 (Anderson & Nagy, 1992; Anglin, 1993; White, Graves, & Slater, 1990). A well-established body of research suggests further that students' reading vocabulary increases by approximately 3,000 to 5,000 words per year, resulting in a reading vocabulary of nearly 25,000 words by the eighth grade and over 50,000 by the end of high school (Graves, 2000). Clearly, the approximately 20 words per day that a student must learn to acquire 4,000 new words in a school year cannot be taught directly. Anderson (1999) maintained that students learn much of their vocabulary from their reading.

While we concur that reading is a powerful instrument for independent word learning, we theorize that social and environmental influences also can be used not only as sources of vocabulary acquisition, but also as tools to heighten awareness and motivation for discovering the meanings of unknown words. Thus, in addition to academic reading and the reading of romance novels, sports magazines, and mystery books, students can rely on church sermons, television, popular music, and family conversations as vocabulary enhancers. With respect to vocabulary teaching, Ruddell (2001) made the point that

> [O]ne goal of...vocabulary instruction is focused clearly on immediate, short-term learning needs,

with emphasis on identifying what students know and preparing them for the reading and learning to follow. The other goal involves development and extension of students' [word learning] through integration of new ideas into their existing knowledge base and assimilation of new words into working vocabularies.... One is short, sweet, and to the point; the other is extended, exploratory, and wide ranging. (p. 141)

We thought that VSS had the potential not only to reduce the limitations of traditional word learning instruction with regard to student choice and motivation (e.g., out of context, commercially produced word lists; definition by synonym-explanation; "learning" by memorization), but also to increase students' word awareness and strategic abilities for independent learning. Through our work with these struggling readers, we hoped to advance recent research examining the effects of social interactions on word learning while at the same time providing an enriched learning environment for these students, similar to the kind of instruction generally reserved for high-achieving students (Vogt, 1989, 2000).

The VSS Study

The study was conducted for one semester in a small, midwestern U.S. rural community during the 1998–1999 school year. The study involved three classes of middle school students enrolled in an intensive 45-minute daily reading intervention program. Classes consisted of one group of six students in seventh grade, one group of five students in eighth grade, and one group of six students in eighth grade. All 17 participants were Caucasian, representative of the predominantly white, middle-class composition of the community. All were reading 2 to 4 years below grade level at the beginning of the school year as measured by the Woodcock-Johnson Psycho-Educational Battery. The study documented the vocabulary development of these students as they engaged in the systematic use of the Vocabulary Self-Collection Strategy (VSS) as one component of the intervention.

Each student selected one word per week (on Mondays) that he or she wanted to study and nominated it for the class list. The students were allowed to select words from any source including content classes, academic or recreational reading, television, conversations, popular music, or anywhere else they encountered a word that was important to them. In the nomination process, students told (a) where they found their word, (b) what they thought it meant, and (c) why they thought it should be on the class list. The teacher nominated a word each week and supplied the same rationale information. As the class decided on its final list of words for the week, definitions were refined through discussion, and when appropriate, through additional reference to a dictionary or other source.

When final definitions were established, students recorded the words and the definitions in their vocabulary journals. Vocabulary study during the week included discussion, semantic mapping, semantic feature analysis, and other interactive word activities. At the end of each week, students were tested on their ability to spell each word, explain its meaning, and write a meaningful sentence using the word. Every 3 weeks each class devoted a portion of instructional time to reviewing past word lists, and students were tested on five words randomly selected from the weekly lists.

Results and Analysis

Data sources included the following:

1. The lists of words collected each week for vocabulary study. Lists were analyzed to determine the progression of words selected, ties to content areas or other aspects of students' lives, level of word difficulty, and other patterns that emerged.

2. End-of-week and 3-week-interval test results. Test results were analyzed to determine short- and long-term retention of word meanings and spellings.

3. Journal entries. Every Friday, the teacher and students recorded in their journals reflections related to any aspect of the

VSS process and individual and group insights or reactions. Journal entries were analyzed to ascertain student response to the instructional approach, their attitudes toward vocabulary learning, and their reflections on themselves as learners. Teacher entries were examined to determine teacher response to VSS, her analysis of student engagement and participation in vocabulary learning, and the congruence of her reflections with student reflections.

4. Comparison of VSS weekly words and test scores with weekly language arts spelling words and test scores. Word lists that made up the seventh- and eighth-grade spelling curriculum were obtained along with 9 weeks of spelling test scores for each student.

Lists of Words Collected Each Week for Vocabulary Study. Table 1 shows the lists of words collected by each class of students for vocabulary study during the 9 weeks of data collection. By any measure, these class lists of words meet the criterion of "significant difficulty" for seventh- and eighth-grade students. In fact, we find the lists and the learning of them truly an "extraordinary," "tremendous," "exhilarating," and "magnificent" accomplishment for these students who, at the beginning of the school year—and undoubtedly throughout their school lives—had been labeled "at risk." To identify and learn the words on any one of these lists would be considered a fine accomplishment for any group of middle school students, even the most advanced.

Analysis of the words students selected reveals the strong influence of content-area subjects on students' choices of words to learn: *Verdun, rendezvous, Gondwanaland, sovereignty, Grenada, federation, Australia, international, ambassador, emissary,* and *affluent* from the social studies curriculum; *potassium, magnetosphere, fluorocarbons, fluorescent, carbohydrate, asthenosphere, volcano, geothermal, ultraviolet, radiation, nocturnal, laccolith, oxidation,* and

minute from science classes; *terracotta* from art class. Student comments support this conclusion. Sources given for words brought to class were "in my science book," "for geography—we had to learn it," "American Studies class," and so forth. The heavy influence of content areas on student choices is an important milestone in their development as strategic readers and writers: Where once they seemed impervious to unknown words in their reading, they now have figured out that locating words in their content class reading and bringing them to the VSS activity will yield multiple rewards—learning a new word for their reading class and increasing their knowledge and accomplishment in content classes.

Many other places and activities were listed as sources for new words as well—home, school, music, conversations, and outside reading. Table 2 shows a sample of the sources and reasons for word choices for Weeks 4 and 9. This sample confirms the impact of school classes on choices, as well as other sources for finding new words—magazines, novels, exhibits, movies, "lots of places." This supports a recent move by educators beyond traditional text-based definitions of literacy to include multiple literacies and multiple texts, such as graffiti, online zines, artwork, crafts, music, cable television, soap operas, cartoons, and logos on clothing (Moje, Young, Readence, & Moore, 2000). The challenge is to find ways to bring these multiple literacies and texts into the service of school and community goals. VSS does just that.

In addition, Table 2 shows students' motivations for choosing words. Their reasons fit the categories Haggard (1980) found to be potent catalysts for adolescents to learn new words: Peer group usage—"Melissa used it in another class and I just loved it." Strong emotion—"Justin asked me to please use it as my word this week instead of the one I planned to use.... He thought it was a beautiful word." Immediate usefulness—"I had to know for journal writing," "Jamie and I were talking about the Taco Bell commercial and she said the dog was a Chihuahua." Adultness/sound/interestingness of word—"It's a cool word with two *z*'s," "I liked what it meant and how it sounds," "Bigger word for *often*." In addition,

Table 1
VSS Words Collected for Study

Week	Group 1	Group 2	Group 3
1	Verdun potassium intricate rendezvous Gondwanaland inaugurated *eureka	ajar curriculum insensate melancholy epilepsy magnetosphere *eureka	considerate drag racing *extraordinary* interesting maintenance chaos *eureka
2	dazzle resin sovereignty peripheral fluorocarbons convection *comprehension	paunch foreign flourished epochs lustrous premonition *comprehension	conscientious fluorescent respect Mustang nebula assistance *comprehension
3	interpret carbohydrate occupation asthenosphere impression *ambiguous	convergent conglomerate persevere Grenada betrayal *ambiguous	prolong nocturne magnanimous responsible disastrous cousin exercise *ambiguous
4	federation spelunking sophisticated confidential occasionally frequent *strategies	census humor retention dormant composite volcano volcano *strategies	incompetent Titanic revival sarcastically Australia embezzle adventurous *strategies
5	geothermal determination conceive mundane significant quadrilateral *oblivious	lacquer recapitulate dupe international distribution pinnacle *oblivious	tedious aisle cantaloupe abbreviate hoarse electronics impossible *oblivious
6	optimistic plight systematic multisyllabic silhouette impulsive *intriguing	winterizing ultraviolet radiation mortality aisle areobic *intriguing	nocturnal alias conscience *tremendous* *exhilarating* *magnificent* *intriguing

(continued)

Table 1
VSS Words Collected for Study (*Continued*)

Week	Group 1	Group 2	Group 3
7	laccolith	omission	eloped
	enthusiasm	inscrutable	lieutenant
	miscellaneous	inhumanity	conscious
	pessimistic	oxidation	incredible
	ambassador	terracotta	discrimination
	bequeath	gaunt	prejudice
	*hypnotize	*hypnotize	*hypnotize
8	loathe	emissary	serene
	phenomenon	demoralize	disrupt
	tranquil	ecstatic	cautious
	impertinent	vacant	reminisce
	minute	rhythmic	ethics
	*odious	*odious	*odious
9	pneumonia	placid	dynasty
	affluent	dingy	galaxy
	mesmerize	nebulous	Chihuahua
	incidentally	magnanimous	centaur
	self-sustaining	malign	droid
	acquaintance	*esthetically	affluent
	*contemporary		*contemporary

* Teacher nominated

these students added the category of General usefulness—words found in many places or that they believed would have some future usefulness for them—"It's part of history and in the news, and in the movies," "We'll need it in eighth grade." Overall, student remarks in Weeks 4 and 9 reflect a curiosity and word awareness not present at the beginning of the program. This curiosity is what Beck, McKeown, and Omanson (1987) referred to as "word awareness" that signals students' ability and intent to extend word learning beyond the classroom (pp. 157–158). Many students reported engaging family members and friends in discussions of word meanings, and often used references—such as the dictionary—as the final arbiter of such discussions. This is behavior not normally associated with at-risk learners.

End-of-Week and 3-Week-Interval Test Results.
Test results for VSS words yielded a 94% correct mean score over the 9-week period. This translates to an A– grade and is all the more impressive because it includes the level of correctness students achieved on the tests of randomly selected words from 3 prior weeks. Thus, test data support anecdotal evidence that students in the study were achieving well above their usual level on tests of word knowledge and spelling for the VSS words.

Journal Entries. Analysis of 69 student journal entries yielded patterns of student response to VSS. Responses were classified by two researchers working independently using a single-code, forced-choice model; differences were resolved through discussion and consensus. The six response categories that emerged—noticing, choosing, using metacognition, valuing, learning, and transforming—mark the growing development of these students into strategic, independent

Table 2
Examples of Students VSS Entries From Weeks 4 and 9

Word	Where found	Rationale for choosing
federation	Book for geography	It's important to history.
spelunking	In a science magazine	Sounded interesting. I'd love to do it. I thought others might like it.
sophisticated	In my journal writing. It means worldly, wise.	I wanted to write the word. I needed to know how it's spelled.
confidential	In a book	It's a big part of people's lives with their friends. Keeping secrets is important.
occasionally	Text for geography	It's often misspelled.
frequent	In a science magazine	Bigger word for *often*.
census	Black women of the old west	I knew it but not how to spell it. They're going to count everyone again in the year 2000.
dormant	Heard in science class	I asked Mr. D what it meant. We need to know about volcanoes.
incompetent	In a book	It occurs often. I used to always have to look it up last year.
Titanic	Seventh grade went to exhibit	It's part of history, and in the news, and in the movies.
revival	Saw it as I was looking up another word for spelling	I like the way it sounds.
Australia	Lots of places	I want to move there.
embezzle	Saw it in a movie	It's a cool word with two z's. I bet other kids don't know what it means.
adventurous	The word described a character.	If you're daring, it's a good descriptive word.
pneumonia	In a friend's autobiography	I never knew what the word was in Fall. The spelling is so hard.
affluent	Melissa used it in another class and I loved it.	I'm interested in words in other classes.
mesmerize	Written in my autobiography	I think there are lots of times when I do this (get mesmerized).
incidentally	*Outdoor Life*	I like it. I didn't know it.
acquaintance	In a magazine called *Jump*	It's tricky with the *ac* & *qu*.
placid	In a book for reading class	I liked what it meant and how it sounded.
dingy	In a poem in a magazine	Heard of the word but didn't know what it meant.
nebulous	In science, Mr. D used it and I said, "Isn't that some kind of organism?" He said, "No, it means vague or confused."	Thought it was a cool word, and I wanted to know what it meant.

(continued)

Table 2
Examples of Students VSS Entries From Weeks 4 and 9 (*Continued*)

Word	Where found	Rationale for choosing
magnanimous	My cousin came over and we gave her some lead ropes and bridles for her horse. She said, "That was magnanimous of you."	I thought it was a neat word, and I asked her what it meant.
esthetically	In our story	Justin asked me to please use it. He thought it was a beautiful word.
galaxy	In a space book	I thought it was a good word because of *Star Wars* coming out.
Chihuahua	In a discussion with a friend	Jamie and I were talking about the Taco Bell commercial and she said the dog was a Chihuahua.
centaur	My older brother talked about it.	You'll need it in eighth grade.

word learners. Explanation of the categories and sample responses follow:

1. Noticing—What makes a word good? In this category, students reflect on how they chose the words for VSS. One student wrote, "I pick a word that is hard to spell and has a tricky definition—that's not too hard and not too easy and has more than one meaning."

2. Choosing—What do I like about this choice? Students uniformly liked choosing their own words. One student wrote, "I think we should keep on being able to pick our own words because then we will want to study them more efficiently. If we get something handed out or picked by the teacher, we don't want to study something we don't like."

3. Using metacognition—What are my strategies? In this category, students articulated the personal strategies they use to learn new words. Typical of these responses are the following: "Whenever I see or hear a new word I ask myself what it could mean.... I can say just about any words, but I have not a clue what they mean. So lately I've been paying my full attention to different or odd words." "I

have been learning more and asking more about what the word is. If I find a word I don't know what it means, I ask for help or I look it up in the dictionary."

4. Valuing—Why is this important? Students gave highly personal reasons why VSS was important to them. For example, one student wrote, "All that matters is if we can spell or not. All I want is to spell right."

5. Learning—How am I improving? Journal entries in this category focused on self-evaluation. "I am learning that the more you look at words and the more you become familiar with them you will get better at spelling them. I think that when you pick a word that you are not very familiar with and you become familiar with it you can tell you are learning."

6. Transforming—How am I changing the way in which I see the world? Student journals reflect high levels of word awareness and new-found curiosity about unknown words. "I hear words from all over the place. I mean there are millions of words just sitting out there I don't know." "I heard three of our words this week. Mr. D used the words *mortal* and *intriguing* to describe the Civil War. My pastor used *aerobic* when I was at Confirmation last night."

Overall, student journal entries reveal that they have become quite sophisticated in their ability to seek out vocabulary learning opportunities and to reflect on themselves as word learners. Further, students reported noticeable transfer to their reading and writing as VSS progressed ("I'm reading better"), and an increase in their intrinsic interest in vocabulary acquisition.

Comparison of VSS Weekly Word Test Scores With Weekly Language Arts Word Test Scores. As indicated earlier, the VSS tests yielded an overall mean of 94% correct; the weekly spelling test scores averaged 76% correct. A 9-week comparison of means of students' scores (based on percent correct) on weekly VSS scores and on weekly spelling test scores in language arts class confirmed that students performed statistically significantly better on VSS lists than on the lists from the curriculum (effect size = 1.41). These data support VSS as an effective means for vocabulary development. The 76% correct level on traditional weekly spelling tests is quite in line with experiential and anecdotal evidence—with traditional word/spelling lists at-risk students achieve at about a C level; on VSS lists their achievement soars to an A– level. One explanation could be that the comparison is unfair because of the presence of 20 words on typical spelling lists and 7 or 8 words on VSS lists; however, if that is the case, then perhaps the conclusion could be drawn that it is much better for students to learn 7 or 8 words well than 20 words superficially. A more balanced explanation is that students learn words that they have chosen and that are meaningful to them at a rate that far exceeds their learning of decontextualized words chosen by unknown others.

Conclusions and Recommendations

The results of this study provide strong support for the Vocabulary Self-Collection Strategy as an effective means both for increasing the depth and breadth of student vocabulary knowledge and for developing students' abilities to be strategic, independent word learners. VSS word lists demonstrate that when given the opportunity to select their words, students will consistently choose important, challenging, interesting words to learn. In addition, VSS and comparative test scores reveal that they will learn self-chosen words and their spellings, retain that learning over time, and devote more effort to learning their own words than they will to commercially packaged word lists.

Much of the strength and lasting power of learning with VSS can be attributed to the textured and ongoing language transactions that are its hallmark. Rosenblatt's notion of "acquisition of a linguistic-experiential capital" (1994, p. 1083) suggests that socially mediated learning results in an accumulation of knowledge and experience that then serves as both a repository for what has been learned and a scaffold for new learning. This is called the "Matthew Effect" (Stanovich, 1986)—the literacy rich get richer and the poor get poorer—and those students who acquire this "linguistic-experiential capital" then have greater wherewithal to gain more knowledge in an exponential growth pattern. Activity theory raises some interesting questions about how the general context of social negotiation in VSS mutually transforms internal and external activities (Engestrom, 1996). VSS evidently jump-starts learners' linguistic-experiential capital; at-risk students suddenly become "rich" with the capital necessary for academic success and are thereby able to add to their own knowledge base and their own effectiveness as learners.

The teacher's role in guiding students' acquisition of linguistic-experiential capital is as vital as it is complex. It is the teacher who creates opportunity for students to function in their individual Zones of Proximal Development; it is the teacher who orchestrates activities so that language transactions and experiences support student learning; and it is the teacher who decides on a minute-by-minute basis how to keep it all working and running. Gavelek and Raphael (1996) discussed the many decision-making points for teachers, in what Harré (1984) called the "Vygotsky Space," as teachers decide when and how social interactions in the classroom will occur. Raphael, Brock, and Wallace (1997) stated,

> The context of peer talk...provides students the opportunity to see how language is used as a symbol system for understanding and interpreting text and to engage in their own language practices (both social and individual) related to meaningful talk about text. (pp. 180–181)

VSS provides a sturdy framework for teachers to structure vocabulary learning that builds on language interactions and peer talk in classrooms.

The importance of this study appears to be twofold. First, it is yet another piece of evidence in support of social constructivist learning theory and the value of language interactions in classrooms (McCormack, 1997; Rosenblatt, 1994; Vygotsky, 1978, 1986). Second, it contributes to our growing information base regarding the effect of social interactions on word learning (see Fisher, Blachowicz, Costa, & Pozzi, 1992; Stahl & Vancil, 1986). Social constructivist learning theories suggest that the relationship between meaning construction and experienced or anticipated social transactions is direct and powerful; yet we have devoted relatively little attention to those aspects of meaning construction embodied by vocabulary development in our systematic studies of literacy learning (Ruddell, 1994). Studies such as this add to that knowledge base and give direction for further research. We believe that additional studies of VSS are warranted in many different class settings and conditions, including content area classes, diverse populations, and students who are English language learners. In the meantime, the Vocabulary Self-Collection Strategy is a useful addition to secondary classrooms.

Afterword

Martha: In the course of writing this article, I watched over a 3-week period Ken Burns's masterful *Jazz* documentary that appeared on PBS television. In Episode 7, Dave Brubeck was recalling how he had been discovered to have musical talent when he was in the Army and subsequently became an entertainer for the troops during World War II. He began his story, "We were in Verdun." A bolt of electricity shot through me as I watched and I thought, "That's one of our *words*!" And I could picture the word *Verdun* at the top of the Week 1, Group 1 list. It was exciting and wonderful to hear someone use one of the words from our list. Now, I hadn't even been in the room when the words were chosen, but this is a measure of the power of VSS: I *had* read the journals and the students' and teacher's commentary on why the words should be learned, and over a period of time I included myself in the ownership group.

Brenda: Three thousand miles away, I had exactly the same reaction as I, too, watched Episode 7 of *Jazz*. I was immediately transported back to my classroom and back to our VSS discussion of *Verdun* and could picture the Group 1, Week 1 list.

That's what happens when the words students are responsible for learning are learned in an environment in which personal choice is paramount and shared experience and activity predominate. Thus, instructional practice that creates such an environment—such as VSS—is worthy of greater attention from all of us.

References

Anderson, R.C. (1999). Research foundations to support wide reading. In V. Greaney (Ed.), *Promoting reading in developing countries* (pp. 55–77). Newark, DE: International Reading Association.

Anderson, R.C., & Nagy, W.E. (1992, winter). The vocabulary conundrum. *American Educator*, pp. 14–18, 44–47.

Anglin, J.M. (1993). Vocabulary development: A morphological analysis. *Monographs of the Society for Research in Child Development*, 58(10, Serial No. 238).

Beck, I.L., McKeown, M.G., & Omanson, R.C. (1987). The effects and uses of diverse vocabulary techniques. In M.G. McKeown & M.E. Curtis (Eds.), *The nature of vocabulary acquisition* (pp. 147–163). Hillsdale, NJ: Erlbaum.

Burns, K. (Producer). (2001, January). *Jazz*. [Television miniseries]. New York: Public Broadcasting Service.

Engestrom, Y. (1996). Interobjectivity, ideality, and dialectics. *Mind, Culture, and Activity: An International Journal*, 3, 259–265.

Fisher, P.J.L., Blachowicz, C.L.Z., Costa, M., & Pozzi, L. (1992, December). *Vocabulary teaching and learning in middle school cooperative literature study groups.* Paper presented at the National Reading Conference, San Antonio, TX.

Gavelek, J.R., & Raphael, T.E. (1996). Changing talk about text: New roles for teachers and students. *Language Arts, 73,* 182–192.

Graves, M.F. (2000). A vocabulary program to complement and bolster a middle-grade comprehension program. In B.M. Taylor, M.F. Graves, & P. van den Broek (Eds.), *Reading for meaning: Fostering comprehension in the middle grades* (pp. 116–135). Newark, DE: International Reading Association.

Haggard, M.R. (1980). Vocabulary acquisition during elementary and post-elementary years: A preliminary report. *Reading Horizons, 21,* 61–69.

Haggard, M.R. (1982). The vocabulary self-collection strategy: An active approach to word learning. *Journal of Reading, 26,* 203–207.

Haggard, M.R. (1986a). The vocabulary self-collection strategy: Using student interest and world knowledge to enhance vocabulary growth. *Journal of Reading, 29,* 634–642.

Haggard, M.R. (1986b). The vocabulary self-collection strategy: Implications from classroom practice. In M.P. Douglass (Ed.), *Reading: The quest for meaning, 50th yearbook of the Claremont Reading Conference* (pp. 340–351). Claremont, CA: Claremont Reading Conference.

Haggard, M.R. (1989). Engaging students' interest and willing participation in subject area learning. In D. Lapp, J. Flood, & N. Farnan (Eds.), *Content area reading and learning* (pp. 95–110). Boston: Allyn & Bacon.

Harré, R. (1984). *Personal being: A theory for individual psychology.* Cambridge, MA: Harvard University Press.

McCormack, R.L. (1997). Eavesdropping on second graders' peer talk about African trickster tales. In J.R. Paratore & R.L. McCormack (Eds.), *Peer talk in the classroom: Learning from research* (pp. 26–44). Newark, DE: International Reading Association.

Moje, E.B., Young, J.P., Readence, J.E., & Moore, D.W. (2000). Reinventing adolescent literacy for new times: Perennial and millennial issues. *Journal of Adolescent & Adult Literacy, 43,* 400–410.

Raphael, T.E., Brock, C.H., & Wallace, S.M. (1997). Encouraging quality peer talk with diverse students in mainstream classrooms: Learning from and with teachers. In J.R. Paratore & R.L McCormack (Eds.), *Peer talk in the classroom: Learning from research* (pp. 176–206). Newark, DE: International Reading Association.

Rosenblatt, L.M. (1978). *The reader, the text, the poem: The transactional theory of the literary work.* Carbondale, IL: Southern Illinois University Press.

Rosenblatt, L.M. (1994). The transactional theory of reading and writing. In R.B. Ruddell, M.R. Ruddell, & H. Singer (Eds.), *Theoretical models and processes of reading* (4th ed., pp. 1057–1092). Newark, DE: International Reading Association.

Ruddell, M.R.-H. (1992). Integrated content and long-term vocabulary learning with the vocabulary self-collection strategy (VSS). In E.K. Dishner, T.W. Bean, J.E. Readence, & D.W. Moore (Eds.), *Reading in the content areas: Improving classroom instruction* (3rd ed., pp. 190–196). Dubuque, IA: Kendall/Hunt.

Ruddell, M.R. (1994). Vocabulary knowledge and comprehension: A comprehension-process view of complex literacy relationships. In R.B. Ruddell, M.R. Ruddell, & H. Singer (Eds.), *Theoretical models and processes of reading* (4th ed., pp. 414–447). Newark, DE: International Reading Association.

Ruddell, M.R. (2001). *Teaching content reading and writing* (3rd ed.). New York: John Wiley & Sons.

Ruddell, M.R., & Shearer, B.A. (1999, December). *The vocabulary self-collection strategy (VSS) in a middle school reading intervention program.* Paper presented at the 49th annual meeting of the National Reading Conference, Orlando, FL.

Stahl, S.A., & Vancil, S.J. (1986). Discussion is what makes semantic maps work in vocabulary instruction. *The Reading Teacher, 40,* 62–67.

Stanovich, K. (1986). Matthew effects in reading: Some consequences of individual differences in the acquisition of reading. *Reading Research Quarterly, 21,* 360–407.

Tolman, C. (1999). Society versus context in individual development. Does theory make a difference? In Y. Engstrom, R. Miettenin, & R. Punamaki (Eds.), *Perspectives on activity theory* (pp. 70–86). New York: Cambridge University Press.

Vogt, M.E. (1989). *The congruence between preservice teachers' and inservice teachers' attitudes and practices toward high and low achievers.* Unpublished doctoral dissertation, University of California, Berkeley.

Vogt, M.E. (2000). Content learning for students needing modifications: As issue of access. In M. McLaughlin & M.E Vogt (Eds.), *Creativity and innovation in content area teaching* (pp. 329–351). Norwood, MA: Christopher-Gordon.

Vygotsky, L.S. (1978). *Mind in society: The development of higher psychological processes* (M. Cole, V. John-Steiner, S. Scribner, E. Souberman, Eds. and Trans.). Cambridge, MA: Harvard University Press. (Original work published 1934)

Vygotsky, L. (1986). *Thought and language* (A. Kozulin, Ed. and Trans.). Cambridge, MA: MIT Press. (Original work published 1934)

White, P.G., Graves, M.F., & Slater, W.H. (1990). Growth of reading vocabulary in diverse elementary students: Decoding and word meaning. *Journal of Educational Psychology, 82*(2), 281–290.

Windschitl, M. (1999). The challenges of sustaining a constructivist classroom culture. *Phi Delta Kappan, 80,* 751–755.

Questions for Reflection

• What can you do to make word learning more authentic? How can you connect vocabulary instruction to your students' real-life interests in order to create enthusiasm and motivate their internalizing new words and making them their own? How can you use VSS for teaching content/subject matter vocabulary?

• This article describes the use of VSS with at-risk middle schoolers. How do you think the strategy could be used with older or younger students? With a range of ability levels? How might it need to be adapted for use with different student populations?

• How do you think VSS instruction can contribute to students' word consciousness?

Words Are Learned Incrementally Over Multiple Exposures

Steven A. Stahl

We live in a sea of words. Most of these words are known to us, either as very familiar or at least as somewhat familiar. Ordinarily, when we encounter a word we don't know, we skip it, especially if the word is not needed to make sense of what we are reading (Stahl, 1991). But we remember something about the words that we skip. This something could be where we saw it, something about the context where it appeared, or some other aspect. This information is in memory, but the memory is not strong enough to be accessible to our conscious mind. As we encounter a word repeatedly, more and more information accumulates about that word until we have a vague notion of what it "means." As we get more information, we are able to define that word. In fact, McKeown, Beck, Omanson, and Pople (1985) found that while four encounters with a word did not reliably improve reading comprehension, 12 encounters did.

What happens when someone sees a word for the first time in a book? Consider the following paragraph from the *Atlantic Monthly*:

America's permanent election campaign, together with other aspects of American electoral politics, has one crucial consequence, little noticed but vitally important for the functioning of American democracy. Quite simply, the American electoral system places politicians in a highly vulnerable position. Individually and collectively they are more vulnerable, more of the time, to the vicissitudes of electoral politics than are the politicians of any other democratic country. Because they are more vulnerable, they devote more of their time to electioneering, and their conduct in office is more continuously governed by electoral considerations. (King, 1997)

Although I had seen the word *vicissitudes* before, I did not know its meaning. From the context, one can get a general picture of what it means, something like "serendipitous happenings." My *Random House Dictionary* (1978) says "unexpected changing circumstances, as of fortune," so I was fairly accurate in my guess.

When a word is encountered for the first time, information about its orthography (or spelling) is connected to information from the context, so that after one exposure a person may have a general sense of the context in which it appeared ("It has something to do with..."), or a memory of the specific context ("I remember seeing it in an automobile manual"), but not a generalizable sense of the meaning of the word. Dale and O'Rourke (1986) talk about four "levels" of word knowledge:

1. I never saw it before.
2. I've heard of it, but I don't know what it means.
3. I recognize it in context—it has something to do with...
4. I know it.

In ordinary encounters with a word in context, some of the information that is remembered will be reinforced. The information that overlaps between encounters is what is important about the word. Other information will be forgotten. The forgotten

From Stahl, S.A. (2003). Words are learned incrementally over multiple exposures. *American Educator*, 27(1), 18-19, 44. (Adapted from *Vocabulary Development*, part of From Reading Research to Practice: A Series for Teachers, Brookline Books, 1999) Reprinted with permission from the Spring 2003 issue of the *American Educator*, the quarterly journal of the American Federation of Teachers, AFL-CIO.

information is more incidental. With repeated exposures, some connections become strengthened as that information is found in repeated contexts and become the way the word is "defined."

Consider the word *vicissitudes* in the above context. The concept of *vicissitudes* will likely be linked to other concepts in the context, such as "politicians," "electoral politics," or possibly to the whole scenario presented. Because of the syntax, we know that *vicissitudes* does not directly mean "politics," but is a characteristic of politics. As the word is encountered repeatedly, it will be associated with other concepts, possibly "romance" or "getting a job." (Or as the mother of one of my students told her repeatedly while growing up, "Beware of the vicissitudes of life.") These become the strong components of the concept, such as might be represented in a dictionary definition (McKeown, 1991). If the links to other concepts are not repeated, they may recede in importance. Given the core meaning of the word *vicissitudes*, the fact that the subject of the essay is politics is incidental and likely would be forgotten with repeated exposures.

As a person encounters the word again and again, word meaning grows at a relatively constant rate, dependent on the features of the context. That is, people show as much absolute gain in word knowledge from an unknown word as they show from a word of which they have some partial knowledge, all other things being equal (Schwanenflugel, Stahl, & McFalls, 1997). We found that students made the same amount of growth in word knowledge from a single reading, whether they began by knowing something about a word or not. Thus, vocabulary knowledge seems to grow gradually, moving from the first meaningful exposure to a word to a full and flexible knowledge.

One does not always need to know a word fully in order to understand it in context or even to answer a test item correctly. Adults possess a surprising amount of information about both partially known and reportedly unknown words. Even when people would report never having seen a word, they could choose a sentence in which the word was used correctly at a level above chance or discriminate between a correct synonym and an incorrect one (Durso & Shore, 1991). This suggests that people have some knowledge even of words that they reported as unknown, and that this knowledge could be used to make gross discriminations involving a word's meaning. Curtis (1987) found that people who reported only a partial knowledge of a word's meaning ("I've seen it before") could make a correct response to multiple-choice questions.

When a person "knows" a word, he knows more than the word's definition—he also knows how that word functions in different contexts. For example, the definition of the verb smoke might be something like "to inhale and puff the smoke of (a cigarette, etc.)" (Random House, 1978). However, the verb smoke describes distinctly different actions in the following sentences:

a. He smoked a cigarette.

b. The psychologist smoked his pipe.

c. The hippie smoked a marijuana cigarette.

d. The 13-year-old smoked his first cigarette.

These all fit under the general definition, but the actions vary from a typical smoking action in (a), to a puffing in (b), to a deeper and longer inhaling in (c), to an inhaling followed by coughing and choking in (d). Children cannot learn this information from a dictionary definition. Instead, they need to see the word in many different contexts, to see how the word meaning changes and shifts.

Thus, to understand the word in (d) we need to know that 13-year-olds are generally novices at smoking and that smoking can make one cough, if one is not used to it. Some words are embedded in a single knowledge domain, such as *dharma* or *jib*. To understand *dharma*, one must understand at least some basic concepts associated with Hinduism or Buddhism. To understand *jib*, one must know something about sailing. These words are so tied to their knowledge domains that they cannot be defined outside of them. (Some people, e.g., Johnston, 1984, have used vocabulary tests to measure domain knowledge.) Most words can be used in multiple domains but have distinct meanings within those domains. The word *obligation*, for example, has a series of related meanings, depending on whether the obligation is a moral one, or a payment due on a loan, and so on. Anderson and Nagy (1991) argue that words are polysemous, containing groups of related meanings, rather than a single fixed meaning. These meanings have a family resemblance to each other. Consider the word *give* in these different contexts (Anderson & Nagy, 1991):

> John gave Frank five dollars.
>
> John gave Mary a kiss.
>
> The doctor gave the child an injection.
>
> The orchestra gave a stunning performance.

All of these involve some sort of transmitting, with a giver, a recipient, and something, tangible or intangible, that is given. But the act of giving is radically different in each case.

A full and flexible knowledge of a word involves an understanding of the core meaning of a word and how it changes in different contexts. To know a word, we not only need to have *definitional knowledge*, or knowledge of the logical relationship into which a word enters, such as the category or class to which the word belongs (e.g., synonyms, antonyms, etc.). This is information similar to that included in a dictionary definition. In addition, we also need to understand how the word's meaning adapts to different contexts. I have called this *contextual knowledge*, since it comes from exposure to a word in context. This involves exposure to the word in multiple contexts from different perspectives. Children exposed to words in multiple contexts, even without instruction, can be presumed to learn more about those words than students who see a word in a single context (Nitsch, 1978; Stahl, 1991).

References

Anderson, R.C., & Nagy, W.E. (1991). Word meanings. In R. Barr, M.L. Kamil, P. Mosenthal, & P.D. Pearson (Eds.), *Handbook of Reading Research, Vol. II*. White Plains, N.Y.: Longman.

Curtis, M.E. (1987). Vocabulary testing and vocabulary instruction. In M.G. McKeown & M.E. Curtis (Eds.), *The nature of vocabulary acquisition*. Hillsdale, N.J.: Erlbaum.

Dale, E., & O'Rourke, J. (1986). *Vocabulary building*. Columbus, Ohio: Zaner-Bloser.

Durso, F.T., & Shore, W.J. (1991). Partial knowledge of word meanings. *Journal of Experimental Psychology: General, 120*, 190–202.

Johnston, P. (1984). Prior knowledge and reading comprehension test bias. *Reading Research Quarterly, 19*, 219–239.

King, A. (1997). Running scared. *Atlantic Monthly, 279*(1), 41–56.

McKeown, M.G. (1991). Learning word meanings from dictionaries. In P. Schwanenflugel (Ed.), *The psychology of word meanings*. Hillsdale, N.J.: Lawrence Erlbaum Associates.

McKeown, M.G., Beck, I.L., Omanson, R.C., & Pople, M.T. (1985). Some effects of the nature and frequency of vocabulary instruction on the knowledge of use of words. *Reading Research Quarterly, 20*, 522–535.

Nitsch, K.E. (1978). *Structuring decontextualized forms of knowledge*. Unpublished Ph.D., Vanderbilt.

Random House Dictionary. (1978). New York: Random House.

Schwanenflugel, P J., Stahl, S.A., & McFalls, E.L. (1997). *Partial word knowledge and vocabulary growth during reading comprehension* (Research Report No. 76). University of Georgia, National Reading Research Center.

Stahl, S.A. (1991). Beyond the instrumentalist hypothesis: Some relationships between word meanings and comprehension. In P. Schwanenflugel (Ed.), *The psychology of word meanings* (pp. 157–178). Hillsdale, N.J.: Lawrence Erlbaum Associates.

Questions for Reflection

- Think about yourself as a reader. What do you typically do when you encounter an unknown word?

- If word learning benefits from multiple exposures to new words, in what ways can you ensure students receive those multiple exposures without their becoming contrived or forced? How can you ensure that the new words are used in a variety of different contexts to reveal depth of meaning?

Words Are Wonderful: Interactive, Time-Efficient Strategies to Teach Meaning Vocabulary

Margaret Ann Richek

In order to comprehend, students must know the meanings of the words they read. Yet too often, vocabulary instruction is tedious and ineffective. In this article I suggest ways to help students experience success and enjoyment in learning vocabulary. These strategies have been used from kindergarten through college; in whole classes, small groups, and special settings; in Spanish and English; and internationally. The engagement that students experience results in enhanced learning as well as a sense of excitement about words. Two strategies, Semantic Impressions and Word Expert Cards, help teachers to introduce words. Four additional techniques—Anything Goes, Connect Two, Two in One, and Find That Word—provide the motivation and practice that help students become comfortable using new vocabulary in reading, writing, and speaking.

How Important Is Meaning Vocabulary?

The influence of meaning vocabulary is one of the most enduring findings of educational research. Vocabulary knowledge is among the best predictors of reading achievement (Daneman, 1991). The National Reading Panel (National Institute of Child Health and Human Development [NICHD], 2000) has affirmed the prominence of vocabulary in the reading process. Differences in children's vocabularies develop even before school begins and are key to inequality of educational attainment (Hart & Risley, 1995).

While a substantial amount of general vocabulary is acquired through wide reading, it is also important for teachers to address word learning directly (Baumann, Kame'enui, & Ash, 2003). The school curriculum is filled with challenging new words. Novels, social studies texts, and science experiments all have vocabulary that needs to be mastered before students can comprehend and learn. Direct instruction in word meanings is effective, can make a significant difference in a student's overall vocabulary, and is critical for those students who do not read extensively (Beck, McKeown, & Kucan, 2002).

One instructional practice is to have students look words up in a dictionary, copy or restate definitions, and then create sentences using the words. However, students often cannot understand the definitions that dictionaries, even children's dictionaries, present (McKeown, 1993). I have seen fifth graders copy "the state in which" as the complete definition of a noun. Students may not know how to choose the appropriate definition for a word that has multiple meanings. When working from misinterpreted definitions, the sentences students create are often unfortunate and frustrating to read.

Reprinted from Richek, M. (2005, February). Words are wonderful: Interactive, time-efficient strategies to teach meaning vocabulary. *The Reading Teacher, 58*(5), 414–423. doi: 10.1598/RT.58.5.1

How can teachers more effectively teach meaning vocabulary? Studies show that words should be processed deeply and repeatedly by students (Mason, Stahl, Au, & Herman, 2003; NICHD, 2000). Words are typically learned gradually (Baumann et al., 2003), and the more actively and deeply students process words, the better they learn them (Blachowicz & Fisher, 2000; Stahl & Fairbanks, 1986). Activities using words in games, connecting words, and manipulating words creatively result in excellent student learning (Beck et al., 2002). When students are having fun, they are motivated to learn.

Ways to Introduce Words

The task of learning words is large and important, so why not make it fun, interactive, and empowering as well? Two word introduction strategies that foster engaged learning are Semantic Impressions and Word Expert Cards.

Semantic Impressions

In this strategy, originally called Story Impressions (McGinley & Denner, 1987), students internalize meanings by using words in a certain order to compose their own story before they read a published story. To do this, the teacher chooses key words from a story or book chapter and lists them in the order (or approximate order) they appear in the published story. Try to choose words that are central to the plot, for these are the ones students will later need for successful comprehension. However, an occasional "fun" word can be included. The list is usually from 5 to 20 words long.

Write the words vertically on a board or overhead. Then briefly discuss each one, asking if anyone knows what it means or can use it in a sentence. Typically, when a class pools its knowledge, something is known about each word. You can build upon this, refining concepts and supplementing definitions. However, definition work should not be time consuming because students may need words redefined as they compose their Semantic Impressions story.

Next, tell the students that they are going to compose a story using these words. The words must be used in the order they appear, but after a word has been introduced it may be used again. Other forms of the word may be used; for example, *important* instead of *importance* may be written into the story.

Then, working as a group, students compose a sensible—if at times fanciful—story using the words. With teacher guidance, the class creates a narrative that has a beginning, middle, and end. If the story gets off track, gently coach the students to think about a problem and a solution and to compose a story. Primary students often personalize their creations by using class members as story characters. Because the words have been chosen from an existing narrative, students will be able to compose a meaningful story without the forced use of words. In fact, I have found that the stories flow quite naturally. At times, you will need to clarify the meaning of a word before students can use it. At other times, so many different scenarios will be advanced that you will need to help students choose from a wealth of ideas. As the group gives its story, write it on a board or an overhead for all to see. The process can almost always be completed within 20 minutes and thus requires no more time than more commonly used strategies for word introduction. When it is finished, the class may choose to give their creation a title.

After completing a Semantic Impressions story, reread it, helping the class to revise and edit. This usually begins with fixing mechanical problems in spelling, punctuation, and grammar. However, it often proceeds to adding "juicy" details and adjectives, combining short sentences, paragraphing, and providing motives for actions in the story. My classes have added prequels and epilogues. Of course, this work provides experience and modeling for revision.

Semantic Impressions is vocabulary learning at its most active. Students internalize words they will later read by weaving them into personalized narrative. The rich associations to this narrative make word meanings memorable. New concepts are clarified as students use them. In short, Semantic Impressions provides active, engaged, and joyful vocabulary learning. Table 1

Table 1
Directions for Semantic Impressions

- Choose between 5 and 20 words that are central to the plot of a narrative (story, chapter book).

- List these words, in the order they appear in the story, on a chalkboard or overhead. (The order of one or two may be changed if desired.)

- Tell students that as a group they will compose a sensible story based on these words. Advise them that the story should have a beginning, middle, and end (or problem and resolution).

- Briefly go over the meaning of each word on the list, encouraging student contributions.

- Discuss three rules:
  1. Words must be used in order.
  2. Once a word is used, it can be reused.
  3. The form of words (plurals, tenses, parts of speech) can be changed.

- As students give oral contributions, write their Semantic Impressions story on the chalkboard or overhead. (Note that the word list, as well as the story, is displayed.)

- As you take down oral student contributions, help students to formulate a cohesive narrative with a sensible flow. Student sentences may be combined.

- When the story is finished, the class may choose to edit it.

- Have the students read, or listen to, the published narrative.

presents reading specialist Rachel Hogan's directions for teachers using Semantic Impressions.

It should be noted that Semantic Impressions has benefits beyond learning vocabulary. The strategy improves students' abilities to write and revise sensible narratives. They develop pride of authorship in a story that contains "their" words. They anticipate how words will be used in the story they will read. Finally, as students read the published story, they deepen word meanings by comparing the use of words in the two narratives.

As students become familiar with the process, I add new challenges. Sometimes, I use particularly difficult story words. Working with third graders to introduce a story about the eruption of Mt. Vesuvius in Italy, I included the words *shepherds*, *weavers*, and *peddlers* on the list to deepen students' knowledge of life in ancient times. Using a trade book, *The Ballad of Belle Dorcas* (Hooks, 1990), to supplement fourth-grade social studies, I included the terms *Tidewater Region* and *Deep South*, allowing students to review important geographical concepts.

Many classes want to make books from their Semantic Impressions stories. These books become welcome additions to the classroom library. For primary students, I write each sentence of the story on a separate sheet of paper and then assign two students to illustrate each page. For intermediate-grade students, class members illustrating books must first agree on the setting and appearance of the characters so that the pages of their book will be consistent.

After doing a class Semantic Impressions story, students often ask if they can compose their own. To do this, they work independently or in pairs, creating other original stories from the word list. This provides additional practice with vocabulary. As students become more skilled, teachers can make the task more advanced. Teacher Gary Riskin asked his second graders to compose Semantic Impressions stories in specific genres, such as mystery and adventure.

Although Semantic Impressions is usually done in preparation for reading, it also is excellent preparation for a listening experience.

Children can do a Semantic Impressions story and then experience a teacher read-aloud.

What do Semantic Impressions stories look like? To introduce *Cloudy With a Chance of Meatballs* (Barrett, 1978) for a reading lesson, I chose the following words and phrases:

1. pancakes
2. weather
3. rain
4. snow
5. prediction
6. sanitation department
7. took a turn for the worse
8. damaged
9. abandon
10. new land
11. supermarket

Working with two classes of third-grade students who spoke English as a second language, the following stories emerged:

Class one: "A Day of Snow"

Yesterday I woke up at 5 A.M. and I ate *pancakes*. That morning the *weather* was very cold. It was so cold that the *rain* became ice and *snow* covered the streets. The weather *prediction* was wrong because they had predicted a sunny day. The *pancakes* didn't fill me, so I was still hungry. I called the *sanitation department* to move the *snow* so I could go out and buy food. The *weather took a turn for the worse* so the s*anitation department* got stuck in the *snow*. Their truck's motor was *damaged* by the *snow*, so they had to *abandon* it. A day later, the *snow* melted. When the *snow* melted, the place looked like a *new land*. I was very happy because I could go to the *supermarket*.

Class two: "A Lady Who Loved Pancakes"

Once upon a time there was a little lady who loved *pancakes*. When she ate them, she could tell what the *weather* would be. One day she ate *pancakes* and said "Today it will *rain*." When people heard, they got out their umbrellas and went inside. Later it got colder and started to *snow*. Her *prediction* was wrong, and people got mad. The next day, the *sanitation department* started to remove the *snow*. The people's anger *took a turn for the worse* and they *damaged* her house. So she had to *abandon* the city and move to a *new land*. She built a house next to a *supermarket*. One day she wanted to taste something else like *pancakes*, so she asked the man at the *supermarket* for a similar food. The man said "Why don't you try waffles?" She ate waffles, *predicted* the *weather* again, and she was right. Afterwards, she continued to eat waffles and always *predicted* the *weather* right.

Semantic Impressions is an effective, as well as time-efficient, strategy. In one study, two third-grade classes of equivalent achievement were compared in their abilities to learn vocabulary in *Brave Irene* (Steig, 1986). Overall achievement at the school in this study was slightly below national norms, with 45% of children achieving at or above grade level on the Iowa Test of Basic Skills. The school has a diverse population, with a significant number of students who speak English as a second language. Third-grade teachers Jennifer Toomey and Jolene Biesack participated. One used the Semantic Impressions strategy for word introduction; the other introduced the words through discussion using word cards. They each spent about 20 minutes on the strategy. A multiple-choice posttest of words showed that the Semantic Impressions group knew 91% of the words, as compared to a 73% mastery rate for the discussion group. A two-sample t test revealed that the difference between the two treatments was highly significant ($t = 3.96$, $df = 39$, $p < .001$). To make sure that this effect was not due to differences in the general vocabulary knowledge of the students, an analysis of covariance was performed using the vocabulary subtest percentile of the Iowa Test of Basic Skills, an indicator of general vocabulary mastery, as a covariate for each student. This analysis of covariance also showed a highly significant difference between the two classes ($t = 3.91$, $df = 35$, $p < .001$) and indicates that, when student achievement is controlled for, the Semantic Impressions strategy remains effective.

As students weave Semantic Impressions stories that contain challenging words, they broaden their vocabularies, prepare to read with comprehension, and deepen their understandings of narrative elements. Most of all, they experience vocabulary learning that is fun.

Word Expert Cards

When students read a novel or a unit in social studies or science, they often need to master many words. How can this be done effectively? A system first published by Lansdown (1991) gives each student the job of being a Word Expert for just a few of the many words to be learned. In this strategy, students construct cards, gaining experience in interpreting dictionary definitions. Then, students teach one another the words. Finally, when students see the words in the context of a novel or a unit of study, meanings are reinforced and deepened. Word Expert Cards combine direct vocabulary instruction, word study in context, and peer teaching.

The teacher begins by identifying a master list of key words. Choose words that are of general use, as well as those important to the novel or unit of study. My list generally contains 50 to 100 words. Before the novel or unit of study begins, each student is assigned two or three Expert words from the list. Each student has different words so, in total, all of the words are assigned. I also give students a page number from the novel or text where they can locate their words.

Students then start making Word Expert Cards for their two or three personal words. A piece of construction paper is folded in half and the student begins work on the inside of the card. (At times, I ask students to use scratch paper and copy work onto their card only after I have approved it.) First, the student writes the word. Then he or she copies a sentence from the book that contains the word. (The page number given by the teacher helps the student to locate the word.) Next, the student looks up the word in a developmentally appropriate dictionary and finds the part of speech and meaning that matches the way the word is used in the copied sentence. The student will sometimes need to determine the root form of a word to locate a definition. For example, to find the word *smuggling*, the entry for *smuggle* must be used. The student puts the definition in his or her own words. Finally, the student writes a personal sentence for the word. Throughout the process, students are encouraged to consult one another. (See Table 2 for Susan Ali's directions for Word Expert Cards.)

Table 2
Directions for Word Expert Cards

- Use the page number to locate the word in the story.
- Copy the sentence containing the word inside the card.
- Use a dictionary to look up the definition for each word; you may discuss it with others.
- On scratch paper, write the part of speech and the definition in your own words that matches the use of the word in the story.
- On scratch paper, write your own sentence using the word.
- Get the definition and sentence approved for accuracy by the teacher.
- Copy onto the inside of your card the approved definition, part of speech, and sentence.
- Write the vocabulary word on the front outside of the card in big bold letters.
- On the front of the card, illustrate the vocabulary word neatly and creatively. Get your illustration approved.
- Write your name, word, and class period on the back side of the card.
- Completed cards must be turned in by (date).

As students work on their cards, the teacher roams the room, helping them. Teacher monitoring only takes a few minutes per student, but it is vital to the process. It is difficult for students to use dictionaries effectively, so the teacher's hands-on coaching in locating and interpreting definitions is essential. The teacher is also indispensable for helping students to choose the word meaning that matches the word's use in the copied sentence. A student with a sentence like "They came to a road that *skirted* the top of a deep ravine" will usually need help in locating the appropriate meaning. By checking student sentences, the teacher also helps to clarify word use.

In composing Word Expert Cards, students give each word a personal interpretation. Sentences are often pertinent to their lives. Fifth graders write such sentences as "My brother likes to *caterwaul* because he is a baby" and "I *reconsidered* if I should say I'm sorry to my brother." Clarifying definitions can be an active process. Working with sixth graders preparing to read *Journey of the Sparrows* (Buss, 1991), we made noises to demonstrate *cooed* and *chuckled* and actions for *squirming* and *straining*. Students also consulted one another about these word meanings.

When the inside of the card is finished, the student writes the word in bold print on the outside. Then he or she makes an illustration that shows the meaning. Students' artistic interpretations often relate to personal experiences and are easy to explain to others. One college student illustrated *aspiring* with a picture of a woman in a business suit, carrying a briefcase. A fifth grader drew herself in open-mouthed astonishment to show *marvel*. On the back outside of the card goes the name of the Word Expert who made it.

It generally takes one to two class periods for students to make the cards. Two Word Expert Cards are shown in Figures 1 and 2. The first was made by third grader Levi Todd for the novel *The Indian in the Cupboard* (Banks, 1980); the second was made by seventh-grader Cora Nowicki for a science unit on cellular structure. When working with younger students, I may simplify directions, for example eliminating the part of speech requirement.

**Figure 1
Third-Grade Word Expert Card
for a Novel (Outside Shown on Top;
Inside on Bottom)**

Note. By Levi Todd.

When the cards have been approved, students use them to teach their words to their classmates. In doing this, students come to feel ownership over their own words as well as a growing comfort with the many other words that their classmates teach them. Learning is, of course, reinforced as students go on to read a novel or textbook in which the vocabulary appears in context.

How does the peer-teaching process work? The teacher should initially allocate a single class period. Students usually work in pairs. The first student teaches his or her word to a partner by first showing the outside of the card and asking the partner to determine the meaning from the illustration. The Word Expert next reveals the information on the inside of the card, step by step, asking the partner to try to figure out the meaning, first from the Expert's original

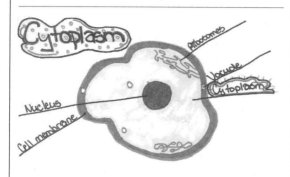

**Figure 2
Seventh-Grade Word Expert Card
for Unit on Cellular Structure (Outside
Shown on Top; Inside on Bottom)**

Cytoplasm

Sentence where found – All of the functions
for cell expansion, growth and replication
are carried out in the cytoplasm of a cell.
Part of Speech – Noun
My definition – A substance like jelly
that is the living matter of a cell around
the nucleus.
My sentence – The cells of every living
thing, including human beings, are filled
with cytoplasm.

Note. By Cora Nowicki.

grader, assigned the word *gallant*, who started bowing and opening doors for me.

After one day of peer teaching, I start the novel or unit of study. Then, for several days, students do about 10 minutes of paired vocabulary learning. Each student gradually learns each word from a peer. As this process unfolds, students also meet the words in their novels or texts.

I have used this strategy in the second grade and beyond. One third-grade teacher used the cards to teach such social studies concepts as *reservoir* and *satellite*; another instructor employed them to refine complex 11th-grade mathematical concepts.

Word Expert Cards help students to learn important and conceptually challenging words. They combine direct instruction in vocabulary and dictionary skills with contextual learning in reading. The guided peer teaching fosters social skills; it is a joy to watch a roomful of animated students excitedly explaining difficult words.

Data collected by Lansdown (1991) suggested that Word Expert Cards are effective. On a pretest, average knowledge of words appearing in a novel ranged from 16% to 28% in six classes of sixth and seventh graders. At the end of the novel unit, class means for words learned ranged from 92% to 97%.

Strategies for Practice and Review

Because words are learned gradually, only practice can ensure that students acquire enough knowledge to use them comfortably in reading, writing, speaking, and listening. The review activities in this section require the active, deep, and flexible processing most conducive to learning vocabulary. However, these strategies take only a few minutes each and can be fit easily into the teaching day.

To start, you will need to display the words your class is studying. They can be put on a word wall (Cunningham, 2000) where the words are listed on cards under the alphabet letter they begin with. Or words may simply be listed so all can see. If you don't have much wall space, try

sentence, next from the sentence copied from the book, and finally from the definition. This process enables students to practice using contextual clues. Then the students reverse teacher and learner roles.

After the pairs have completed their teaching, generally in 7 to 10 minutes, students rotate to another partner and repeat the process. Using this method each student truly becomes a confident Expert on his or her own words. In fact, I find that the class can almost always identify the Expert for each word. These Experts provide guidance when questions arise about their words. In this way, knowledge is distributed throughout the class, with each student participating in the teaching process. At times, Experts start to live their words. I remember with a chuckle one misbehaving eighth hanging lists of words from clothespins attached to the ceiling.

Next the word lists are used in practice activities. Four engaging activities are Anything Goes, Connect Two, Two in One, and Find That Word. Each is appropriate for use *after* words have been introduced.

Anything Goes

For this game, I simply point to a word on a list or word wall and ask students questions about it. The following are examples of questions:

1. What is the meaning of this word?
2. Can you give me two meanings of this word?
3. Can you use this word in a sentence?
4. What is the difference between these two words?
5. Can you use this word and another word in a sentence?
6. Can you spell a past tense, plural, or gerund form of this word?
7. What is the part of speech (or two parts of speech) of this word?
8. What is the root of this word?
9. Give me all of the prefixes and suffixes you see in this word.

Working with fifth graders, I elicited three meanings of the word *depression* using question two above. Then, using question four, I asked for the difference between *captive* and *captor*. A few minutes later, I referred to the word *cubing* on the word wall and asked them to spell *cube*, which was not on the word wall. After this, using question seven, I asked for the two parts of speech of *cube*. If one student answered incorrectly, he or she was able to ask a classmate for help. The 15 questions I asked took six minutes, but they motivated my students and consolidated their word learning.

Fourth-grade teacher Carrie Froeter created a word wall using important words from social studies, English, science, and mathematics. (The school was the same one where the Semantic Impressions data was gathered.) The Anything Goes strategy was used six times, for 10 minutes each time. Students then took a multiple-choice test assessing knowledge of six words used in the game and six words that had been studied but not used in the game. The words were of equal frequency in English and, in Carrie's opinion, had been emphasized equally in the subject units. Results showed that the words reviewed in Anything Goes had a 77% mastery rate; in contrast, the words not reviewed had a 43% mastery rate. On a one-sample t test, these scores were significantly different ($t = 7.29$, $df = 39$, $p < .001$).

Connect Two

In this strategy [Blachowicz & Lee, 1991], students are challenged to find similarities between two words. Although words can simply be listed in random order and connected, I often construct two columns of about 10 words apiece. Then, I ask students to think of something that a word in column one has in common with a word in column two. For example:

Column one	Column two
bayonet	musket
disgrace	exuberant
muffled	cunning
exposed	pondered
insignificant	ruefully
splendid	courier
roll	hoarse
magazine	incense
ravine	restrained

When we start, the similarities students observe are often superficial. They may point out that *disgrace* and *pondered* have the same number of letters. To move students beyond this, I point out similarities in meaning or in structure. Soon, students demonstrate deeper processing. Examples from this fifth-grade class were that *muffled* and *restrained* are both actions in which people hold back something, that *magazine* and *musket* both have to do with guns, and that *exposed* and *exuberant* can both be used as adjectives. The explanations that students verbalize are especially helpful in deepening their thinking.

Two in One

Writing a sentence for each new vocabulary word is a time-honored, if pedestrian, activity. With a slight twist, it can be turned into a compelling review: Ask students to put *two* (or more) words into each sentence. This slight change adds tremendous engagement. Present students with a list and ask them to make up sentences that include multiple words. You should allow them to change word forms, using, for example, *glancing* or *glanced* instead of *glance*. To increase the level of thinking as well as conversational use of the words, I ask students to work in pairs or small groups. After about five minutes of composing, each group reads the sentence (or sentences) to the class. You should circulate while the students work and help them refine sentences.

This simple activity has many instructional benefits. By using two words in one sentence, students form conceptual connections between them. In being allowed to use different forms of a word, students practice using base words and their derivatives. Learning word derivatives is one of the best sources of vocabulary growth (Nagy & Scott, 2000). Finally, the Two in One task is invariably met with enthusiasm. Even first graders will soon ask if they can use *three* words in a sentence.

Find That Word

In this strategy, inspired by Word Wizard (Beck et al., 2002), students seek out the words they are studying in their environment. They may find these words in free reading, other subject area books, speech, radio, television, or through computer searches. When the students read or hear a word used, they write down the sentence containing it and bring it in to class. Then, perhaps for about 10 minutes, twice per week, I allow students to come up and read their sentences to the class. The sentences for any week are put on display, so students can refer to them.

Find That Word dramatically increases student awareness and appreciation for vocabulary words. Students also see how words are used in different contexts, which provides a dimension of correct use that cannot be gained through dictionary definition alone. After a few sessions of Find That Word, students often become so enthusiastic that they stop me in the hall to show me words they have located in books. I usually keep a running count of how many accumulated sentences the class has brought in. One third-grade class collected 381 sentences in four weeks!

To encourage students' word finding, I will deliberately use these words in my speech. Members of the class enthusiastically copy my sentences. Because I also want to encourage students to use words, I have devised a special point system. Each word found in reading or in adult speech is worth 1 point; however, each sentence originally spoken by a student (and, of course, recorded by another class member) is worth 2 points. With some groups, I encourage editing skills by quickly checking whether copied sentences have any grammatical or spelling errors. If they do, I ask students to consult with one another and fix the problems before the sentence can be read aloud. The following is a recent sample of words recorded by sixth graders:

> The alligator is very *aggressive*. (from a television channel)
>
> I *glanced* through the curtains. (from a novel)
>
> If you happen to *stumble* across a word, write it down. (from my speech)
>
> We're *whimpering*. (from a student in class—double credit)
>
> Put your hands over your *nostril* as if you are praying. (from a mother advising how to stanch a student's nosebleed)

An English as a Second Language primary teacher used Find That Word to reinforce common nouns like *bed*, *table*, and *television*. Each child was assigned one word to listen for. In a social studies unit, third-grade teacher Lauren Viscardi's students brought in such sentences as

"The census shows we're an *immigrant* nation," found in a magazine. Lisa Kadam's advanced sixth graders did the Find That Word strategy with word such as *conspirators*, which were found in Shakespeare's play *Julius Caesar*. Ms. Kadam asked students to compare the way that word and others were used in the Find That Word sentence and in the play (Herzberg & Forman, 2001).

Putting These Ideas to Work

These six strategies help students to learn words by processing them actively in rich instruction and to retain words through engaging review, as suggested by the National Reading Panel (NICHD, 2000). The benefits of such vocabulary instruction can extend throughout the entire school curriculum. Semantic Impressions has been used with social studies narratives and biographies. It develops facility in narrative writing and editing. Word Expert Cards are suitable for any curriculum area that features extensive terminology, including social studies, science, mathematics, health, and English as a Second Language, as well as reading and literature.

The review strategies are invaluable across the school curriculum. Teacher Carrie Froeter used Anything Goes to review words across four subject areas. Connect Two and Two in One have commonly been used in social studies and science, as teachers ask students to synthesize knowledge by forming relationships between words that encapsulate important concepts. Find That Word reinforces vocabulary in a variety of subjects by asking students to record encounters of words in their environments. This process demonstrates the relevance of school learning to the outside world.

The six strategies also offer assessment opportunities to the teacher. By observing students, the teacher can find words that seem difficult to use in Semantic Impressions or challenging to define and teach in Word Expert Cards. This vocabulary can receive additional instructional focus. Student confidence and comfort in the four review strategies provide invaluable hints to words that are difficult or, conversely, those that are easily mastered. I may keep checkmarks on cards or a piece of paper to monitor successful student use of words for Anything Goes, Connect Two, Two in One, and Find That Word. Words that are used often and successfully are gradually eliminated. Words that students struggle with, or that are infrequently chosen for use, receive more instruction.

The strategies presented in this article have helped my students to learn meaning vocabulary effectively and enthusiastically. They have even empowered students to seek out unknown words. My students start to see vocabulary learning as a source of enjoyment rather than as a boring or threatening burden. They look forward to learning new words because words are wonderful!

References

Anderson, R.C., & Freebody, P. (1981). Vocabulary knowledge. In J. Guthrie (Ed.), *Comprehension and teaching: Research reviews* (pp. 77–117). Newark, DE: International Reading Association.

Banks, L.R. (1980). *The Indian in the cupboard*. Garden City, NY: Doubleday.

Barrett, J. (1978). *Cloudy with a chance of meatballs*. New York: Macmillan.

Baumann, J.F., Kame'enui, E.J., & Ash, G.E. (2003). Research on vocabulary instruction: Voltare redux. In J. Flood, D. Lapp, J.R. Squire, & J.M. Jensen (Eds.), *Handbook of research on the teaching of the English language arts* (2nd ed., pp. 752–785). Mahwah, NJ: Erlbaum.

Beck, I.L., McKeown, M.G., & Kucan, L. (2002). *Bringing words to life: Robust vocabulary instruction*. New York: Guilford.

Blachowicz, C.L.Z., & Fisher, P. (2000). Vocabulary instruction. In M.L. Kamil, P.B. Mosenthal, P.D. Pearson, & R. Barr (Eds.), *Handbook of reading research* (Vol. 3, pp. 503–523). Mahwah, NJ: Erlbaum.

[Blachowicz, C.L.Z., & Lee, J. (1991). Vocabulary development in the whole literacy classroom. *The Reading Teacher, 45*, 188–195.]

Buss, F.L. (1991). *Journey of the sparrows*. New York: Penguin Putnam.

Cunningham, P.M. (2000). *Phonics they use* (3rd ed.). New York: Longman.

Daneman, M. (1991). Individual differences in reading skills. In R. Barr, M.L. Kamil, P.B. Mosenthal, & P.D. Pearson (Eds.), *Handbook of reading research* (Vol. 2, pp. 512–538). White Plains, NY: Longman.

Hart, B., & Risley, T.R. (1995). *Meaningful differences in the everyday experience of young American children*. Baltimore: Paul H. Brookes.

Herzberg, D. (Producer) & Forman, K.W. (Director). (2001). *Vocabulary strategies that boost students' reading comprehension* [Motion picture]. (Available from the Bureau of Education & Research, PO Box 96068, Bellevue, WA 98009).

Hooks, W.H. (1990). *The ballad of Belle Dorcas*. New York: Knopf.

Lansdown, S. (1991). Increasing vocabulary knowledge using direct instruction, cooperative grouping, and reading in junior high school. *Illinois Reading Council Journal*, *19*(4), 15–21.

Mason, J.A., Stahl, S.A., Au, K.H., & Herman, P.A. (2003). Reading: Children's developing knowledge of words. In J. Flood, D. Lapp, J.R. Squire, & J.M. Jensen (Eds.), *Handbook of research on the teaching of the English language arts* (2nd ed., pp. 914–930). Mahwah, NJ: Erlbaum.

McGinley, W.J., & Denner, P.R. (1987). Story impressions: A prereading/writing activity. *Journal of Reading*, *31*, 248–254.

McKeown, M.C. (1993). Creating effective definitions for young word learners. *Reading Research Quarterly*, *28*, 16–31.

Nagy, W., & Anderson, R.C. (1984). How many words are there in printed school English? *Reading Research Quarterly*, *19*, 304–330.

Nagy, W.E., Anderson, R.C., & Herman, P.A. (1987). Learning word meanings from context during normal reading. *American Educational Research Journal*, *24*, 237–270.

Nagy, W.E., & Scott, J.A. (2000). Vocabulary processes. In M.L. Kamil, P.B. Mosenthal, P.D. Pearson, & R. Barr (Eds.), *Handbook of reading research* (Vol. 3, pp. 269–284). Mahwah, NJ: Erlbaum.

National Institute of Child Health and Human Development. (2000). *Report of the National Reading Panel. Teaching children to read: An evidence-based assessment of the scientific research literature on reading and its implications for reading instruction* (NIH Publication No. 00-4769). Washington, DC: U.S. Government Printing Office.

Stahl, S., & Fairbanks, M. (1986). The effects of vocabulary instruction: A model-based meta-analysis. *Review of Educational Research*, *56*(1), 72–110.

Steig, W. (1986). *Brave Irene*. New York: Farrar Straus Giroux.

Sternberg, R.B. (1987). Most vocabulary is learned from context. In M.G. McKeown & M.E. Curtis (Eds.), *The nature of vocabulary acquisition* (pp. 89–105). Mahwah, NJ: Erlbaum.

Questions for Reflection

• Semantic Impressions is described initially as a whole-class activity, but sometimes classroom management benefits from different sorts of student groupings. How could the activity be modified for use entirely in small groups or by individual students? What would be gained—or lost—in such grouping structures?

• Think about the diversity of students in your class. For the Word Expert Cards activity, how might you best form student pairs for the peer teaching component? For example, how might you guide students to support the English-language learners in your class? How will you ensure that your lower achieving students have appropriate support?

Teaching Elementary Students to Use Word-Part Clues

Thomas G. White, Joanne Sowell, and Alice Yanagihara

Much of the vocabulary explosion that begins around 4th grade is due to words with a prefix, suffix, or both (Nagy & Anderson, 1984). To prepare children for this onslaught of affixed words, educators and basal publishers routinely endorse the teaching of prefixes and suffixes. Long lists of affixes are everywhere, accompanied by countless workbook exercises. It is easy for students (and perhaps teachers) to lose sight of the goal: actively *using* word-part clues to derive all or part of the meaning of unfamiliar words.

In a climate that generally scorns the teaching of isolated skills, we would not argue for the elimination of affix teaching. Instead we would limit the number of affixes to be taught, and emphasize application of affix knowledge to unfamiliar words.

To teach use of word-part clues, answers to two questions are needed. First, which prefixes and suffixes need to be taught, and when? Second, just how should this be done?

Which Prefixes?

Which prefixes should be taught? No firm answers to this question exist. Only Stauffer (1942) did an actual count of prefixes, but he used a corpus of words that may not be representative of printed materials in use in schools today, and included such initial elements as *ad-*, *ab-*, and *com-*. In most cases, these elements are not true prefixes because no familiar English word is left

when they are "peeled off"—e.g., removing *ad-* from *adjacent* leaves "jacent" (Marchand, 1969; Stotsky, 1977). Moreover, they are probably not useful to students who have just begun to learn about prefixes.

We believe that frequency of occurrence is an important factor to weigh in decisions about prefix teaching. Table 1 shows the results of a count of prefixed words appearing in the *Word Frequency Book* (Carroll, Davies, & Richman, 1971), a large corpus representing printed American school English for grades 3–9. Observe the separate counts for *in-* meaning "not" and *in-* meaning "in or into." We regard these as different prefixes rather than different meanings of the same prefix.

What is striking about these data is that a handful of prefixes account for a large percentage of the prefixed words. The prefix *un-* alone accounts for 26% of the total. More than half (51%) of the total is explained by the top three prefixes, *un-*, *re-*, and *in-* "not." And with just four prefixes, *un-*, *re-*, *in-* "not," and *dis-*, one could cover approximately three-fifths of the prefixed words (58%).

Thus, four prefixes appear to be strong candidates for instruction if their meanings are not already known. In fact, we found in another study that three of these "big four" prefixes were unknown by the majority of a sample of 3rd and 4th graders on at least one test, while *un-* meaning "not" was known by just 63% of the students (White, Speidel, & Power, 1987).

Reprinted from White, T.G., Sowell, J., & Yanagihara, A. (1989). Teaching elementary students to use word-part clues. *The Reading Teacher, 42*(4), 302-308.

Table 1
The Most Common Prefixes in Printed School English for Grades 3-9

Rank	Prefix	Number of different words with the prefix*	Percentage
1	*un-*	782	26
2	*re-*	401	14
3	*in-, im-, ir-, il-,* "not"	313	11
4	*dis-*	216	7
5	*en-, em-*	132	4
6	*non-*	126	4
7	*in-, im-,* "in or into"	105	4
8	*over-* "too much"	98	3
9	*mis-*	83	3
10	*sub-*	80	3
11	*pre-*	79	3
12	*inter-*	77	3
13	*fore-*	76	3
14	*de-*	71	2
15	*trans-*	47	2
16	*super-*	43	1
17	*semi-*	39	1
18	*anti-*	33	1
19	*mid-*	33	1
20	*under-* "too little"	25	1
	All others	100 (estimated)	3
Total		2,959	100%

* From John B. Carroll, Peter Davies, and Barry Richman, *The American Heritage Word Frequency Book*, Boston, MA: Houghton Mifflin, 1971.

Which Suffixes?

Suffix frequencies have been studied before, too. Harwood and Wright (1956) counted suffixes, but excluded common inflectional suffixes such as *-s* and *-ing*.

Table 2 shows the 20 most frequent suffixes occurring in a random sample of 2,167 suffixed words drawn from 60 randomly selected pages of the *Word Frequency Book*. A word was considered suffixed if an English base word was left when the (apparent) suffix was removed (thus *deity* was not regarded as a suffixed word). If a word had two or more suffixes, each was counted.

It was not possible to distinguish plural *-s/-es* (e.g., *students*) and third singular *-s/-es*

(e.g., *reads*) due to ambiguous cases (*leaves*). Comparative *-er* and agentive *-er*, however, were distinguished.

It is plain from Table 2 that the distribution of suffixes, too, is not uniform. The first 10 suffixes listed comprise 85% of the sample. Plural and/or third person singular *-s/-es* alone account for about a third (31%) of the sample. Three inflectional suffixes, *-s/-es*, *-ed*, and *-ing*, account for 65%. In light of this, middle elementary teachers would do well to concentrate on *-s/-es*, *-ed*, and *-ing*.

We now have a good idea of the prefixes and suffixes that deserve emphasis. How do we teach students to use affix knowledge?

Table 2
English Suffixes Ranked by Frequency of Occurrence

Rank	Suffix	Number of occurrences in sample	Percentage
1	-s, -es	673	31
2	-ed	435	20
3	-ing	303	14
4	-ly	144	7
5	-er, -or (agentive)	95	4
6	-ion, -tion, -ation, -ition	76	4
7	-ible, -able	33	2
8	-al, -ial	30	1
9	-y	27	1
10	-ness	26	1
11	-ity, -ty	23	1
12	-ment	21	1
13	-ic	18	1
14	-ous, -eous, -ious	18	1
15	-en	15	1
16	-er (comparative)	15	1
17	-ive, -ative, -itive	15	1
18	-ful	14	1
19	-less	14	1
20	-est	12	1
	All others	160	7
Total		2,167	100%*

The sample consisted of the 2,167 suffixed words appearing in 60 randomly selected pages in John B. Carroll, Peter Davies, and Barry Richman, *The American Heritage Word Frequency Book*, Boston, MA: Houghton Mifflin, 1971.

* The total actually exceeds 100% due to rounding upward on items in ranks 13-20.

Prefix Pitfalls

Teachers need to be aware of three complications in teaching application of prefix meanings.

First, most prefixes are not consistent in meaning. Each of the "big four" (*un-*, *re-*, *in-*, and *dis-*) has at least two distinct meanings. For *un-* and *dis-*, there is both a negative meaning— "not" as in *unhappy*, and a so-called "reversative" meaning—"do the opposite," as in *untie*. *In-* means both "not" (as in *incorrectly*) and "in or into" (*insight*). *Re-* can mean either "again" (*replaying*) or "back" (*replacement*).

The second difficulty is false analysis. This can occur when removal of a "prefix" leaves no recognizable base word (e.g., *intrigue*) or a word

that is unrelated in meaning to the whole word that existed prior to removal (e.g., *invented*). For *re-*, *in-*, and to a lesser extent *dis-*, there is for students a relatively high risk of false analysis.

In fact, about three-fourths of the words beginning with the letters *re-* and *in-* are not prefixed words at all, and about half of the words beginning with *dis-* are not true prefixed words. To make matters worse in the case of *in-*, the student must cope with alternate spellings that have the same meaning, namely, *im-*, *ir-*, and *il-*.

The third and last pitfall is that if students consider *only* word-part clues (affixes and roots) when dealing with unfamiliar prefixed words, they may be misled about the true meaning of

Table 3		
Possible Prefix Lessons, With Suggested Grade Levels		
Lesson	**Grade level**	**Content**
1	4	The concept of a prefix: instances and noninstances
2	4	Prefixes meaning "not": *un-*; *dis-*
3	4	Prefixes meaning "not": *in-, im-, ir-, non-*
4	5	A prefix meaning "again" or "back": *re-*
5	5	Alernative meanings of *un-*; *dis-*; *in-, im-*
6	5	Three more useful prefixes: *en-, em-; over-; mis-*

a word. For example, they may think that *un-assuming* means "not supposing" instead of modest, or that *indelicate* means "not fragile" instead of offensive. White, Power, and White (1988; see also Nagy & Anderson, 1984) estimate that about 15–20% of the prefixed words in printed school materials are like this.

Although teachers should be wary of these problems, they need not be overly discouraged. We believe the above complications can be treated effectively in a set of thoughtfully constructed lessons, described below and outlined in Table 3.

Lessons on Prefixes

Stotsky (1977) found a good deal of confusion over what a prefix is in the six basal series she reviewed. In light of this, we would begin Lesson 1 by explicitly defining and teaching the concept of a prefix by presenting examples and nonexamples.

Thus, the teacher writes "What is a prefix?" on chart paper and, below it, the following: (1) A prefix is a group of letters that go in front of a word. (2) It changes the meaning of a word. (3) When you peel it off, a word must be left.

Feature (3) is demonstrated by constrasting genuine prefixed words (*unkind, refill,* etc.) with tricksters (nonexample words like *uncle* and *reason*). Students taught in this way may begin with a clear idea of what a prefix is.

As shown in Table 3, Lesson 2 teaches the negative meanings of *un-* and *dis-*, and Lesson 3 teaches the negative meanings of *in-* and *non-*.

The reason for choosing *non-* instead of *re-* or perhaps *en-* at this early stage is partly convenience, since *non-* has the same meaning as *in-*, and partly that *non-* has a very favorable ratio of prefixed to nonprefixed words beginning with the same letters.

Notice also that only two of the alternate forms of *in-* are included in this lesson. We found just 9 prefixed words beginning with *il-* in the *Word Frequency Book*, so *il-* does not seem worth the effort.

Lesson 4 focuses on the two meanings of *re-*, "again" and "back." Lesson 5 returns to *un-, dis-,* and *in-*, teaching their less common meanings: the reversative meaning of "do the opposite" for *un-* and *dis-*, and "in or into" for *in-* or *im-*. Finally, Lesson 6 presents three more useful prefixes and their meanings: *en- (em-), over-,* and *mis-*.

Before teaching Lessons 2–6, we would prepare sentences containing prefixed words on chart paper or overhead transparencies. Some of the roots of the prefixed words would be familiar and some unfamiliar. At least half of the prefixed words would be suffixed, because most prefixed words do have a suffix also (White, Power, & White, 1988).

Imagine this sentence is displayed for students:

> John didn't come home when he was told; he disobeyed his father.

The teacher would ask "What word looks as if it has a prefix?" and "When you peel off *dis-*, is there a word left?"

The rest of the dialogue might go something like this: "What does *obey* mean? Did John obey his father? So what does *dis-* mean here? And *disobeyed* means what? Does that makes sense? Remember, when you try to figure out words with a prefix, you should always check to see that the meaning makes sense."

Examples of words which reveal that a simple "prefix + base" analysis does not always work could be included in the lessons: "Does *disarm* mean 'something that is not an arm'?"

How Many/Which Grade Levels

Once Lessons 1–6 have been completed, should there be more lessons covering additional prefixes? We think not. The 9 prefixes and meanings in these lessons cover more than three-quarters (76%) of the prefixed words in the *Word Frequency Book*. The remaining 24% are best taught as the need or opportunity arises. For example, when the word *subarctic* crops up in a geography lesson, the teacher should point out that *sub-* is a prefix that means, among other things, "below."

To limit prefix instruction to 9 prefixes is not the usual advice teachers receive. Johnson and Pearson (1978), for instance, present a list of 19 prefixes. Stotsky (1977) lists 25 prefixes that were included in two or more of the six basals she investigated. And Fry, Polk, and Fountoukidis (1984) display a list of 77 prefixes without commenting on appropriate grade levels.

As to the question of grade levels, our recommendation, for average and below average students, is to complete Lessons 1–3 by the end of grade 4 and Lessons 4–6 by the end of grade 5.

Brighter students reading above grade level might begin earlier, perhaps at the end of grade 3, and move through the lessons more rapidly.

These suggestions are based on White, Power, and White's (1988) estimates of the benefits of teaching 3rd and 4th graders to apply the "big four" prefix meanings to unfamiliar words. In these estimates, several factors are taken into account: the frequency of prefixed words in 3rd and 4th grade reading material, amount of reading, and knowledge of the meaning of root words.

Suffix Removal and Roots

The meaning of English suffixes is often abstract or redundant with contextual cues because they serve a mostly grammatical purpose. For this reason, many reading educators assume that with a few exceptions such as *-less* and *-able*, suffix meanings need not be taught, or that at best it is not useful or appropriate to teach suffix meanings until grade 6 or later (see, e.g., Thorndike, 1941).

Nevertheless, middle elementary students should know how to dismantle suffixed words so they can identify familiar and meaningful base or root words. Thus, the primary focus of suffix teaching during the middle elementary years is suffix removal and root identification.

A simple procedure for teaching these skills is as follows. In an initial lesson, teach the concept of a suffix in the same manner as the prefix concept (above). In the next lesson or two, present suffixed words that show no spelling change from the base word: *blows, boxes, talking, faster, lasted, sweetly, comical, rainy*, etc. For each word, simply (1) ask students whether there is a suffix, (2) have them write the suffix in a blank next to the word, and (3) ask them to take the suffix off and then write the root word below the suffixed word.

We suggest, in addition, one or more lessons illustrating each of the three major kinds of spelling change that occur in suffixation: (1) consonant doubling (*thinner, swimming, begged, funny*), (2) *y* to *i* (*worried, flies, busily, reliable, loneliness*), and (3) deleted silent *e* (*baking, saved, rider, believable, refusal, breezy*).

The same three steps as above are followed, except now the teacher explains that sometimes when you take the suffix off a word, there is something left that looks like a word you know, but to make it right you must take off a letter (in the case of consonant doubling), change a letter (*i* back to *y*), or add a letter (silent *e*).

In view of the data in Table 2, it is recommended that these lessons contain numerous examples of words that end with one of three inflectional suffixes: *-s/-es, -ed*, or *-ing*. However, not all root identification practice should consist of inflectionally suffixed words. At minimum, words illustrating the following derivational (i.e., part-of-speech-altering) suffixes probably should be included as well: -ly, -er, -ion, -able, -al, -y, and -ness.

These 7 suffixes round out the top 10 suffixes that accounted for 85% of our sample of suffixed words. In addition, we found that at least one-quarter of a sample of 147 dialect speaking 3rd and 4th graders did not recognize them as suffixes. The 10th suffix, -ness, was recognized by 91% of these students, but it may be worth reviewing anyway.

Evidence for Effectiveness

Two instructional studies have validated the approach we are advocating. In one study, we constructed a set of lessons and materials to: (a) teach the meanings of 9 prefixes and their application to novel prefixed words, and (b) provide suffix removal and root identification practice on words ending with -s/-es, -ed, -ing, and 10 other common suffixes.

A 3rd grade teacher at a private school enrolling Hawaiian and part Hawaiian children used the lessons with her top three reading groups twice weekly for 7–8 weeks. Following instruction, four tests were given to these students and a control group: a root identification test, a multiple choice test of knowledge of prefix meanings, and two transfer tests.

Transfer Test 1 required students to apply knowledge of prefix meanings to unfamiliar prefixed words, given the meaning of a base word. For example: "If *scrupulous* means 'lawful or honest,' then *unscrupulous* means..." followed by four more choices.

On a more stringent Transfer Test 2, students were asked to define 10 prefixed words occurring in sentence contexts. Most of these were rare words occurring once or less in the *Word Frequency Book* (e.g., *irreversible*, *nonconforming*, *rekindle*, *unendurable*).

The results, summarized in Table 4, were very favorable. On each test, the scores of students who received the lessons were significantly higher than those of students in the control group.

In the second study, Nicol, Graves, and Slater (1984) used lessons very much like ours to teach 4th, 5th, and 6th graders 8 prefix meanings in three half hour lessons. Students receiving this instruction showed substantial gains on a transfer test like Transfer Test 1 (above): 80% correct versus 57% for a noninstructed group. These gains were maintained on a delayed posttest given three weeks later.

Deliberate, Systematic Teaching

We suggest that, for middle elementary students, deliberate or systematic (as opposed to opportunistic) affix teaching can be limited to 9 frequently occurring prefixes and 10 frequently occurring suffixes. These affixes are sufficient to cover about 75% of the prefixed words and 85% of the suffixed words in printed school English for grades 3–9.

Table 4
Percentage of Correct Responses by 3rd Graders on Posttests

Test	Instructed group*	Control group†
Identification of root words	71%	53%
Prefix meanings	84	43
Transfer test 1–applying prefix knowledge to unfamiliar words	82	54
Transfer test 2–defining 10 unfamiliar prefixed words in context	23	6

* N=16, 17, 17, 17 for the four tests, respectively.
† N=19, 20, 20, 15 for the four tests, respectively.

We stress that the goal of prefix and suffix instruction is *use* of word-part clues to derive the meaning of unfamiliar words. An application strategy can be directly and effectively taught through lessons such as the ones described here.

Almost 50 years ago E.L. Thorndike wrote, concerning the teaching of derivational suffix meanings to secondary students and adults, that "a reasonable amount of deliberate and systematic teaching, if based on adequate knowledge and planned and carried out wisely, can retain [the] merits [of incidental learning], economize time in learning the mother tongue, and give some useful ideas about language in general (1941, p. 65). This quotation seems to apply, as well, to the teaching of prefix meanings and root identification to middle elementary students. One of the key phrases is "reasonable amount."

The second key phrase in the Thorndike quote is "useful ideas about language." Effective teachers, we submit, will not only teach application of word-part clues in lessons like ours but will also encourage use of a word-part strategy throughout the day in circumstances that reveal its value to students.

References

Carroll, J.B., Davies, P., & Richman, B. (1971). *The American Heritage word frequency book*. Boston, MA: Houghton Mifflin.

Fry, E.B., Polk, J.K., & Foutoukidis, D. (1984). *The reading teacher's book of lists*. Englewood Cliffs, NJ: Prentice Hall.

Harwood, F.W., & Wright, A.M. (1956). Statistical study of English word formation. *Language, 32*(2), 260–273.

Johnson, D.D., & Pearson, P.D. (1978). *Teaching reading vocabulary*. New York: Holt, Rinehart & Winston.

Marchand, H. (1969). *The categories and types of present-day English word-formation* (2nd ed.). Munich, West Germany: C.H. Beck.

Nagy, W.E., & Anderson, R.C. (1984). How many words are there in printed school English? *Reading Research Quarterly, 19*(3), 304–330.

Nicol, J.E., Graves, M.F., & Slater, W.H. (1984). *Building vocabulary through prefix instruction*. Unpublished paper, University of Minnesota, Minneapolis.

Stauffer, R.G. (1942). A study of prefixes in the Thorndike list to establish a list of prefixes that should be taught in the elementary school. *Journal of Educational Research, 35*(6), 453–458.

Stotsky, S.L. (1977). *Teaching prefixes: Facts and fallacies. Language Arts, 54*(8), 887–890.

Thorndike, E.L. (1941). *The teaching of English suffixes*. New York: Teachers College, Columbia University, Bureau of Publications.

White, T.G., Power, M.A., & White, S. (1988). *Morphological analysis: Implications for teaching and understanding vocabulary growth*. Unpublished paper, Kamehameha Schools/Center for Development of Early Education, Honolulu, HI.

White, T.G., Speidel, G.E., & Power, M.A. (1987, April). *An empirical basis for teaching morphological analysis to middle elementary students*. Paper presented to the American Educational Research Association, Washington, D.C.

Questions for Reflection

- Do your students know the meaning of the most frequently occurring prefixes in printed school English for grades 3–9 (Table 1)? Can they apply their knowledge of these prefix meanings to unfamiliar words?

- Can your students identify root words by removing the most common English suffixes (Table 2)?

- For upper elementary students, the authors recommend lessons covering the nine most frequently occurring prefixes and "opportunistic" teaching of the meanings of the other prefixes in Table 1. How should affix teaching (if any) be different for younger or older students? What about Greek and Latin prefixes?

Breaking Down Words to Build Meaning: Morphology, Vocabulary, and Reading Comprehension in the Urban Classroom

Michael J. Kieffer and Nonie K. Lesaux

Ms. Jenkins (all names are pseudonyms) reads a newspaper article regarding a recent poll of public opinion about the U.S. President with her fourth-grade class. She stops to pose a question, "What does *popularity* mean?" The room is silent for a few moments as the 9- and 10-year-olds put their minds to work. Antonio, a student known more for the frequency of his answers than their accuracy, raises his hand. "It's like something about the president." "OK," Ms. Jenkins notes. "Can anyone add to what Antonio said?"

Ms. Jenkins faces a sea of furrowed brows and blank stares. She glances at the clock on the wall and begins to wonder if they will make it through the text before lunch. After a long silence, Brenda responds. "It's what the people think about the President, like how much they like him," she suggests. "Great, Brenda. You're right, how did you figure that out?" "Well," Brenda pauses. "I looked at it for a while, trying to find a word inside it that I do know like you told us to do last week—and I found the word *popular*. A popular kid is, you know, a kid that people like, so I figured that *popularity* must have to do with that." "Good work, Brenda, in attacking that word to find a part that you know. Did anyone try something different?" After a longer pause, Rafael raises his hand, "Well, I did what Brenda did. But when you say *popular* I think of Spanish, and it's *como popular.* And when on

television they say *el Presidente es popular*, it means they like him."

The scene above resonates with many teachers we know. As students read challenging texts, especially those in the content areas, they encounter increasingly complex words. When confronting a novel word, many students are like Antonio—they have a vague notion of what the word means, but they lack a specific understanding of it, and others may not recognize the word at all. As a result, students' comprehension of a text may suffer. Without a firm grasp on the definition of a key word such as *popularity*, many students like Antonio are likely to miss the meaning of the passage. Even when teachers provide appropriate scaffolding with respect to decoding these words by reading them aloud, students with limited vocabularies may not be able to access the meaning of the text (Anderson & Freebody, 1981; RAND Reading Study Group, 2002).

Research evidence confirms what many teachers know—students who reach fourth grade with limited vocabularies are very likely to struggle to understand grade-level texts (e.g., Chall & Jacobs, 2003; National Institute of Child Health and Human Development, 2000; RAND Reading Study Group, 2002; Biancarosa & Snow, 2004). Unfortunately, this is often the case in urban or low-income schools in the United States. Even before they arrive at school, students in low-income neighborhoods tend to have smaller vocabularies

Reprinted from Kieffer, M.J., & Lesaux, N.K. (2007). Breaking down words to build meaning: Morphology, vocabulary, and reading comprehension in the urban classroom. *The Reading Teacher, 61*(2), 134–144. doi: 10.1598/RT.61.2.3

than their counterparts in high-income schools, and this gap tends to increase with time (Hart & Risley, 1995; Molfese, Modglin, & Molfese, 2003; Organization for Economic Co-operation and Development, 2000). Along with many others, Rupley, Logan, and Nichols (1998/1999) argued that vocabulary is an essential and often overlooked component in any balanced literacy program, a sentiment increasingly recognized in recent years (Cassidy & Cassidy, 2005/2006).

A large and rapidly growing segment of students in urban schools in the United States are English-language learners (ELLs). These learners are particularly likely to lack the English vocabulary they need to comprehend difficult texts (August, Carlo, Dressler, & Snow, 2005). An increasing number of ELLs are students who immigrated before kindergarten age or who are the U.S.-born children of immigrants (August & Hakuta, 1997). By the fourth grade, most of these students have acquired the basic, interpersonal English they need to communicate with their classmates and teachers, but continue to lack the academic English vocabulary to comprehend content area texts. These learners, along with many of their native English-speaking classmates, require thoughtful, targeted instruction in academic English vocabulary in upper elementary school.

Despite their limited vocabularies, some students have effective strategies for learning new words, and these strategies can and should be taught to others. Effective word-learners attack unknown words, break them into their meaningful parts, hypothesize meanings for the larger words, and then check their meanings against the context of the text as well as their own background knowledge (Anderson & Nagy, 1992; Freyd & Baron, 1982). In the process, they use their knowledge of high-frequency root words to access low-frequency words. For example, Brenda can use the root word *popular*, a word that is commonly heard on the playground, to access the more infrequent word *popularity*. Because many of the difficult words that students encounter contain root words that are more commonly known, this strategy can be very powerful. Spanish-speaking ELLs, like Rafael,

who have a developed knowledge of their first language, can use their knowledge of word parts in that language to understand English words. In each of these cases, the children are using their ability to think about the forms of language to derive meaning.

Considering the limited vocabularies of many students in urban schools, equipping them with effective strategies for learning new words is essential. Instruction that provides these strategies is crucial for ELLs and for many of their classmates in urban schools who face similar struggles with reading comprehension.

In this article, we describe what reading research can tell educators about the role of word-attack strategies in reading comprehension. In particular, our recent study with urban fourth- and fifth-graders in California suggests that breaking down words into meaningful parts is important for both Spanish-speaking ELLs and their native English-speaking classmates. We first explain what research says about vocabulary and reading comprehension, then describe the findings of our study, and finally suggest some general principles and specific activities with which teachers can improve their students' abilities to break down words to build up meaning.

What Does the Research Say?

Vocabulary, Comprehension, and the Fourth-Grade Slump

Decades ago, reading researcher Jeanne Chall identified a trend well known to teachers—many students succeed in learning to read and comprehend simple texts in the early grades, yet struggle to comprehend grade-level texts in the upper elementary years (Chall, 1983). Although it is not entirely clear what causes this "fourth-grade slump" or what factors put urban students at greater risk for these difficulties, there is a general consensus among researchers that vocabulary (Freebody & Anderson, 1983; RAND Reading Study Group, 2002), increasing word length and complexity (Juel, 1988), and differences in exposure to print each play a role (Cunningham & Stanovich, 1991). As the vocabulary demands of texts increase in the upper elementary and middle school grades, many students struggle with comprehension. A particular source of difficulty is their academic vocabulary—the words necessary to learn and talk about academic subjects. This academic vocabulary plays a more prominent role as students read to learn about science and social studies concepts in upper elementary and middle school.

Our own research and teaching in urban schools supports the importance of academic vocabulary in students' success or struggles. First author Michael Kieffer found that his students in an urban middle school lacked much of the vocabulary to read grade-level texts. Urban students with below average vocabularies need thoughtful and strategic vocabulary instruction.

Vocabulary and reading comprehension have a reciprocal relationship—as greater vocabulary leads to greater comprehension, better comprehension also leads to learning more vocabulary words (Stanovich, 1986)—and this relationship has major implications for the teaching of reading (Rupley, Logan, & Nichols, 1998/1999). Although most research in this area has been conducted with native English speakers, current studies suggest that a similar reciprocal relationship between reading and vocabulary exists for ELLs (García, 1991; Proctor, August, Carlo, & Snow, 2005).

Researchers emphasize the importance of vocabulary yet also point out that knowing a word well involves the combination of several different types of knowledge. In his clear and concise volume on vocabulary development, Stahl (1999) suggested that knowing a word means not only knowing its literal definition but also knowing its relationship to other words, its connotations in different contexts, and its power of transformation into various other forms. Students who can master these different aspects of knowing a word have strong depth of vocabulary knowledge, and students who are familiar with many words have breadth of vocabulary knowledge. Antonio, having been previously exposed to the word *popularity*, has a vague notion of what it means, but he lacks this depth of knowledge about the word;

with only a superficial understanding of this key word, his comprehension will likely suffer.

Closing the Word Gap

Although teachers and researchers agree on the importance of academic vocabulary, less consensus exists concerning how such vocabulary can be learned. Some emphasize wide-ranging free reading as the primary vehicle through which words are learned. For example, Anderson and Nagy (1992) argued that the word-learning task is enormous—they estimated that students reading on grade level learn between 2,000 and 3,000 new words a year—and therefore concluded that most words must be learned through context. In support of this argument, researchers described the strong correlation between students' volume of reading and their vocabulary knowledge (Cunningham & Stanovich, 1991).

Other researchers insist that explicit instruction (of at least some of the low- and medium-frequency words likely to challenge students) is crucial for vocabulary learning. Beck, McKeown, and Kucan (2002) argued that the information provided by context is often too limited or misleading to be reliable in effectively supporting students' learning of new words. The National Reading Panel (National Institute of Child Health and Human Development, 2000) supported this view, finding that direct instruction of vocabulary improves comprehension. They found insufficient evidence to prove that extensive reading programs such as Silent Sustained Reading improved vocabulary, at least when implemented without complementary instructional techniques.

A balanced approach to vocabulary instruction combines explicit instruction of a limited number of well-chosen words with instruction in strategies with which students can acquire words independently (Graves, 2006; Stahl, 1999; Stahl & Nagy, 2006). Implementing such an approach ultimately requires that teachers know how to teach specific words and know which strategies are the most efficient and effective for students to use when learning words independently. Not all strategies for learning words are made equal, nor will all strategies work for all learners. To identify those word-learning strategies that will best equip students to comprehend text, researchers have investigated the strategies that successful learners use naturally.

One way to identify effective strategies is to examine students' use of various strategies and to analyze how these strategies relate to students' performance on reading comprehension assessments. Although the average vocabulary level of students in urban schools is often below the national average, great differences exist among students' individual levels, suggesting that some urban school students are more successful in learning vocabulary than others. By examining what strategies average and above average word learners use regularly, differentiating them from below average word learners, one may be able to identify the tools that could help move all students forward in their vocabulary and comprehension. In our own research, we found that one such tool is morphology.

Morphology: What Is It and Why Does It Matter for Reading?

The word *morphology* can be broken down (morphologically) into two meaningful parts (known as *morphemes*): *morph-* meaning shape and *-ology* meaning the study of. Thus, morphology, in its most generic form, is the study of shape. In language and reading, morphology refers to the study of the structure of words, particularly the smallest units of meaning in words: morphemes. Morphemes are generally one of the two following types:

1. Bound morphemes, which are prefixes and suffixes that cannot stand alone as words, such as *geo-*, *re-*, and *-ity*

2. Unbound morphemes, which are roots within more complex words that can stand alone as words, such as *popular*

Bound morphemes that are suffixes are one of the two following types:

1. Inflection morphemes such as *-ed* and *-s* that change the tense or number of a word without changing its part of speech

2. Derivational morphemes such as *-ity* and *-tion* that change a word's part of speech

For example, adding *-ity* changes *popular* from an adjective to the noun *popularity*. When an inflectional morpheme is added, as in walk*ed*, we call the new word inflected whereas when a derivational morpheme is added, as in informa*tion*, we call the new word derived.

An understanding of word structure can be a powerful tool for students faced with the daunting task of acquiring academic vocabulary. A large number of the unfamiliar words that students encounter in printed school English could be understandable if students knew the more common root word and could break the complex word down (Nagy & Anderson, 1984). Because texts contain many of these complex but decipherable words, children's abilities to attack and dissect them are essential to their understanding of these texts.

Children develop awareness of morphology throughout their childhood and into their adolescence. Young children generally understand how inflectional morphemes (such as *-s* on plurals or *-ed* on past-tense verbs) are attached to words, whereas children in upper elementary school continue to develop understanding of how derivational morphemes connect to words (such as *-ity* on *popularity*; Tyler & Nagy, 1989). This development follows a relatively predictable sequence, although the rate at which students progress through the sequence varies considerably between children. As a result, students at a given grade level can be at very different levels in their awareness of morphology. Teachers can get some sense of where their students are on this developmental continuum by administering a developmental spelling inventory (for an example, see Bear, Invernezzi, Templeton, & Johnston, 2000).

A few studies have shown that understanding of derivational morphology is related to reading comprehension (Carlisle, 2000; Freyd & Baron, 1982; Nagy, Berninger, & Abbott, 2006). Because the ability to attack and dissect words is our particular focus, we will use the terms *morphology* and *breaking down words* interchangeably in the remainder of this article. Although there are many ways in which students can understand morphology, the ability to use morphology to attack novel words is the most promising for improving reading comprehension.

What Did We Investigate and What Did We Find?

Because the relationship between morphology and reading comprehension had primarily been studied among native English speakers in suburban contexts, we wondered whether this relationship also held up among Spanish-speaking English-language learners and native English speakers in an urban context. This research seems particularly important given the apparent difficulties that these populations have with acquiring vocabulary and comprehending academic text.

Our study examined how students' ability to break down words related to their vocabulary knowledge and reading comprehension in fourth and fifth grade. We also examined how this relationship changed between fourth and fifth grade. We collected data from 111 students (87 Spanish-speaking ELLs and 24 native English speakers) in a large urban district in southern California in both fourth and fifth grade. Students' understanding of morphology was assessed by asking them to extract the root word from a complex word to complete a sentence (e.g., students were given *popularity* and asked to complete "The girl wanted to be very _____"; see Table 1 for a list of the words used on the task). Students were also given a range of standardized tests assessing reading comprehension, word reading fluency, and vocabulary. We assessed reading comprehension with the Woodcock Language Proficiency Battery—Revised, Passage Comprehension subtest, which is a cloze test in which students provide a word to complete a passage; and the Gates-MacGinitie Reading Comprehension Test (1989), which is a traditional multiple-choice test. We assessed word reading fluency with the Test of Oral Word Reading Efficiency, Sight Word Efficiency subtest (1999), which is a timed test in which students read as many words of increasing difficulty as they can in 45 seconds. Vocabulary was assessed with the Peabody Picture Vocabulary Test (3rd edition),

which is a multiple-choice measure of receptive vocabulary knowledge in which students hear a word and choose an appropriate picture.

Following an analysis of these relationships in the context of reading development and instruction, we have two major findings about comprehension and vocabulary to report.

Morphology and Comprehension

We found that morphology was related to reading comprehension in both fourth and fifth grade, and became more important as students grew older. Students with greater understanding of morphology also have higher reading comprehension scores when holding constant their word reading fluency. Although this relationship was significant in fourth grade, it grew stronger in fifth grade, such that students' understanding of morphology was a better predictor of reading comprehension than their vocabulary level. In addition, we found that this relationship was the same for Spanish-speaking ELLs as for native English speakers in an urban setting. That is, morphology was equally important for reading comprehension in both populations of students.

Vocabulary and Morphology

Students with larger vocabularies tended to have greater understanding of morphology. As with the relationship between reading and vocabulary development, the relationship between vocabulary and morphology appears to be reciprocal. Understanding morphology may help students broaden their vocabularies, and vocabulary growth may improve students' understanding of morphology. This suggests that teaching morphology may work well with other types of context-rich and thoughtful vocabulary instruction to improve students' reading and language outcomes.

As shown in Table 1, some of the items on the morphology task were more difficult for students than other items. The following three factors influenced the difficulty of the items:

1. Whether they required a change in sound to go from the derived word to the root (e.g., *popularity* to *popular*)

Table 1
Items on Fourth-Grade Morphology Test in Order From Least to Most Difficult
With Spanish-English Cognates in Bold and Cognate Suffixes in Italics

Derived word	Root word	Root frequency (from www.wordcount.com)	Changes required
Runner	Run	High	Spelling
Growth	Grow	Medium	None
Dryer	Dry	High	None
Swimmer	Swim	Low	Spelling
Fourth	Four	High	None
Teacher	Teach	Medium	None
Discus*sion*	**Discuss**	Medium	Sound *Originality*
Originality	**Original**	High	Sound
Popularity	**Popular**	High	Sound
Baker	Bake	Low	Spelling
Courag*eous*	Courage	Medium	Sound
Fifth	Five	High	Sound, Spelling
Posses*sion*	**Possess**	Low	Sound
Activity	**Active**	Medium	Spelling
Divi*sion*	**Divide**	Medium	Sound, Spelling
Width	Wide	High	Sound, Spelling
Deci*sion*	**Decide**	Medium	Sound, Spelling
Availability	Available	High	Sound, Spelling
Glori*ous*	**Glory**	Medium	Spelling
Strength	Strong	High	Sound, Spelling
Fam*ous*	**Fame**	Low	Spelling
Admis*sion*	**Admit**	Medium	Sound, Spelling
Density	**Dense**	Low	Spelling
Furi*ous*	**Fury**	Low	Spelling

2. Whether the word required a change in spelling (e.g., from *swimmer* to *swim*)

3. The frequency of the root word

As shown in Table 1, items that required both spelling and sound changes (e.g., *strength* to *strong*) were among the most difficult. Items that also included less frequent root words (e.g., from *furious* to *fury*) tended to also be difficult for students. The easiest items had common root words and did not require changes in spelling (e.g., *dryer* to *dry*, *growth* to *grow*). This finding suggests that teachers may need to point out to students how some derived words relate to their roots. Although students may automatically see the connection between *dry* and *dryer*, they may

need to be taught to recognize that *strength* and *strong* are related. The findings also suggest that for some words, students need to be taught the meaning of the root even before they learn about its relationship with the derived word. Teaching students to recognize *fury* within *furious* can only be helpful if they first learn the meaning of *fury*.

The conclusion that students with greater understanding of morphology are more successful at learning academic vocabulary and comprehending text is a strong argument for including morphology instruction in language and literacy programs, especially in urban settings. This conclusion also raises important instructional questions regarding how teachers ought to go about teaching morphology in the context of general vocabulary instruction.

So, What Does Good Morphology Teaching Look Like?

We recommend four principles for teaching morphology to improve students' vocabulary and reading comprehension. These recommendations are based on the research findings described above, the frameworks and programs put forth by vocabulary experts in the field, and our own experiences working in urban schools.

Principle 1: Teach Morphology in the Context of Rich, Explicit Vocabulary Instruction

Our findings suggest that understanding morphology is related to, but also distinct from, overall vocabulary. Therefore, it makes sense that morphology strategies should be taught within the context of a comprehensive program of vocabulary improvement, but as a *distinct* component of that program. Although a complete discussion of effective vocabulary instruction is not possible here, it is worth summarizing some of the key elements that make up rich, explicit vocabulary instruction, with an emphasis on how morphology may fit into such a program.

Vocabulary instruction has been conceptualized in several different ways. In their classic meta-analysis on vocabulary instruction, Stahl and Fairbanks (1986) found that the most effective approaches provided multiple exposures to words, introduced the words in meaningful contexts, and involved students in deep processing of the words' meanings. By synthesizing results from 52 studies on the topic, they found that these methods had substantial effects not only on vocabulary knowledge, but also on students' reading comprehension.

Similarly, Beck, McKeown, and Kucan (2002) defined what they call "robust vocabulary instruction" as vigorous, strong, and powerful instruction that "involves directly explaining the meanings of words along with thought-provoking, playful, and interactive follow-up" (p. 2). They suggested that teachers choose useful, academic words that appear in a wide variety of texts, provide student-friendly explanations for them, create instructional contexts that supply useful information about new words, and engage students in actively dealing with word meanings. Although they did not address morphology in particular, they highlighted the importance of teaching relationships among words. Teachers should emphasize the relationships among words based on their shared roots, prefixes, or suffixes.

In his recent book, Graves (2006) suggested that a comprehensive vocabulary program would include activities that serve the following four functions:

1. To provide students with "rich and varied language experiences" (p. 38)
2. To teach a relatively small number of well-selected individual words directly
3. To teach word learning strategies, including morphology, dictionary skills, and the use of context clues
4. To foster "word consciousness," that is, students' "awareness of and interest in words and their meanings" (p. 119)

In this framework, understanding of morphology is firmly contextualized alongside other strategies for word learning.

Addressing the specific needs of ELLs, Carlo et al. (2004) suggested four principles that underlie an effective vocabulary program for these learners.

1. New words should be taught in meaningful contexts.
2. Words should be encountered in a variety of contexts.
3. Word knowledge involves depth of meaning as well as spelling, pronunciation, morphology, and syntax.
4. Native Spanish speakers should have access to the text's meaning in Spanish.

From this perspective, morphology is considered both a component of knowing a word well and a strategy for learning new words.

Principle 2: Teach Students to Use Morphology as a Cognitive Strategy With Explicit Steps

Our findings, along with those of other researchers, suggest that using morphology to manipulate words is best understood as a cognitive strategy to be learned, not simply a set of rules to be memorized. Like other strategies related to reading comprehension, this is a strategy that is best taught with the cognitive steps of the task in mind. To break a word down into morphemes, a student must complete the following four steps:

1. Recognize that he or she doesn't know the word or doesn't have a deep understanding of the meaning of the word.
2. Analyze the word for morphemes she or he recognizes (both roots and suffixes). As our findings indicate, this process may be more difficult if the word is not transparent, particularly if it requires a change in both sound and spelling.
3. Hypothesize a meaning for the word based on the word parts.
4. Check the hypothesis against the context.

Teachers should teach these four steps explicitly, model them several times with various words, and provide students with time to practice them. In so doing, teachers can scaffold this process, gradually releasing the responsibility to the students (see Clark & Graves, 2005, for a thoughtful discussion of scaffolding in comprehension instruction).

Principle 3: Teach the Underlying Morphological Knowledge Needed in Two Ways—Both Explicitly and in Context

Although the ability to break words down into morphemes is best taught as a cognitive strategy, it also requires a certain amount of knowledge about language. Along with the four steps described above, this knowledge needs to be taught explicitly. There are three types of knowledge of language that students need to know to use morphology effectively:

Knowledge of Prefixes and Suffixes. Teachers can teach prefixes and suffixes in a variety of ways. Teachers should engage students in grouping words by prefix or suffix. They can then discuss what these words share in meaning or part of speech. In this way, students can articulate their own meanings of prefixes and suffixes. Providing a cumulative word wall with these prefixes and suffixes grouped by meaning will reinforce these lessons. Teachers can also develop students' word consciousness by encouraging them to seek out and analyze new examples of word parts to add to the wall. Like other vocabulary items, learning prefixes and suffixes will require practice and reinforcement. Table 2 displays the 20 most common prefixes and suffixes, adapted from Blevins (2001). Students may know many of the high-frequency affixes but need to learn the low- and medium-frequency affixes.

Knowledge of How Words Get Transformed. Students should be taught the changes in sound and spelling that are often required to extract roots from derived words. To do so, teachers can group words by root to show how a single word can take many forms. This can expand students' written vocabulary by providing them with several forms for a known word. For instance, Kinsella (2002) and others have advised teachers to create a word chart that displays these various forms of key words selected from a text that students are reading. Table 3 displays an example of such a word chart, with words drawn by us from a newspaper article about current events. As with the word wall grouped by prefixes and suffixes, students can be engaged in finding and adding forms of these words themselves.

Knowledge of Roots. Students' abilities to extract roots from derived words can be a powerful strategy for acquiring new vocabulary, but only if students know the meanings of the roots.

Table 2
Most Common Prefixes and Suffixes in Order of Frequency

Highest frequency	High frequency	Medium frequency
Prefixes		
un- (not, opposite of)	over- (too much)	trans- (across)
re- (again)	mis- (wrongly)	super- (above)
in-, im-, ir-, il- (not)	sub- (under)	semi- (half)
dis- (not, opposite of)	pre- (before)	anti- (against)
en-, em- (cause to)	inter- (between, among)	mid- (middle)
non- (not)		
under- (too little)		
in-, im- (in or into)		
Suffixes		
-s (plurals)	-ly (characteristic of)	-al, -ial (having characteristics of)
-ed (past tense)	-er, -or (person)	-y (characterized by)
-ing (present tense)	-ion, -tion (act, process)	-ness (state of, condition of)
	-ible, -able (can be done)	-ity, -ty (state of)
		-ment (action or process)
		-ic (having characteristics of)
		-ous, -eous, -ious (possessing the qualities of)
		-en (made of)
		-ive, -ative, -itive (adjective form of a noun)
		-ful (full of)
		-less (without)

Note. Adapted from Blevins (2001).

Table 3
Sample Completed Word Form Chart With Words Drawn From a Newspaper Article

Noun	Adjective	Verb	Adverb
politics, politician	political		politically
strategy	strategic	strategize	strategically
provision	provisional	provide	provisionally
representation	representative	represent	
finance	financial	finance	financially
acceptance	(un)acceptable	accept	(un)acceptably

Although some roots are known to upper elementary students, it appears that others (such as *dense* and *fury*) may not be. Thus teachers need to teach a selected number of these roots as well. Clearly, this is a big task, given the huge number of roots that exist. As a starting point, teachers can teach some of the most common Latin and Greek roots (see Table 4). However, like other vocabulary words, these roots should be not be presented as a list to be memorized, but rather they should be taught in meaningful contexts when they are most useful for students to comprehend particular

Table 4
Common Latin and Greek Roots

Root	Definition	Examples
Common Latin roots		
Audi	Hear	Audience, auditorium, audible, audition
Dict	Speak	Dictate, predict, contradict, verdict, diction
Port	Carry	Import, export, portable, porter, transport
Rupt	Break	Abrupt, bankrupt, erupt, interrupt, rupture
Scrib/script	Write	Describe, inscribe, prescribe, scribe
Spect	See	Inspect, respect, spectacles, spectator
Struct	Build	Construct, destruct
Tract	Pull, drag	Attract, detract, contract, subtract
Vis	See	Visible, supervise, vision, visionary
Common Greek roots		
Auto	Self	Automobile, automatic, autograph, autobiography
Bio	Life	Biography, biology, biodegradable, biome
Graph	Written or drawn	Graphic, telegraph, seismograph
Hydro	Water	Dehydrate, hydrant, hydrodynamic
Meter	Measure	Barometer, centimeter, diameter, thermometer
Ology	Study of	Geology, biology, archeology
Photo	Light	Photograph, photocopy, photosynthesis, photoelectric
Scope	See	Microscope, periscope, stethoscope, telescope
Tele	Distant	Telephone, telescope, telecast, telegram

Note. Adapted from Blevins (2001).

texts. For instance, many of these roots such as *therm* and *hydro* may be best suited to science lessons built around expository text. For other resources on teaching morphological knowledge, see Bear et al. (2000).

Principle 4: For Students With Developed Knowledge of Spanish, Teach Morphology in Relation to Cognate Instruction

Teaching Spanish-speaking students to recognize and use cognates (words with similar spelling and meaning in two languages, such as *information* and *información*) has the potential to be a very powerful way for students to use their first language as an asset to improve their English reading comprehension. This strategy is particularly promising because many academic English words are similar in form and meaning to everyday Spanish words (e.g., *tranquil* is a rare, low-frequency English word while *tranquilo* is a common, frequently used Spanish word). But as with any technique or instructional strategy of promise, there are also pitfalls. Research suggests that this strategy may not work automatically for all students because students may lack proficiency in Spanish or may not have enough literacy in Spanish to recognize similarities in spelling (Nagy, García, Durgunoglu, & Hancin-Bhatt, 1993; Nagy & García, 1993). Even students with well-developed Spanish skills will need targeted instruction to learn how to recognize cognate relationships and use them to build reading comprehension in English.

One step to making cognate instruction effective is to teach the understanding of morphology in relation to teaching cognates. This is not difficult to do, given the prevalence of cognates among derived words (see the bold items in Table 1 for examples) and among Latin and Greek roots (virtually all of the roots in Table 4 have some cognate relationship with Spanish words). Teachers can further subdivide their word wall to have a section for cognates and encourage students to find them. Students can also be taught to use common suffixes that are themselves cognates (see italicized suffixes in Table 1 for examples). They can be taught to recognize the regular relationships between English and Spanish suffixes (-idad in Spanish almost always translates to -ity in English, as in originalidad and originality).

Putting It All Together to Build Meaning

As we have suggested, morphology is just one part of a comprehensive vocabulary and reading comprehension program for upper elementary students. However, it is important that we do not ignore such a potentially powerful tool to add to students' toolkits for extracting and constructing meaning from texts. As the insights of Brenda and Rafael reveal, this tool can be essential in our students' path toward becoming successful readers and writers.

Notes

This research was supported by National Institute for Child Health and Human Development Grant 1 R03 HD049674-01 awarded to Nonie K. Lesaux, and in part by a Harvard Graduate School of Education Dean's Summer Fellowship awarded to Michael J. Kieffer. The authors wish to acknowledge the Spencer Foundation's support of Lesaux during the writing of this article.

References

Anderson, R.C., & Freebody, P. (1981). Vocabulary knowledge. In J.T. Guthrie (Ed.), *Comprehension and teaching: Research reviews* (pp. 77–117). Newark, DE: International Reading Association.

Anderson, R.C., & Nagy, W.E. (1992). The vocabulary conundrum. *American Educator, 16*(4), 14–18.

August, D., Carlo, M., Dressler, C., & Snow, C. (2005). The critical role of vocabulary development for English language learners. *Learning Disabilities Research and Practice, 20,* 50–57.

August, D., & Hakuta, K. (1997). *Improving schooling for language-minority children: A research agenda.* Washington, DC: National Academy Press.

Bear, D., Invernezzi, M., Templeton, S., & Johnston, F. (2000). *Words their way: Word study for phonics, vocabulary, and spelling instruction.* Columbus, OH: Merill/Macmillan.

Beck, I.L., McKeown, M.G., & Kucan, L. (2002). *Bringing words to life: Robust vocabulary instruction.* New York: Guilford.

Biancarosa, G., & Snow, C.E. (2004). *Reading next—A vision for action and research in middle and high school literacy: A report to Carnegie Corporation of New York.* Washington, DC: Alliance for Excellence in Education.

Blevins, W. (2001). *Teaching phonics and word study in the intermediate grades: A complete sourcebook.* New York: Scholastic.

Carlisle, J.F. (2000). Awareness of the structure and meaning of morphologically complex words: Impact on reading. *Reading and Writing: An Interdisciplinary Journal, 12,* 169–190.

Carlo, M.S., August, D., McLaughlin, B., Snow, C.E., Dressler, C., Lippman, D.N., et al. (2004). Closing the gap: Addressing the vocabulary needs of English-language learners in bilingual and mainstream classrooms. *Reading Research Quarterly, 39,* 188–215.

Cassidy, J., & Cassidy, D. (2005/2006, December/January). What's hot, what's not for 2006. *Reading Today, 23,* 1.

Chall, J.S. (1983). *Stages of reading development.* New York: McGraw Hill.

Chall, J.S., & Jacobs, V.A. (2003). Poor children's fourth-grade slump. *American Educator, 27*(1), 14–15, 44.

Clark, K.F., & Graves, M.F. (2005). Scaffolding students' comprehension of text. *The Reading Teacher, 58,* 570–580.

Cunningham, A.E., & Stanovich, K.E. (1991). Tracking the unique effects of print exposure in children: Associations with vocabulary, general knowledge, and spelling. *Journal of Educational Psychology, 83,* 264–274.

Freebody, P., & Anderson, R.C. (1983). Effects of vocabulary difficulty, text cohesion, and schema availability on reading comprehension. *Reading Research Quarterly, 18,* 277–294.

Freyd, P., & Baron, J. (1982). Individual differences in acquisition of derivational morphology. *Journal of Verbal Learning and Verbal Behavior, 21,* 282–295.

García, G.E. (1991). Factors influencing the English reading test performance of Spanish-speaking Hispanic children. *Reading Research Quarterly, 26,* 371–392.

Graves, M.F. (2006). *The vocabulary book: Learning and instruction.* New York: Teachers College Press.

Hart, B., & Risley, T.R. (1995). *Meaningful differences in the everyday experiences of young American children.* Baltimore: P.H. Brookes.

Juel, C. (1988). Learning to read and write: A longitudinal study of 54 children from first through fourth grades. *Journal of Educational Psychology, 80,* 437–447.

Kinsella, K. (2002, January 12). *Academic reading and writing scaffolds for underprepared secondary students.* Professional development workshop, Long Beach, CA.

Molfese, V.J., Modglin, A., & Molfese, D.L. (2003). The role of environment in the development of reading skills: A longitudinal study of preschool and school-age measures. *Journal of Learning Disabilities, 36,* 59–67.

Nagy, W.E., & Anderson, R.C. (1984). How many words are there in printed school English? *Reading Research Quarterly, 19,* 304–330.

Nagy, W.E., Berninger, V.W., & Abbott, R.D. (2006). Contributions of morphology beyond phonology to literacy outcomes of upper elementary and middle-school students. *Journal of Educational Psychology, 98,* 134–147.

Nagy, W.E., García, G.E., Durgunoglu, A.Y., & Hancin-Bhatt, B. (1993). Spanish-English bilingual students' use of cognates during reading. *Journal of Reading Behavior, 25,* 241–259.

National Institute of Child Health and Human Development. (2000). *Report of the National Reading Panel. Teaching children to read: An evidence-based assessment of the scientific research literature on reading and its implications for reading instruction* (NIH Publication No. 00-4769). Washington, DC: U.S. Government Printing Office.

Organization for Economic Co-operation and Development. (2000). *Literacy in the information age: Final report of the international adult literacy survey.* Paris: Author.

Proctor, C.P., August, D., Carlo, M., & Snow, C.E. (2005). Native Spanish-speaking children reading in English: Toward a model of comprehension. *Journal of Educational Psychology, 97,* 246–256.

RAND Reading Study Group. (2002). *Reading for understanding: Toward an R&D program in reading comprehension.* Santa Monica, CA: RAND.

Rupley, W.H., Logan, J.W., & Nichols, W.D. (1998/1999). Vocabulary instruction in a balanced reading program. *The Reading Teacher, 52,* 336–346.

Stahl, S.A. (1999). *Vocabulary development.* Cambridge, MA: Brookline Books.

Stahl, S.A., & Fairbanks, M.M. (1986). The effects of vocabulary instruction: A model-based meta-analysis. *Review of Educational Research, 56,* 72–110.

Stahl, S.A., & Nagy, W.E. (2006). *Teaching word meanings.* Mahwah, NJ: Erlbaum.

Stanovich, K.E. (1986). Matthew effects in reading: Some consequences of individual differences in the acquisition of literacy. *Reading Research Quarterly, 21,* 360–407.

Tyler, A., & Nagy, W.E. (1989). The acquisition of English derivational morphology. *Journal of Memory and Language, 28,* 649–667.

Questions for Reflection

- Vocabulary instruction is often considered the domain of the reading/language arts teachers among a school's faculty. Yet, as children move up through the grades, some of the most complex vocabulary demands they encounter are in texts from other subject areas. How might you work with teachers across content areas to develop an approach to vocabulary instruction to support learners in all their classes?

- The authors suggest that teaching morphology can help both native English speakers and English-language learners, but also that teaching cognates will be most helpful for students with developed knowledge of Spanish. Think about the language learners in your class and school. What do you know about their native languages and their past educational experiences? What different approaches might you need to use with, for example, a student who reads at grade level in French or a Korean-speaking student who has been taught only in English?

Developing Word Consciousness

Judith A. Scott and William E. Nagy

Word consciousness *refers to the knowledge and dispositions necessary for students to learn, appreciate, and effectively use words. Word consciousness involves several types of metalinguistic awareness, including sensitivity to word parts and word order. In this chapter, we focus on the need for students to be aware of differences between conversational and written language, and of the pervasive power of word choice as a communicative tool in the latter. Specific activities for promoting word consciousness developed by a team of upper elementary teachers are described. We argue that word consciousness is not just a tool for the appreciation of literature or for effective writing but is essential for vocabulary growth and for comprehending the language of schooling.*

To effectively promote vocabulary growth, teachers not only must aim to help students learn specific words (although this is often an important goal) but also must develop vocabulary knowledge that is *genuine*—that is, knowledge and dispositions that will transfer to and enhance students' learning of other words as well. One part of generative vocabulary knowledge is word-learning strategies, which are discussed in Part II (Chapters 6–10) of this book [*Vocabulary Instruction: Research to Practice*, edited by James F. Baumann and Edward J. Kame'enui]. In this chapter, we focus on a different aspect of generative word knowledge, word consciousness, and on one aspect of word consciousness in particular—an awareness of the difference between the conversational and written registers, and the powerful role that word choice plays in the latter. Later in the chapter, we provide examples of specific ways that teachers can promote word consciousness in their classrooms.

Vocabulary knowledge has been identified as one of five essential components of reading in recent federal documents (RAND Reading Study Group, 2002; NICHD Report of the National Reading Panel, 2000). Although teaching specific words is one important component of promoting vocabulary growth, one cannot teach students all of the words that they need to learn. Hence, as Baumann, Kame'enui, and Ash (2003) point out, teaching specific words is only one of three important instructional objectives in a comprehensive program of vocabulary instruction. The other two objectives are to "teach students to learn words independently" and to "help students to develop an appreciation for words and to experience enjoyment and satisfaction in their use" (p. 778). In recent papers, Graves and his colleagues (Graves, 2000; Graves & Watts-Taffe, 2002) have advocated a four-part vocabulary program: wide reading, teaching individual words, teaching word learning strategies, and fostering word consciousness.

Reprinted by permission of the publisher from Scott, J.A., & Nagy, W.E. (2004). Developing word consciousness. In J.F. Baumann & E.J. Kame'enui (Eds.), *Vocabulary instruction: Research to practice* (pp. 201-217). New York: Guilford.

Although word consciousness can be thought of as one component of a vocabulary curriculum (Graves, 2000), the word component may suggest a compartmentalization that is not intended. We are not suggesting that word consciousness should be added as one of several different kinds of vocabulary activities, but rather that teachers need to take word consciousness into account throughout each and every day. Although developing an appreciation for words is among the most intangible of all goals in vocabulary learning (Graves, 1987), this goal is critical for both the development of conscious control over language use and the ability to negotiate the social language of schooling.

What Is Word Consciousness?

Word consciousness can be defined as interest in and awareness of words (Anderson & Nagy, 1992; Graves & Watts-Taffe, 2002). Despite the apparent simplicity of this definition, it is probably best to conceptualize word consciousness as a cluster of rather diverse types of knowledge and skills.

Word Consciousness as Metalinguistic Awareness

Word consciousness is first of all a type of *metalinguistic awareness*, that is, the ability to reflect on and manipulate units of language—in this case, words. However, one can make further distinctions in the types of metalinguistic awareness that contribute to word consciousness.

Most basic may be the concept of *word* as a term referring to identifiable units in written and spoken language. Teachers in primary grades should not assume that their students have a complete understanding of this basic term. Roberts (1992) described the gradual development of this concept in kindergarten, first-, and second-grade children, finding that students' tacit knowledge of this concept remained ahead of their ability to explain it.

There are several specific types of metalinguistic awareness that may contribute to word consciousness. One is *morphological awareness*:

awareness of word parts and how they contribute to the overall meaning of a word. Anglin's (1993) findings suggest that morphological awareness makes an important contribution to vocabulary growth—most obviously, to the explosive increase between first and fifth grade in the number of prefixed and suffixed words that children can explain.

Syntactic awareness is the ability to reflect on and manipulate the order of words in a sentence. It can be tested, for example, by a sentence anagram task, asking students to reassemble scrambled words back into a meaningful sentence. One way syntactic awareness may contribute to vocabulary growth is through its contribution to the process of inferring the meanings of new words from context. For example, a different set of words would fit in the blank in *He saw the _____ car* versus *He saw the car _____*. The errors of children who fail to successfully infer the correct meaning of a word in context often show a disregard for the syntactic structure of the sentence (McKeown, 1985; Werner & Kaplan, 1952).

Similarly, syntactic awareness seems to contribute to the successful use of definitions. The errors of children who fail to correctly use information in a definition often show a disregard for the structure of the definition (Miller & Gildea, 1987; Scott & Nagy, 1997).

Though *metasemantic awareness* is not a commonly used term, it should also be clear that children's ability to reflect on the meanings of words also contributes to their vocabulary knowledge and use. Knowledge of terms such as *antonym* and *synonym* is part of word consciousness, as is the ability to deal with *figurative language* and *metaphor*.

Knowledge and Beliefs About Word Learning

Word consciousness also involves knowledge and beliefs about word learning, and the various instructional practices and tools used to achieve it. That is, one can ask "What is it that teachers and students should know about word learning?" We believe that the following should be included in such a list (see Nagy & Scott, 2000, for a more complete discussion of these points):

- Word knowledge is complex: Knowing a word is more than knowing a definition.
- World learning is incremental: It is a process that involves many small steps.
- Words are heterogeneous: Different kinds of words require different learning strategies.
- Definitions, context, and word parts can each supply important information about the meaning of a word, but each of these sources has significant limitations.

Furthermore, there are general principles of learning that have important implications for vocabulary instruction. To take a very specific example, there is a substantial body of research showing that distributed practice is more effective than massed practice for learning vocabulary, at least when it involves memorizing definitions (Willingham, 2002).

Knowledge about the nature and use of definitions is also important to vocabulary learning. Children's ability to produce definitions in conventional form shows substantial growth between kindergarten and fourth grade (Watson & Olson, 1987), but even sixth grade children's ability to understand definitions of novel words is limited in certain ways (Scott & Nagy, 1997). Fischer (1990, 1994) suggests that one reason that high school foreign language students make ineffective use of bilingual dictionaries is an overly simplistic concept of definition—that is, they simply look for cross-language synonyms. On a more positive note, Schwartz and Raphael (1985) reported benefits in word learning when students used a graphic organizer that restructured definitional information.

Word Consciousness and the Difference Between Spoken and Written English

So far we have presented word consciousness as a multifaceted and rather complex topic. However, we believe that there is one aspect of word consciousness that is fundamental: helping students become aware of the differences between spoken and written English and, in particular, the role that precision of word choice plays in effective writing.

In every language, there are multiple *registers*—levels or styles of usage appropriate to different situations, topics, and audiences. Although there are a variety of registers in both written and spoken English, for the purpose of this chapter, we will focus on the differences between the oral language typical of face-to-face conversation and the written language typical of books. The difference in modality (the fact that the former is spoken and the latter written) is only one of the differences between these two registers; there also are differences in vocabulary, in syntax, in the purposes for which language is used, and in the tools used to accomplish these purposes. Snow (1994) argued that the difference in modality is not the only difficulty facing children learning to read and in fact that learning to decode is far less of a problem than learning to cope with the differences in the way that the oral and written registers are used.

One of the important ways that oral and written language differ is in terms of their vocabulary. Written language typically uses a far richer vocabulary than oral language (Hayes & Ahrens, 1988). However, this difference is not because writers tend to have larger vocabularies than talkers; rather, it has to do with how oral and written language are used, and what constitutes effective communication in each. In particular, it has to do with the different role of word choice in these two registers.

Precise choice of words is not an essential skill in conversation. Careful word choice can play a role in some types of oral language, for example, in storytelling. In conversation, however, there are simply too many other factors that are more important, or at least more easily available. One can use prosody (pitch, stress, and phrasing), gesture, and facial expression to nuance the meaning of a word. In conversation, one must have strategies for getting and holding the floor, and these strategies are not dependent on the precision of word choice. In conversation, communicative effectiveness depends heavily on making use of shared beliefs, knowledge, and experiences. "You know who" can say more than a detailed description. The demands of producing and understanding speech at a relatively rapid rate also discourage the use of uncommon words (Chafe & Danielewicz, 1987).

Written language, on the other hand, is typically decontextualized. That is, when one is reading a novel, for example, there is less information offered by the context than there is when one is engaged in a conversation with a friend. The author obviously cannot point to objects in the readers' physical context and use words such as *this* or *that*. Nor can the author use gestures, facial expressions, or intonation. Nor can the author make detailed assumptions about what knowledge he or she might share with the reader (Rosenblatt, 1978). Communication is, therefore, much more dependent upon the language itself, and one of the primary linguistic tools used by writers is precision in their choice of words. In writing, therefore, unlike in conversation, word choice is one of the most important, if not the most important, tool for expressive power.

Children are familiar with the rules of conversation, but even if they have learned the mechanics of reading and writing, they are not necessarily familiar with how decontextualized language functions. They have to be initiatied into the pragmatics of written language—how it is used to effectively accomplish communicative purposes—as well as the mechanics (Snow, 1994). If children do not understand the communicative power of precise word choice, it is hard to see how they will come to understand the distinctions in meanings among related words or be motivated to learn words. Written language is an arena in which vocabulary is the currency, but you have to know that if you are going to make the effort to invest in it.

Word Consciousness and Motivation

We have already suggested that understanding the difference between written and oral language and the expressive power of word choice in written language are foundational to word consciousness. They are also fundamental in terms of motivation. Learning words can be viewed as valuable if you know what to do with them and if you know how to use them as tools.

One key principle of motivation is success. Students are unlikely to enjoy a task that they cannot perform adequately. On the other hand, being able to perform a task successfully is itself a powerful motivator. Thus, scaffolding students' success is an important factor in effective instruction.

Language, including vocabulary, is at least as emotionally laden as any other part of the curriculum. Making a linguistic error, for example, a spelling error, can be humiliating. Not knowing what a word means or using a word incorrectly can also pose a serious risk. Learning the literate register is learning a new dialect of English, and dialect differences are also associated with very visceral reactions.

How does a teacher create an environment in which it is possible for a student to take linguistic risks and in which students can achieve a level of success high enough to motivate them to continue taking these risks? In the remainder of this chapter, we give some examples.

Promoting Word Consciousness in the Classroom

In this section, we describe activities developed during a 7-year, teacher research project called The Gift of Words (Henry et al., 1999; Scott, Asselin, Henry, & Butler, 1997; Scott, Blackstone, et al., 1996; Scott, Butler, & Asselin, 1996; Scott & Wells, 1998; Skobel, 1998). In this project, we found that teachers could influence word consciousness in their students, including the perceptions that students have about the use of words with an academic or literate tone, by providing an enriched focus on word use during reading, writing, and discussions.

The underpinning of the project was the work of Vygotsky, as developing conscious awareness and control of language was one of his central themes (Minick, 1987). Vygotsky (1978) also provided the foundation for understanding teacher and student interactions as mediated assistance, which facilitates students' learning and motivation. In this process, teachers help children become consciously aware of their use of oral and written language by controlling instruction strategically to focus attention on different aspects of reading and writing. Instruction is also mediated in that the teacher creates future contexts in which children can consciously apply what they are learning in new ways (Moll & Whitmore, 1993). In vocabulary acquisition, as in all aspects of learning, it is essential for students to be actively engaged in and to take increasing responsibility for their own learning.

Teaching Word Consciousness and Generative Knowledge of Words

The Gift of Words project grew out of the collaborative experiences and ideas from a core group of practicing elementary teachers and university participants who met and worked together for 7 years. As teachers invested time and energy in word learning strategically throughout the day, their students began to use words differently. The vocabulary-group teachers were able to develop students' willingness to experiment with words and to risk using them in new ways (Scott, Butler, & Asselin, 1996, 1997; Skobel, 1998). One teacher articulated a general agreement that she would "lay any money down that there isn't a single kid in my class...that isn't more aware of words" (Henry et al., 1999, p. 264). Another veteran teacher agreed, saying, "Without question, the kids were excited about words in a way that, in my teaching, I have never seen before. And, it's not that I have ignored words before; it is just that this year, [the focus] was major" (Henry et al., 1999, p. 264).

The vocabulary-group teachers chose to focus explorations with vocabulary learning in different curricular areas. A focus on vocabulary within literature circles has been described elsewhere (Scott & Wells, 1998). Four other teachers looked at vocabulary development that occurred in the context of writing. Precise understanding of words is not necessary in many situations during reading. It's relatively easy to skip over a word when you're reading. It's much more difficult to skip a word in writing, and in writing the use of different words or phrases can create a different register or tone. The motivation for learning and using words is enhanced when children are trying to express themselves in writing because they are trying to communicate with others. In writing word choice is an important tool because students are trying to convey specific thoughts or ideas to amuse their audience or to describe a setting, a character, or a chain of events. We saw word consciousness developing out of the perceived need to use words well.

Reading and writing are reciprocal processes, and modeling has been shown to be an effective instructional strategy for each. The underlying tenet of the program was that modeling word consciousness with a focus on language use in general, as opposed to a particular set of words, will help students develop a mind-set for learning to pay attention to words.

The Gift of Words project was based on the premises that (1) students need to learn to value words in order to spend time and energy trying to learn them; and (2) both wide reading and direct instruction are important. Through wide reading, children are exposed to a variety of words and word usage. Through direct instruction and discussion, students can become more conscious of specific words, learn how these words fit with other words, and deepen their knowledge or morphology and syntax. The teachers used words encountered in stories and poems as the text for instruction to model conscious attention to language. In the development of word consciousness, they used the instructional cycle shown in Figure 12.1.

Well-written novels and poems provided the foundation for the project. Emerging writers need to study master writers, just as emerging musicians and artists study the masters in their fields. Introducing well-crafted text with rich use of vocabulary allowed students to internalize how various authors used words and provided models that could be critiqued and analyzed.

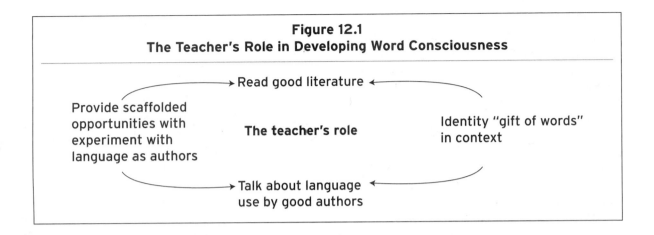

Figure 12.1
The Teacher's Role in Developing Word Consciousness

Read good literature

Provide scaffolded opportunities with experiment with language as authors

The teacher's role

Identity "gift of words" in context

Talk about language use by good authors

Any piece of good literature will work, but some authors paint pictures with words more aptly than others. Our teachers started by using Newbery Medal books, Children's Choices, and other novels by renowned authors such as Katherine Paterson, Avi, Jack London, Jerry Spinelli, Lois Lowry, Karen Cushman, Natalie Babbitt, and Paul Fleischman.

Books and poems read aloud to the classes became a way to analyze word use together. The following phrases, for example, were identified as Gifts of Words: the phrases the author used to paint a particularly vivid picture or a descriptive phrase that added texture and tone to the writing.

- "joy jiggling inside..." *Bridge to Terabithia* (Paterson, 1977, p. 101)

- "The house felt as lifeless as a tomb." *The Half-A-Moon Inn* (Fleischman, 1980, p. 10)

- "His long chin faded into an apologetic beard." *Tuck Everlasting* (Babbitt, 1975, p. 17)

The Gifts of Words phrases provided the opportunity to talk about meaning and analyze word choice. The words were not necessarily difficult or academic in tone, but attention to metaphors, similes, and descriptive language created an entry point for discussion about word meaning and word use. For instance, the teacher could

relate *apologetic* to the known word *apology*, talk about noun and adjective forms, and ask students how a *beard* could be *apologetic*.

Talk About Language Use by Good Authors.
An important aspect of any teaching is to take the implicit and make it explicit for students. Talking, for instance, about why you, the teacher, like a particular phrase or how the words in a good lead sentence grabbed your attention provides the metacognitive link between an author's word choice and the response of the reader. A teacher can discuss how authors make comparisons and build a sense of character in their books. The attention given to the way words are used by experienced authors can foster attention to language use in students' writing and the purposeful exploration of words.

Provide Scaffolded Opportunities to Experiment With Language as Authors.
Scaffolded opportunities occur when a teacher or a more competent person helps students by giving them support when they need it and taking it away as they become more capable independent learners (Bruner, 1986; Diaz, Neal, & Amaya-Williams, 1990). The teachers provided different sets of scaffolded opportunities for their students. However, in all the classrooms, students started their explorations by borrowing phrases from the authors they were reading and inserting them in their own writing.

Bakhtin (1981) claimed that the word in language is half someone else's. It only becomes one's own when the speaker or writer appropriates the word, adapting it to his or her own semantic and expressive intention. This notion, called ventriloquism (Wertsch, Tulviste, & Hagstrom, 1993), assumes that any written or spoken utterance contains both the voice of the current speaker and the voices of those who have used the same words or patterns of discourse within the context in which the word or pattern of discourse was learned. Wertsch et al. developed this idea to address how students learn to "ventriloquate" through new social languages. They theorized that students need to actively appropriate the way that others converse in order to form changes in their own patterns of interaction. According to Wertsch et al., this occurs when students are encouraged and given the opportunity to appropriate or ventriloquate new social languages.

For many students, the language of novels constitutes a new social language. Thus, we need to provide children with a chance to learn to value and appropriate such language and make it their own. In this project, the vocabulary, phrases, and sentences found in children's literature were used as springboards that students could adapt in their own attempts to communicate in writing.

The Gift of Words Bank—a collection of rich descriptive phrases—made such phrases available for students to appropriate in their own writing. Ms. Cross, a grade 5 and 6 teacher, had students collect Gift of Word phrases from their own independent reading of novels, from the novels read aloud, and from poems and short stories. Once they had an adequate collection, each student received four or five Gift of Words phrases that had been written out on long sentence strips. They categorized their phrases into action, feelings, settings, personalities, and a miscellaneous category. These were then bound together and hung on the wall. As students were writing their own stories and poems, they could borrow these collections and either insert a phrase directly into their own writing or use the phrase as a model. In several of the students' stories, characters

"burst out of bed as though the sheets were afire" (Fleischman, 1980, p. 1).

Students were also taught how to use the phrases analogically to fit into the context of their own story. For example, the phrase "There are more thieves than trees in a place like this," from *The Half-A-Moon Inn* (Fleischman, 1980), became "There is more filth than clean air in a dump like this" in one student's writing. Another changed "She was a great potato of a woman" (Babbitt, 1975, p. 10) to "He was a long string bean of a man."

Another activity that developed word consciousness focused on developing possible settings for the students' stories. Ms. Cross's class discussed the importance of a good setting in a well-written story and brainstormed many different settings together. The students then picked a setting that they might use in their story. Individually, they drew or painted their setting on medium-sized tag board. When they were completed, lined paper was attached to the back, and the class circulated to write a descriptive phrase to describe each picture. Students developed setting phrases such as:

- Bright lights burst out from the tiny windows.
- The dark green grass grew taller than the house itself.
- The river flowed heavily under the lonely bridge.

The various settings were shared in authors' circles and become available for borrowing when students began to write their own stories. A similar process was followed for creating characters.

For Ms. Cross, the main objective for these activities was to prepare the students to write their own stories. She commented:

The students all told me that they would not have been able to write the stories that they did if the class bank of character cards, setting cards, and Gift of Words Bank weren't there for them to use. The more talented writers were able to take their writing that much further and the struggling writers were able to feel successful because of the structured support [that] the writing scaffolds provided for them throughout the writing process. (in Scott, Blackstone, et al., 1996, p. 49)

Another teacher, Ms. Skobel, wrote:

Improving student writing begins with examining how other authors use language effectively. Picture books, poems, and novels are used as the model or the text for student learning. The first aspect of improving student writing [that] I look at is the way other authors use words effectively. Students have little difficulty recognizing the figurative language used in poems and books. It is this awareness of how words are arranged that transforms a "boring" piece into a more powerful piece, *for the reader*. It is the person who is going to read a piece that I try to encourage my students to remember, just as the author we happen to be examining at any given time has thought of their reader. Authors, like painters, try to create an image for their audience; a painter with paints, an author with words. (1998, p. 23)

Word consciousness can also be developed through the critique of texts where rich description is not a primary component of the writing. In Ms. Blackstone's class, the students commented that the author did an inadequate job of describing the characters or setting in her picture book *Snow White in New York* (French, 1986). The fifth graders then decided to rewrite the book, using drama to re-enact the scenes and enhance their writing.

The story was divided into parts and distributed to groups of students. The groups acted out the sections of the story, maintaining the basic plot while they exaggerated the actions. After each segment of the story was presented, the students brainstormed descriptions of the characters' actions and appearances that were recorded on charts. Each group then rewrote their part of the story to include more colorful and powerful language. When writing, they referred to their experience while portraying the character in the story, as well as the words brainstormed by the group. Compiling the segments to create a class book became the final step of the project.

The writing shown in Table 12.1 indicates progress toward sophisticated writing and exploration of word use beyond what the students might have written alone. Although this is not perfect prose, the examples show how students experimented with the use of more complex language structures and vocabulary in the re-creation of the story. This story was chosen by the students, but any short story containing action, student appeal, and limited descriptive language would suffice for this activity.

Wordless picture books can also create opportunities to scaffold children's word consciousness during writing. The plot and structure of the story are given through rich visual representation. The challenge for students is the

---

Table 12.1
Sections of the Picture Book *Snow White in New York* (French, 1986)
as Rewritten by Grade 5 Students

Original version	Rewritten version
"The seven jazz-men, their hearts broken, carried the coffin unsteadily up the church steps" (p. 25).	At Snow White's funeral, the seven heartbroken jazzmen, their hearts shattered, shuffled up the church steps.
"Suddenly one of them stumbled…" (p. 25).	Then suddenly, one of the jazzmen slipped on a rock and skidded like a car pressing on its brakes fast.
"The poisoned cherry that had been stuck in her throat was gone" (p. 26).	The casket landed on the ground with a thud, and the cherry that had been stuck in Snow White's throat burst out.

development of words and phrases that aptly describe the elements already in place.

Our teacher-research group concluded that a focus on words in general as opposed to teaching specific words was critical for creating word consciousness within their classrooms. The teachers wanted to "turn children on to words" so that they would continue to explore and use new words and phrases on their own. As students read a variety of authors' works, they paid attention to the way authors used language and developed an extended vocabulary base; the more they wrote, the more they learned how to manipulate words and phrases to express themselves in the forms of language found most often in academic settings or in literature. As they drew upon and manipulated sophisticated language, the more natural it became to incorporate these forms into their own writing and speaking.

Word Consciousness and Teaching Specific Words

Although we have presented word consciousness in terms of generative vocabulary knowledge, it should be pointed out that word consciousness depends heavily on in-depth knowledge of specific words. We have suggested that understanding the power of word choice is crucial to word consciousness. However, one can only understand the power of word choice if one knows the (sometimes subtle) distinctions in meaning between the words among which one is choosing. A discussion of why one would choose *announce* versus *proclaim* in a given sentence doesn't work if the student has no sense of the difference in meaning between these two words. To help students develop this in-depth knowledge of specific words, in addition to extensive exposure to rich language, there also has to be some intensive instruction on specific words.

Intensive Instruction on Specific Words.
When teaching specific words, a teacher first needs to decide which words are important to teach. Some words and phrases are new labels for known concepts (e.g., *carlin* as a word meaning *old woman*), and other words are new

concepts (e.g., *photosynthesis*) (Graves, 1987). If one thinks of words as interconnected webs of meaning, hooking a new label onto a developed concept or expanding the web to include terms closely related to known words (e.g., *glance* as a form of *looking*) is much easier than creating an entirely new web to form a new concept. Direct explicit instruction may be most useful in developing understanding of a new concept or in identifying subtle differences.

In-Depth Development of New Concepts.
Let us examine for a moment two examples of exemplary direct and explicit instruction from a recent study of 23 ethnically diverse classrooms (Scott, Jamieson-Noel, & Asselin, 2003). In the first example, the teacher developed a thorough understanding of the concept of *symmetry* in a sixth-grade math class. She modeled symmetry, she had pairs of students use their bodies to form symmetrical and nonsymmetrical images, and students cut folded paper to create examples of symmetry. Their examples were used to discuss types of symmetry and nonsymmetrical contrasts. When it was time to use the textbook to do the math exercises, they had a well-developed concept of the word.

In the second example, another teacher helped students create a whole-class semantic map of terms related to *racism*. As they talked about these concepts and suggested ways they could be visually represented, ideas were recorded on chart paper. From this discussion, students created individual posters using pictures from magazines to represent the concept of racism. As they chose each picture, they were evaluating its depiction of the vocabulary terms introduced during the lesson.

Both of these teachers followed guidelines from recent research regarding appropriate direct and explicit vocabulary development (Blachowicz & Fisher, 2000). Specifically, teachers (1) helped students establish multidimensional knowledge about the words they were teaching; (2) encouraged students to connect what they knew and experienced with specific concepts; and (3) provided multiple opportunities to help students develop subtle distinctions between related words that occurred in the same semantic field.

Conclusion

In this chapter, we have discussed word consciousness as part of the vocabulary curriculum, that is, in terms of how it contributes to vocabulary growth. However, we want to be clear that we do not consider word consciousness simply as a motivational trick to encourage students to memorize vocabulary words, an otherwise unpalatable activity. Rather, word consciousness contributes to literacy in a number of respects.

First of all, word consciousness—and especially an understanding of the power of word choice as a communicative tool—is essential for sustained vocabulary growth. Words are the currency of written language. Learning new words is an investment, and students will make the required effort to the extent that they believe that the investment is worthwhile. The world of schooling contains tens of thousands of words that most children never hear in their homes or in everyday conversations. In order to learn these words, they need to become conscious of how words work and ways they can use them as tools for communication.

Second, word consciousness is essential to effective writing. As students learn to negotiate the written word, sensitivity to word choice enhances their ability to communicate their ideas. Richard, a sixth-grade student, said:

> The most useful thing I learned as a writer this year is the Gift of Words.... I like how you take a sentence and transform it, like *"I'm afraid"* to *"heart pounding fear."* I'm going to try to make my work better by using more Gift of Words. Sometimes I don't use them. I don't know why because I can take a sentence and BOOM, it's a lot more powerful. (in Skobel, 1998, p. 23)

Third, word consciousness also contributes to reading comprehension. Word-level fixup strategies (e.g., figuring out the meaning of an unfamiliar word from context) are essential items in one's comprehension strategy toolbox. Morphological and syntactic awareness are

particularly valuable in this realm. In addition, developing enhanced word consciousness contributes to critical reading. Students with enhanced word consciousness become more critical consumers of literature when they pay attention to an author's use of words in the books that they read. More generally, the ability to reflect on the meanings of words is an essential part of understanding decontextualized language. The language of text uses a richer vocabulary than conversation not only because of differences in content but also because the means of effective communication in textbook language are different. Beyond just having larger vocabularies, students need to understand how and why these words are used.

Teachers play a vital role in bringing word consciousness to the fore. We believe that when teachers "up the ante" by using sophisticated vocabulary in their classrooms, teach words fully so that students internalize rich word schemas, and create learning communities in which students can explore word use with a vocabulary coach at their side, they are giving their students tools they need to become successful in the world of schooling and beyond.

References

Anderson, R.C., & Nagy, W. (1992). The vocabulary conundrum. *American Educator, 16*(4), 14–18, 44–47.

Anglin, J.M. (1993). Vocabulary development: A morphological analysis. *Monographs of the Society for Research in Child Development, 58*(10, Serial No. 238).

Babbitt, N. (1975). *Tuck everlasting.* New York: Farrar, Straus & Giroux.

Bakhtin, M.M. (1981). *The dialogic imagination: Four essays by M.J. Bakhtin* (M. Holquist, Ed.; C. Emerson & M. Holquist, Trans.). Austin: University of Texas Press.

Baumann, J.F., Kame'enui, E.J., & Ash, G. (2003). Research on vocabulary instruction: Voltaire redux. In J. Flood, D. Lapp, J.R. Squire, & J. Jensen (Eds.), *Handbook of research on teaching the English language arts* (2nd ed., pp. 752–785). Mahwah, NJ: Erlbaum.

Blachowicz, C., & Fisher, P. (2000). Teaching vocabulary. In M. Kamil, P. Mosenthal, P.D. Pearson, & R. Barr (Eds.), *Handbook of reading research* (Vol. 3, pp. 503–523). Mahwah, NJ: Erlbaum.

Bruner, J. (1986). *Actual minds, possible worlds.* Cambridge, MA: Harvard University Press.

Chafe, W., & Danielewicz, J. (1987). Properties of spoken and written language. In R. Horowitz & S.J. Samuels (Eds.), *Comprehending oral and written language* (pp. 83–113). San Diego, CA: Academic Press.

Diaz, R.M., Neal, C.J., & Amaya-Williams, M. (1990). The social origins of self-regulation. In L. Moll (Ed.), *Vygotsky and education* (pp. 127–154). New York: Cambridge University Press.

Fischer, U. (1990). *How students learn words from a dictionary and in context.* Unpublished doctoral dissertation, Princeton University.

Fischer, U. (1994). Learning words from context and dictionaries: An experimental comparison. *Applied Psycholinguistics, 15*(4), 551–574.

Fleischman, P. (1980). *The Half-A-Moon Inn.* New York: HarperCollins Trophy.

French, F. (1986). *Snow White in New York.* Oxford, UK: Oxford University Press.

Graves, M. (1987). The roles of instruction in fostering vocabulary development. In M. McKeown & M. Curtis (Eds.), *The nature of vocabulary acquisition* (pp. 165–184). Hillsdale, NJ: Erlbaum.

Graves, M. (2000). A vocabulary program to complement and bolster a middle-grade comprehension program. In B. Taylor, M. Graves, and P. van den Broek (Eds.), *Reading for meaning: Fostering comprehension in the middle grades* (pp. 116–135). Newark, DE: International Reading Association.

Graves, M.F., & Watts-Taffe, S. (2002). The place of word consciousness in a research-based vocabulary program. In A. Farstrup & S.J. Samuels (Eds.), *What research has to say about reading instruction* (3rd ed., pp. 140–165). Newark, DE: International Reading Association.

Hayes, D.P., & Ahrens, M. (1988). Speaking and writing: Distinct patterns of word choice. *Journal of Memory and Language, 27*, 572–585.

Henry, S., Scott, J., Wells, J., Skobel, B., Jones, A., Cross, S., & Blackstone, T. (1999). Linking university and teacher communities: A "think tank" model of professional development. *Teacher Education and Special Education, 22*(4), 251–267.

McKeown, M. (1985). The acquisition of word meaning from context by children of high and low ability. *Reading Research Quarterly, 20*, 482–496.

Miller, G., & Gildea, P. (1987). How children learn words. *Scientific American, 257*(3), 94–99.

Minick, N. (1987). Implications of Vygotsky's theories for dynamic assessment. In C.S. Lidz (Ed.), *Dynamic assessment* (pp. 116–140). New York: Guilford Press.

Moll, L.C., & Whitmore, K.F. (1993). Vygotsky in classroom practice: Moving from individual transmission to social transaction. In E. Forman, N. Minick, & C. Addison Stone (Eds.), *Contexts for learning: Sociocultural dynamics in children's development* (pp. 19–42). New York: Oxford University Press.

Nagy, W., & Scott, J. (2000). Vocabulary processing. In M. Kamil, P. Mosenthal, P.D. Pearson, & R. Barr (Eds.), *Handbook of reading research* (Vol. 3, pp. 269–284). Mahwah, NJ: Erlbaum.

National Institute of Child Health and Human Development. (2000). *Report of the National Reading Panel: Teaching children to read* (NIH Publication No. 00-4754). Washington, DC: U.S. Government Printing Office.

Paterson, K. (1977). *Bridge to Terabithia.* New York: Harper Trophy.

RAND Reading Study Group. (2002). *Reading for understanding: Toward a research and development program in reading comprehension.* Prepared for the Office of Educational Research and Improvement (OERI), U.S. Department of Education. Santa Monica, CA: RAND Education.

Roberts, B. (1992). The evolution of the young child's concept of word as a unit of spoken and written language. *Reading Research Quarterly, 27*, 124–138.

Rosenblatt, L. (1978). *The reader, the text, the poem: The transactional theory of the literary work.* Carbondale, IL: Southern Illinois University Press.

Schwartz, R., & Raphael, T. (1985). Concept of definition: A key to improving students' vocabulary. *The Reading Teacher, 39*(2), 198–205.

Scott, J., Asselin, M., Henry, S., & Butler, C. (1997, June). *Making rich language visible: Reports from a multidimensional study on word learning.* Paper presented at the annual meeting of the Canadian Society for the Study of Education, Newfoundland.

Scott, J., Blackstone, T., Cross, S., Jones, A., Skobel, B., Wells, J., & Jensen, Y. (1996, May). *The power of language: Creating contexts which enrich children's understanding and use of words.* A micro-workshop presented at the 41st annual convention of the International Reading Association, New Orleans, LA.

Scott, J., Butler, C., & Asselin, M. (1996, December). *The effect of mediated assistance in word learning.* Paper presented at the 46th annual meeting of the National Reading Conference, Charleston, SC.

Scott, J., Jamieson-Noel, D., & Asselin, M. (2003). Vocabulary instruction throughout the school day in 23 Canadian upper-elementary classrooms. *The Elementary School Journal, 103*(3), 269–286.

Scott, J.A., & Nagy, W. (1997). Understanding the definitions of unfamiliar verbs. *Reading Research Quarterly, 32*(2), 184–200.

Scott, J.A., & Wells, J. (1998). Readers take responsibility: Literature circles and the growth of critical thinking. In K. Beers & B. Samuels (Eds.), *Into focus: Understanding and supporting middle school readers.* Norwood, MA: Christopher-Gordon.

Skobel, B. (1998). *The gift of words: Helping students discover the magic of language.* Unpublished M.Ed. thesis, Simon Fraser University, Burnaby, BC.

Snow, C. (1994). What is so hard about learning to read? A pragmatic analysis. In J. Duchan, L. Hewitt, & R. Sonnenmeier (Eds.), *Pragmatics: From theory to practice* (pp. 164–184). Englewood Cliffs, NJ: Prentice-Hall.

Vygotsky, L.S. (1978). *Mind in society*. Cambridge, MA: Harvard University Press.

Watson, R., & Olson, D. (1987). From meaning to definition: A literate bias on the structure of word meaning. In R. Horowitz & S.J. Samuels (Eds.), *Comprehending oral and written language* (pp. 329–353). San Diego, CA: Academic Press.

Werner, H., & Kaplan, E. (1952). The acquisition of word meanings: A developmental study. *Monographs of the Society for Research in Child Development, 15*(1, Serial No. 51).

Wertsch, J.V., Tulviste, P., & Hagstrom, E. (1993). A sociocultural approach to agency. In E. Forman, N. Minick, & C.A. Stone (Eds.), *Contexts for learning: Sociocultural dynamics in children's development* (pp. 336–356). New York: Oxford University Press.

Willingham, D.T. (2002). Allocating student study time: "Massed" versus "distributed" practice. *American Educator, 26*(2), 37–39, 47.

Questions for Reflection

- The authors describe metalinguistic awareness as involving morphological awareness, syntactic awareness, and metasemantic awareness. How can you determine the level of awareness of your students in each of these three areas? How can you support their growth in each in order to help them achieve metalinguistic awareness and increased word consciousness?

- In your class literature circles or other book discussions, how much attention to you devote to discussing language use and word choice in the books you are reading? How can you ensure that this topic is a routine part of your book discussion activities? What opportunities exist for discussing vocabulary use in texts outside reading and language arts?

For the Love of Words: Fostering Word Consciousness in Young Readers

Michael F. Graves and Susan Watts-Taffe

It's 6:00 in the evening on a typical Tuesday, and Jonathan's mom, Susan (second author), is hurriedly unpacking the groceries she picked up on the way home and trying to get dinner started. (All student names except for Jonathan, who is Susan Watts-Taffe's son, and all teacher names, except for Janice Hadley, who is cited, are pseudonyms.) Meanwhile, Jonathan, who has just finished an honest day's work as a first grader and hasn't seen his mom since morning, is hanging around the kitchen, recounting the events of the day, and, as he does so often, peppering her with questions. Absorbed in her work, Susan is paying only vague attention, until she hears this: "If *dynamite* blows things up, then why did you say 'This is *dynamite*!' when you saw Uncle Mike's new house?" At this, Susan stops, gets out a pad tucked beside the toaster, and adds Jonathan's question to a list of his talk she has been keeping for the past several years. "You know, that's a great question," she says. "Let's talk about it at dinner."

It's language arts time in Janice Hadley's fourth-grade classroom, and Ted and Tonya are "walking the wall," one of their favorite activities (see Hadley, 2004). Janice has come up with several wrinkles on the popular word wall activity, and her current version of it has turned out to be a big hit. Once a week, students bring in their favorite words and hang them on the wall. Then, over the following weeks, other students add sticky notes with various responses to the words—synonyms, antonyms, things they like or don't like about the words, related words,

really anything they wish to add. The words are left up and strung in a row around the room, and one day a week students in pairs walk the wall, quizzing each other on words they find interesting or challenging. By the end of the year, the words circle the room—twice—and walking it becomes an anticipated pleasure.

It's Friday afternoon in Mr. Brainbridge's sixth-grade class, and he has just handed back the second draft of the themes his students have been working on for more than a week. "These are really shaping up well," he tells the class. "Now for the weekend, I want you to take one more look at them." Mild groans erupt, but they don't sound very serious; Mr. Brainbridge makes it a point to assign doable amounts of homework. "Don't worry," he says. "This won't take you long. It's something we have talked about a good deal in class, and it's kind of fun. What I want you to do is consider some of the words you've used in your essays, particularly the adjectives you think are most important to saying what you want to say in the way you want to say it. Find the adjectives you think are important and look them up in a thesaurus. Then, see if you can hone your word choices a bit, you know, really polish them. You can use a regular thesaurus if you like, or you can use an online thesaurus such as thesaurus.reference.com or www.m-w.com. Once you're satisfied with the words you've used, proof your paper one last time, and hand it in to me on Monday. Any questions?"

Each of these people—6-year-old Jonathan and his mother, Susan; fourth graders Ted and

Reprinted from Graves, M.F., & Watts-Taffe, S. (2008). For the love of words: Fostering word consciousness in young readers. *The Reading Teacher, 62*(3), 185-193. doi: 10.1598/RT.62.3.1

Tonya and their teacher Ms. Hadley; and Mr. Brainbridge (and hopefully his students over the weekend)—illustrate some form of word consciousness, an awareness of and interest in words and their meanings. As Anderson and Nagy (1992) have noted, word consciousness involves both a cognitive and an affective stance toward words. Word consciousness integrates metacognition about words, motivation to learn words, and deep and lasting interest in words. As we have noted elsewhere (Graves & Watts, 2002), students who are word conscious are aware of the words around them—those they read and hear and those they write and speak. And as Scott and Nagy (2004) have emphasized, this awareness involves an appreciation of the power of words, an understanding of why certain words are used instead of others, knowledge about the differences between spoken and written language, and a sense of the words that could be used in place of those selected by a writer or speaker.

Word consciousness is an integral feature of Beck and McKeown's robust instruction on individual words (Beck & McKeown, 2007; Beck, McKeown, & Kucan, 2002; Beck, McKeown, & Omanson, 1987). Given the huge number of words that students need to learn—something like 40,000 by the time they graduate from high school according to Stahl and Nagy's (2006) very carefully considered estimate—getting students interested in words and excited about them so that they learn a number of words on their own is crucial. Of course, getting excited about words is most crucial for students who come to school with small vocabularies. The advantage of word consciousness activities is that they are enticing and enjoyable, build on students' existing vocabularies be they large or small, and help students with small vocabularies without limiting those with larger ones.

What we do in this article is go beyond simply listing possible activities; we categorize the various types of word consciousness activities in such a way that you as a teacher have a framework to help you remember the types of activities and prompt you to create novel activities of your own. Before we do that, however, we want to note that word consciousness is only one part

of a comprehensive vocabulary program. As authorities such as Blachowicz, Fisher, Ogle, and Watts-Taffe (2006), Graves (2006), and Stahl and Nagy (2006) have recently pointed out, a comprehensive vocabulary program contains several elements, including frequent and varied language experiences, teaching individual words, and teaching word learning strategies, as well as fostering word consciousness.

A Framework for Fostering Word Consciousness

The framework we propose, a straightforward one with six categories, is as follows:

1. Create a word-rich environment
2. Recognize and promote adept diction
3. Promote wordplay
4. Foster word consciousness through writing
5. Involve students in original investigations
6. Teach students about words

In general, the framework approaches are arranged from those that are less formal and less time-consuming to those that are more formal, more time-consuming, and more academic. It is important to recognize that these categories overlap. Our purpose is not to create a rigid classification system so that each activity you use fits neatly into one and only one category. Rather, our purpose is to assist you in creating your own activities by suggesting various types of activities you might develop. In the remainder of this article, we describe each of the six categories and give examples for each of them.

Create a Word-Rich Environment

Take a moment to look at your classroom from the perspective of one of your students who is seated in her usual spot. What does a 360-degree scan of your classroom reveal? What words do you see posted around the classroom? Now turn your attention to your classroom library. What kinds of books are available? Are they displayed to entice young readers? Are they arranged for easy access? Now close your eyes and listen. As a student in your classroom, what kinds of words do you hear? Are some of the words read aloud and used in class discussion sophisticated words that pique curiosity and stretch vocabulary knowledge? When we think of a word-rich classroom, we think of the words that students *see* in the classroom environment, *read* in a variety of texts, *hear* spoken by the teacher and other students, and ultimately *use* in their own speaking and writing. In this and the next section, we consider these aspects of word consciousness.

First, let's consider your classroom library. It goes without saying that a well-stocked classroom library goes a long way toward promoting interest in words. In addition to variety in genres—including plenty of informational books, some of which are expository—a strong library has books at a variety of reading levels that are characterized by rich and precise vocabulary. One such book for preschool and the early grades is Denise Fleming's *In the Tall, Tall Grass*, which includes words such as *crunch, munch, tug, lug, lunge, loop,* and *swoop.*

Other rich additions to your classroom library include works of fiction and nonfiction that explicitly explore word use, word origins, and the pleasure and power of words. For example, Monalisa Degross's *Donavan's Word Jar*, a chapter book appropriate for second graders, and Roni Schotter's *The Boy Who Loved Words*, a picture book suitable for all ages, tell stories of boys who collect words for the sheer fun of it and then find ways to make a difference in the lives of others with their words. Andrew Clements's *Frindle*, a book that works well in grades 3–5, tells the story of a boy who challenges his teacher's thoughts on definitions by giving a new name (*frindle*) to a familiar thing (a pen). Informational books about words and wordplay, which we discuss in the section on promoting wordplay, are also wonderful additions to the classroom library.

Now let's consider the physical space in your classroom. As Ms. Hadley's word wall experience demonstrates, walls are great places to post words that will boost word consciousness, especially when students are involved in the creation and maintenance of the wall. In one fourth-grade classroom we visited, for example, a Weather Vocabulary wall contained words such as *barometer, tornado, meteorology,* and *precipitation*, each written and illustrated on a large card by a student. Word walls such as these are easily integrated with content area instruction. Synonym word walls might focus on "happy words" (e.g., *glad, content, joyful, delighted*), "sad words" (*unhappy, gloomy, depressed, miserable*), "moving words" (*walk, strut, saunter, stroll*), and so on. Suitable for all grade levels, such word walls encourage students to consider multiple word choice options in their writing and speaking. Word wall brainstorms, which can be done on large sheets of chart paper or on interactive whiteboards that allow you to print copies for students, are a great way to jump-start writing. Suppose students are to write a piece titled "The Most Fun Ever." A whole-class brainstorm focused on "words I think of when I think of having fun" might yield words such as *soccer, playing, outside, friends, amazing,* and *incredible.*

In addition to using walls to display and promote interest in new words, a small area of the classroom can be devoted to words—word card files, wordplay and riddle books, dictionaries and thesauri, and games involving word use. You might name such a space The Word Station, the Lexicon Lounge, or even the Vocabulary Sanctuary. Better yet, have your students name the space. Devoting this special space to further word explorations within an overall environment that is word-rich will lay a strong foundation for the development of word consciousness. However, what is most important is that you scaffold and nurture students' engagement with this environment. This is especially true for students with smaller vocabularies. In the next sections, we describe specific ways for you and your students to engage with the words in their environment.

Recognize and Promote Adept Diction

When children in your classroom speak, what vocabulary models do they use for precision in word choice? When you talk to your students, what are the words you use? In this section, we explore ways to support students as they become increasingly deliberate and skillful in their use of words in speaking and writing. We begin with read-alouds because books are a particularly rich source of interesting and sophisticated words; books, as Stahl and Stahl (2004) pointed out, are "where the words are" (p. 61). Because most vocabulary is learned from context, making it a regular practice to read aloud to students from well-chosen pieces of prose and poetry, both fiction and nonfiction, provides a gold mine for building word consciousness.

In the primary grades, repeated read-alouds, with accompanying discussion of new words, can significantly improve students' word knowledge. Recent research has shown that when direct attention is given to words, preschool and primary-grade children are capable of learning the meanings of sophisticated new words such as *furrow* and *menacing* within the context of repeated read-alouds, even when their current vocabularies are limited (Beck & McKeown, 2007; Biemiller & Boote, 2006). Reading the same text aloud three or four times over the course of a week gives children an opportunity to become very familiar with the text and its surrounding context and to focus on a small set of new words in the text. Tips for discussing such words include the following (Watts-Taffe, 2006):

- Explain the meaning of the new word (or have another student explain it).

- Extend the meaning of the word by providing examples.

- Engage students with the word by helping them to make connections with their own experiences.

In addition to the benefits of talking about the new words found in read-alouds, taking the time to recognize and discuss the adept word choices that authors have made provides a wonderful model for students to follow when they are reading on their own. In literature discussion groups, for example, students might take turns assuming the role of "word hunter" (Scott et al., 1996), the one who pays particular attention to the author's word choices and highlights words to bring to the attention of the group.

Students might keep personal notebooks in which they record new or interesting words they hear or read. They might keep small word card files to remember interesting words related to specific topics or genres. A second-grade student who is enjoying books like *The Bald Bandit* and *The Canary Caper* from Ron Roy's A–Z Mystery Series might have a file called "mystery words," and collect words such as *detective, burglar, disappearance,* and *caper* to refer back to in writing his or her own mystery story. Or, the whole class might contribute words to a general word card file. Files such as these are a very helpful resource as students engage in the writing process, and teachers can refer students to these collections as a way of scaffolding adept diction in writing.

Another way to support students in becoming more proficient in their use of words and to reinforce specific words that may be central to a reading selection or thematic unit (e.g., *apprentice, economy*) is to have students look and listen for particular words outside of school and then record these "sightings" as well as the contexts in which they occurred (e.g., "My Dad said I was his *apprentice* when he was teaching me how to wash the car," or "Last night on the news, they said the *economy* was strong."). Students can bring their sightings to school to share with the entire class.

Promote Wordplay

Stocking your classroom with games and providing time for playing them is an easy way to entertain, as well as challenge, with words. A wide variety of games based on the I Spy series of books by Walter Wick and Jean Marzollo (available at www.briarpatch.com) invite young children (preschool–grade 3) to match outrageous pictures with words and rhyming riddles and require thought about multiple meanings, precision, and creative use of words. For students in grade 4 and above, the word game Balderdash by Gameworks Creations provides an opportunity to create and evaluate definitions, which can enhance students' use of the dictionary. To maximize the educational benefits of these games, play with your students periodically so that you can support them as they attempt to improve. Each year finds more games available that encourage engagement with words and their meanings, including online games like those at pbskids.org/lions/games.

In addition to packaged games, there is a wide array of games that require very little if any materials. Beck and her colleagues (2002) provide examples of many great activities that can be turned into games including Applause, Applause; Word Associations; and Idea Completion. Each of these, we should note, is more appropriate for review than for initial instruction, because each assumes some knowledge of the words' meanings.

Applause, Applause is a fun game in which students indicate, by level of applause, how much (a lot, a little bit, not at all) they would like to be described by certain words. Their clapping, for example, might reveal whether they would like to be described as *joyous*, *menacing*, *hopeful*, *greedy*, *mature*, or *recalcitrant*. Of course, words that might not merit applause in one context may well do so in another. For example, if a student can give a good explanation why he or she applauds the word *recalcitrant*, that's perfectly fine.

Word Associations activities help students to solidify their understandings of new words. In the Word Associations game, students (working individually, in pairs, or in small groups) are asked to pair a new word with another word or phrase and to explain why the pairing works. For the words *catastrophe*, *fragrant*, *hypothesis*, and *fragile*, teams might be asked,

- Which word goes with perfume? (fragrant)
- Which word goes with Hurricane Katrina? (*catastrophe*)
- Which word goes with a problem to be solved? (*hypothesis*)
- Which word goes with a newborn baby? (fragile)

As students work to explain why they've paired the words and phrases as they have, they increase their facility with the new words.

Similarly, Idea Completion games require students to use their own words to explain the meaning of new words as they complete sentence stems such as these:

- Toddlers often think peas are *repulsive* because....
- The detective described Mr. Smith as *suspicious* because....
- The runner had to admit *defeat* when....

In addition to playing games involving words, children have great fun with traditional types of wordplay. Idioms, clichés, and puns are very engaging to students because they contain "hidden" meanings behind the literal meanings. What does it mean, for example, to "shake a leg," "miss the boat," or "fly by the seat of your pants"? Children love to explore phrases such as these by writing down what they mean, drawing pictures to represent the phrases (sometimes depicting the literal meaning and sometimes depicting the figurative meaning), and acting them out. (As you work with idioms be sure to give plenty of support to your English learners, who are likely to find them a challenge.) Puns can also be a lot of fun. Here are a couple of examples from www.punoftheday.com, which is not a source for children but can provide you with some good examples to share with your class:

- I wondered why the baseball was getting bigger. Then it hit me.
- To write with a broken pencil is pointless.

When sharing puns like these, you might want to play Get It?, a simple game in which students try to figure out the double meaning in the pun and then, once they've Got It!, explain their understanding to the class. As with idioms, children have fun depicting puns with illustration and other forms of art. Children with high levels of word consciousness also enjoy creating original puns and other figures of speech.

Finally, wordplay books are both enjoyable and informative for children. Rick Walton's *Why the Banana Split* is full of plays on words, multiple meaning words, and idioms suitable for grades 1–3. Andrew Clements's *Double Trouble in Walla Walla* is a must for anyone who has ever felt like a *nitwit*, stopped for some *chit-chat*, tried to *razzle-dazzle* anyone, or wondered what all the *hubbub* is about. The title of Debra Frasier's *Miss Alaineus: A Vocabulary Disaster* says it all. This delightful story takes readers into a fifth-grade classroom where Tuesday is Vocabulary Day and the students are getting ready for the school's annual Vocabulary Parade. This book excites students about words, and many students across the country have been involved in their own vocabulary parades since it was published. (See www.debrafrasier.com for some examples.)

Foster Word Consciousness Through Writing

Writing provides an extremely powerful and convenient setting for fostering word consciousness for two principal reasons. First, writing is relatively permanent. That is, words written down aren't fleeting in the way speech is fleeting; they are there to ponder and to change if necessary. Second, students often revise their writing, and considering whether to alter word choices is an important and natural part of that revising. Thus, the most frequent way to foster word consciousness through writing is to make careful consideration of word choices a routine part of the revision process. Among the questions students can ask themselves in doing so are the following: Is this the best word to convey my meaning? Is the word precise enough? Is it appropriately formal or informal? Is it a word my reader is likely to be familiar with? Is it a word my reader is likely to find interesting and appealing? Have I used it too frequently; should I perhaps use a synonym?

Another way to foster word consciousness is to engage students in writing activities that are deliberately designed to focus their attention on words. A unit with this goal was created by one

of us and a colleague (Duin & Graves, 1987) and used with fourth- and sixth-grade students. The unit was modeled after the approach Beck and McKeown have worked with (Beck et al., 1987, 2002) but differed from this work in that the emphasis here was on writing. The words used were ones that students might not know or at least might not use in writing but that they might find useful for writing an adventure narrative. They included *fidgety*, *confident*, *energized*, *overwhelmed*, *jaded*, *anxious*, *brisk*, *ingenious*, *resourceful*, and *audacious*. Before the unit began, students wrote a brief narrative about a real or imaginary camping trip, and took a multiple-choice test on the 10 words.

The unit lasted a week. Day one dealt with the first five words. The teacher asked how the students felt when they began exploring something new and mysterious, and put their responses on the board; she then put the first new word, *fidgety*, on the board, and students spelled it, pronounced it, and wrote it in their booklets. The teacher defined the word and then asked students to think of a time when they felt fidgety and to share this recollection with a partner. Next came a word association activity in which students responded to a question about each new word, for example, Would you like to sit next to a *fidgety* person at a movie?

Day two was similar to day one but dealt with the second five words. Day three was a review in which students worked in groups writing Skeleton Stories. Each group was given a sketch of a skeleton with a brief plot description written on its backbone and was asked to write the new words that might be used in the story on the skeleton's shoulder, arm, leg, or foot depending on where they might occur in the story. Figure 1 shows a skeleton with one group's words added. Students shared their completed Skeleton Stories with the class. Day four was used for a pantomime activity in which student pairs acted out the meanings of the words while the rest of the class guessed which words they were presenting.

On the last day of the unit, students wrote a brief narrative describing a real or imagined time when they went exploring, and again took a

Figure 1
Third-Grade Word Expert Card for a Novel (Outside Shown on Top; Inside on Bottom)

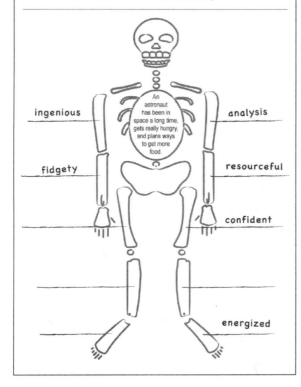

ingenious

analysis

An astronaut has been in space a long time, gets really hungry, and plans ways to get more food.

fidgety

resourceful

confident

energized

Note. By Levi Todd.

multiple-choice test on the 10 words. Results indicated that students who received the instruction knew significantly more of the 10 words after completing the unit, used an average of 6 of the taught words in their postunit narrative as compared with none in their preunit narrative, and wrote postunit narratives that were judged to be of significantly higher quality than those of students who did not complete the unit. The teachers also reported that students really enjoyed the unit, brought it up at various times during the year, and made deliberate efforts to incorporate the taught words and other interesting words in other writing they did during the year.

Involve Students in Original Investigations

Features of words and word usage invite a variety of investigations students can undertake. Following are just a few of the many possibilities:

- The vocabulary used in certain situations or by certain professions
- The vocabulary used by certain individuals
- How students' vocabulary or that of others differs from one situation to another, for example, in school versus on the playground, or when talking as opposed to when writing
- How vocabulary changes over time—words that have entered the language over the past decade
- Terms of address—the use of honorifics such as Mister, Ma'am, Doctor, Professor, and the like—by different people or in different settings
- The use of first names, on television or in the newspaper, for females versus males, for children versus adults

One topic that is always popular and works well for exploration is slang. The following three-part activity is based on some suggestions of Andrews (2006) and our own experiences. This activity, which you might call Your Slang, Your Parents' Slang, and Slang That's Older Still, is a good one for fifth and sixth graders. It proceeds in three stages and is likely to extend over several weeks, with most of the work done outside of class.

Begin the activity by defining slang, giving some examples, and asking students to keep a record of the slang they use, probably over several days. At the end of that time, have students report on what they recorded, and if any student has fewer that 10 slang terms, have him or her borrow some terms from other students. Then, have each student create a list of the 10 terms and their definitions, leaving a space beside each definition where an alternate slang term can be inserted.

Next, have students take their terms and definitions home, ask their parents or caregivers for the slang they would use for each of those meanings, and record their responses. Additionally, for instances in which parents have different slang terms, students should ask them if they still use their original slang terms, use more modern slang terms, or try not to use slang at all, again recording responses.

The final step is reporting and discussion. There are several options here. One is to have each student submit a written report describing the slang he or she used, the adults' slang with the same meaning, and the adults' present use of slang. A second option, and the one we tend to favor, is to have students first meet in groups to discuss what they found, and then to have each student present the results for one slang term to the class. Finally, after either the discussion and oral report or the written report, hold a class discussion about slang and probe students' thinking with some questions such as the following:

- How often do students use slang?
- Are there situations in which they do and do not use slang?
- Is there slang that some students use but others do not? Why?
- Do their parents or caregivers use slang? To what extent is it the same and different from the slang they use?
- What did their parents or caregivers think of the slang they (the students) used? Would they use it?
- What did they (the students) think of the slang the adults used? Would they consider using that slang?
- What is the purpose of slang? What does it accomplish? Why do we have it?

Teach Students About Words

As students interact with words in the various ways we've discussed, it's helpful for them to understand several important characteristics of words and word learning. As Nagy and Scott (2000) have noted, word learning is incremental,

many words have more than one meaning, and word meanings are interrelated.

Word Learning Is Incremental. Research indicates that knowledge of individual words exists on a continuum ranging from known to unknown. Dale (1965) suggested four levels of word knowledge:

1. Never having seen it before
2. Knowing there is such a word but not knowing what it means
3. Having a vague and context-bound meaning for the word
4. Knowing and remembering the word

With each new encounter with a particular word, depth of knowledge increases, moving the word further along on the continuum from unknown to known.

Consider the first grader who heard the word *shabbiest* for the first time when his teacher read aloud from Cynthia Rylant's *Henry and Mudge and the Happy Cat*: "Sitting on the steps was the shabbiest cat Henry had ever seen. It had a saggy belly, skinny legs, and fur that looked like mashed prunes." When asked what the word *shabby* might mean, the boy replied, "When a cat looks bad and all mashed up." In this example, the student has gone from having never heard the word before to having a vague sense of the word's meaning, one that is bound to the particular context of this story. Repeated encounters with this word in a variety of contexts will provide the fuel needed to move this new word along the continuum until the student knows it well, remembers it, and uses it in a variety of appropriate contexts. For further information on the incremental nature of word learning, see Graves (2006) and Nagy and Scott (2000).

In addition to structuring multiple exposures and practice opportunities with new words, it's important for teachers and students to recognize that students' early attempts to articulate their understanding of new words will often reflect partial rather than full knowledge. These early attempts, marked by partial misunderstanding and imprecision, are a crucial component of the word learning process. When students know that word learning requires time and practice, they are more likely to see themselves as competent word learners throughout the entire process, which of course they are!

Many Words Have More Than One Meaning.
It is important for students to realize that many of the words they hear and read have multiple meanings because they will frequently need to figure out which meaning applies in a particular context or learn a new meaning for a known word. Sometimes the different meanings are quite distinct as in *change* (to change your mind) and *change* (coins) or *jam* (a fruit spread to eat), *jam* (squeezing something into a small space), and *jam* (play music). At other times, the differences are more nuanced as in *fishing* (the water sport) and *fishing* (for information) or *multiply* (to increase) and *multiply* (to perform the mathematical operation of multiplication). It's fun to share some examples as we have done here and then ask the students to share some examples from their own experiences. They might be on the lookout for multiple-meaning words to share with the class over a period of weeks. Whenever multiple-meaning words that might cause confusion come up in classroom texts and units of study, be sure to point them out and remind students of the need to check for the meaning that makes sense in the context, even if that means consulting an outside source to learn a new meaning of the word.

Word Meanings Are Interrelated.
A student's knowledge of one word is linked to his knowledge of other words. For example, knowing the meaning of the word *airplane* influences the way in which you come to understand the words *helicopter* and *aircraft*. These words have distinct meanings, but their meanings are related. Think of all of the semantic relationships existing among the words *tree*, *maple*, *birch*, *pine*, *forest*, *rainforest*, *deforestation*, and *habitat*. Now consider how your knowledge of any one word in this set relates to your knowledge of another word in the set. Whether it is by similarity, contrast, extension, specific example, or description, these words are linked in a complex way in our brains. What this means is that the more words your students learn, the easier it is for them to learn even more words.

Concluding Remarks
So there you have it: six broad categories of word consciousness activities designed to prompt you to create myriad ways of engaging young learners with words and enticing them to become lifelong celebrants of the English lexicon. With more than 40,000 words to be learned, this sort of personal and independent interest in words is a vital part of acquiring a powerful vocabulary. We have provided you with a sample of the many ways in which you can create a word-rich environment, recognize and promote your students' diction, promote wordplay, foster word consciousness through writing, involve students in original investigations, and teach students about words. But this is merely a beginning—an invitation, and we hope a bit of a scaffold, to create the sorts of rich and varied word consciousness activities that will lead your students to success with words and to the many other successes that powerful vocabularies will promote.

References
Anderson, R.C., & Nagy, W.E. (1992). The vocabulary conundrum. *American Educator, 16*(4), 14–18, 44–47.

Andrews, L. (2006). *Language exploration and awareness: A resource book for teachers* (3rd ed.). Mahwah, NJ: Erlbaum.

Beck, I.L., & McKeown, M.G. (2007). Increasing young children's oral vocabulary repertoires through rich and focused instruction. *The Elementary School Journal, 107*(3), 251–273. doi:10.1086/511706

Beck, I.L., McKeown, M.G., & Kucan, L. (2002). *Bringing words to life: Robust vocabulary instruction.* New York: Guilford.

Beck, I.L., McKeown, M.G., & Omanson, R.C. (1987). The effects and uses of diverse vocabulary instructional techniques. In M.G. McKeown & M.E. Curtis (Eds.), *The nature of vocabulary acquisition* (pp. 147–163). Hillsdale, NJ: Erlbaum.

Biemiller, A., & Boote, N. (2006). An effective method for building meaning vocabulary in the primary grades.

Journal of Educational Psychology, 98(1), 44–62. doi:10.1037/0022-0663.98.1.44

Blachowicz, C.L.Z., Fisher, P.J.L., Ogle, D., & Watts-Taffe, S. (2006). Vocabulary: Questions from the classroom. *Reading Research Quarterly, 41*(4), 524–539. doi:10.1598/RRQ.41.4.5

Dale, E. (1965). Vocabulary measurement: Techniques and major findings. *Elementary English, 62*(5), 895–901, 948.

Duin, A.H., & Graves, M.F. (1987). The effects of intensive vocabulary instruction on expository writing. *Reading Research Quarterly, 22*(3), 311–330. doi:10.2307/747971

Graves, M.F. (2006). *The vocabulary book: Learning and instruction.* Newark, DE: International Reading Association; New York: Teachers College Press; Urbana, IL: National Council of Teachers of English.

Graves, M.F., & Watts, S.M. (2002). The place of word consciousness in a research-based vocabulary program. In S.J. Samuels & A.E. Farstrup (Eds.), *What research has to say about reading instruction* (3rd ed., pp. 140–165). Newark, DE: International Reading Association.

Hadley, J. (2004, May). *Vocabulary instruction in a Reading First school.* Paper presented at the 49th annual convention of the International Reading Association, San Antonio, TX.

Nagy, W.E., & Scott, J.A. (2000). Vocabulary processes. In M.L. Kamil, P.B. Mosenthal, P.D. Pearson, & R. Barr (Eds.), *Handbook of reading research* (Vol. 3, pp. 269–284). Mahwah, NJ: Erlbaum.

Scott, J.A., Blackstone, T., Cross, S., Jones, A., Skobel, B., Wells, J., et al. (1996, May). *The power of language: Creating contexts which enrich children's understanding and use of words.* Micro-workshop presented at the 41st annual convention of the International Reading Association, New Orleans, LA.

Scott, J.A., & Nagy, W.E. (2004). Developing word consciousness. In J.F. Baumann & E.J. Kame'enui (Eds.), *Vocabulary instruction: Research to practice* (pp. 201–217). New York: Guilford.

Stahl, S.A., & Nagy, W.E. (2006). *Teaching word meanings.* Mahwah, NJ: Erlbaum.

Stahl, S.A., & Stahl, K.A.D. (2004). Word wizards all!: Teaching word meanings in preschool and primary education. In J.F. Baumann & E.B. Kame'enui (Eds.), *Vocabulary instruction: Research to practice* (pp. 59–78). New York: Guilford.

Watts-Taffe, S. (2006, October). *Teaching vocabulary in grades Pre-K through 3: Inspiring the love of words.* Paper presented at the annual conference of the Ohio Council of the International Reading Association, Youngstown, OH.

Questions for Reflection

- This article describes six types of word-consciousness activities. Think for a minute about the activities you use in your classroom and which categories they fall into. Are there some categories in which you offer a rich array of activities and others in which you offer few or none? Why? What is important is not that you fill all the categories but that you mindfully include those word-consciousness activities you think will best assist your students in becoming deeply interested in words.

- Of the six categories of word-consciousness activities presented in the article, creating a word-rich environment probably allows the most creativity. In discussing ways of creating such an environment, the authors suggest a range of different approaches, all focused on the individual classroom. How could this be expanded? Can you think of ways to create a word-rich school? What about ways in which you could suggest students and their parents achieve word-rich environments at home?

English Words Needed:
Creating Research-Based Vocabulary
Instruction for English Learners

Lori Helman

Knowing words in a language is a key component to understanding text and being able to produce it—reading and writing. Many students in the United States come to school with an oral language other than English, and an important charge of the school is to help them become literate in English. To fully carry out this responsibility, educators need to help English learners develop a deep and broad repertoire of basic and academic vocabulary words to use in their reading and writing. As one second-grade teacher shared, "What is one of the biggest challenges for my [English-language learning] students in becoming proficient readers and writers in English? Building up vocabulary and content related to what they're reading." To help with this goal, this chapter provides teachers with the research base on vocabulary learning and instruction with English learners at the elementary grades and suggests effective teaching practices that follow from this literature.

Recent demographic data showed that 9.9 million children in the United States ages 5–17 speak a language other than English at home; of this group, 2.8 million children speak English with difficulty (National Center for Education Statistics, NCES, 2006). Both of these figures represent more than double the number from 1979. Of the students who spoke English with difficulty, approximately 76% spoke Spanish as a home language. To serve all students in

schools, it is imperative that educators become knowledgeable about vocabulary instruction for the sizable group of students learning English. While it is important to consider the needs of students from many language backgrounds, it is also clear that instructional strategies aimed at supporting the learning of Spanish speakers are especially relevant.

English-language learning (ELL) students are at increased risk of experiencing reading difficulty (Snow, Burns, & Griffin, 1998). In fact, the National Assessment of Educational Progress reports a persistent gap in performance on its reading measure between ELL and non-ELL students at the fourth-, eighth-, and twelfth-grade levels (NCES, 2005). An important factor in the reading achievement gap is likely the limited vocabulary knowledge of ELL students (August & Hakuta, 1997; August & Shanahan, 2006; Calderón et al., 2005).

A substantial body of research points to the importance of vocabulary knowledge for adequate reading comprehension in all students (McGregor, 2004; Nagy & Scott, 2000; National Institute of Child Health and Human Development, 2000). Reading comprehension is highly dependent on understanding spoken words (Rayner, Foorman, Perfetti, Pesetsky, & Seidenberg, 2001). Vocabulary knowledge in the early grades is a significant predictor of reading comprehension in middle and high school

Reprinted from Helman, L. (2008). English words needed: Creating research-based vocabulary instruction for English learners. In A.E. Farstrup & S.J. Samuels (Eds.), *What research has to say about vocabulary instruction* (pp. 211–237). Newark, DE: International Reading Association.

(Cunningham & Stanovich, 1997). There is also evidence that learning vocabulary has a positive influence on reading comprehension (Beck, Perfetti, & McKeown, 1982). With the understanding that vocabulary knowledge has been shown to play such a powerful role in reading comprehension for native English speakers, it is time to turn to the vocabulary research with English learners. Does vocabulary play an equally important role with nonnative speakers? If so, what does the research say about how to most effectively teach vocabulary to English learners?

Vocabulary Research With English Learners

An overview of research findings with English learners described the important role of oral English in the success of students in school. As English learners' oral proficiency grew, so did their abilities to use more complex language learning strategies, which led to greater use of academic language and a better grasp of word meanings (Genesee, Lindholm-Leary, Saunders, & Christian, 2005). The report of the National Literacy Panel on Language Minority Children and Youth found that students learning English did not perform as well on measures of reading comprehension as their native-speaking peers, and that oral language proficiency in English and English reading comprehension are positively correlated (August & Shanahan, 2006). A variety of research studies point to the importance of vocabulary knowledge for English learners—the positive effects of more developed vocabularies and the negative effects of low vocabulary knowledge. García (1991) found that students learning English often did not have the knowledge of keywords in English needed to comprehend their texts. Other researchers have echoed the finding that poor reading comprehension for English learners is often related to low vocabulary knowledge (Jiménez, García, & Pearson, 1996; Nagy, 1997; Verhoeven, 1990). In addition, vocabulary knowledge was found to be an important foundation for reading comprehension with English learners (Calderón et al., 2005) and

a significant predictor of writing skills in English (Dufra & Voeten, 1999). In a review of the research, Cheung and Slavin (2005) concluded that the evidence supported the extensive use of vocabulary instruction as a key component of an effective reading program.

Despite the importance of vocabulary knowledge for English learners' proficient reading and writing, a very limited number of studies have examined the instructional practices that may be effective for teaching vocabulary. The National Literacy Panel on Language-Minority Children and Youth found only three experimental studies that dealt with the topic (Shanahan & Beck, 2006). The first study compared vocabulary instruction for first-grade Spanish speakers that was presented in individual sentence contexts versus vocabulary instruction that involved meaning-centered instruction, including words used in longer narratives, picture support, and student-generated dictations. Students who received the more meaningful instruction learned more than double the number of focus words as compared with the control group (Vaughn-Shavuo, 1990).

The second study reviewed by Shanahan and Beck (2006) was conducted with 75 third-grade Mexican American students (Pérez, 1981). Students received packets of activities that helped them work with and understand complex language concepts such as idioms, analogies, compound words, synonyms, antonyms, and words with multiple meanings. Students worked on these activities 20 minutes a day for a 3-month period. Results showed that the treatment group made significantly more growth on a reading inventory than the control group.

The final study involved fifth-grade Spanish speakers who were taught 10–12 words per week over 15 weeks. The treatment had the following characteristics: It was thematic with academically useful words; it included homework and periodic assessments; the words were presented first in Spanish, then in English; students were taught strategies for using information from context, morphology, multiple meanings, and cognates; and it was implemented in a classroom with both ELL and non-ELL students (Carlo et al., 2004). English learners showed significant gains on the intervention, although their pre- and posttest scores were lower than the non-ELL students. Shanahan and Beck (2006) concluded that, while the three studies provided results that are consistent with vocabulary research for native English speakers, "There is a great need for more investigation into what constitutes sound and effective vocabulary instruction for English-language learners" (p. 431).

Several other studies and reflections by the researchers involved provide us with important information about what may lead to effective practices in vocabulary instruction for English learners. Cognates, or words that share related spellings and meanings across two languages (e.g., *pause/pausa*), have been shown to be a useful learning tool for Spanish-speaking students, but the ability to use cognates may require explicit scaffolding for students (Carlo et al., 2004; García, 1991; Jiménez et al., 1996; Nagy, García, Durgunoglu, & Hancin-Bhatt, 1993).

Calderón et al. (2005) implemented a year-long study with 293 Spanish-dominant third graders who were transitioning from Spanish to English instruction. Vocabulary instruction focused on the words both in the decodable texts students read and in grade-level literature. Vocabulary was previewed with technology; teachers also discussed words before, during, and after the story had been read. Students listened to and discussed 50 literature texts throughout the year, focusing on key vocabulary words within the story. Additional oral language activities to build vocabulary included listening for target words outside of class and investigating cognates, multiple-meaning words, and idioms. The authors concluded that carefully designed vocabulary instruction improves vocabulary knowledge in both Spanish and English and that vocabulary practices effective with native English speakers have also proved useful with English learners but must be adapted to their backgrounds. Teachers who participated in the study expressed how helpful it was for them to have the vocabulary words selected and the strategies prepared for them—a task that would have been overwhelming on their own (Calderón et al., 2005).

Biemiller and Boote (2006) reported on a series of vocabulary studies with primary-grade students in classrooms with approximately 50% English learners. The first study found that repeated readings of books lead to a 12% gain in word meanings and that adding explanations of words added 10% for a total gain of 22%. The second study tested a more intensive format for word instruction and transfer with additional words taught and multiple opportunities for review. A greater number of words were learned in the second format, and the authors attribute this to added reviews and the instruction of word meanings.

A recent study by Roberts (2008) found that a home reading program that included storybook reading in the child's first language was as effective as English picture book reading for developing second-language vocabulary. In addition, Beck and McKeown (2007) examined the potential for increasing young low-income children's vocabulary knowledge through rich and focused instruction. While this study was not done with English learners, there was a similar need to help the students increase their vocabulary repertoires to be successful in the school world of academic language. Rich instruction involved focused discussion of read-aloud texts and teaching and encouraging the use of selected sophisticated words. Results showed that the richer the vocabulary instruction, the greater the pre- to posttest gains (Beck & McKeown, 2007).

As researchers discussed why they believe their vocabulary interventions were successful, the following key ideas were expressed:

- Words were presented in meaningful contexts, such as in interesting texts.
- Lessons motivated students and encouraged participation.
- Interventions were in-depth and took place over time with repetition and review.
- Lessons involved discourse around text.
- Vocabulary study built on students' background language such as with previews in the home language and cognate identification.

- Students learned to apply strategies for word learning, such as morphemic analysis.
- Lessons involved scaffolding such as with simplified syntax, visual materials, or oral language practice activities.

Connections Among Vocabulary Research and Second-Language Teaching Principles

Teachers reading the list of key ideas presented above are likely to nod their heads and think, "That fits with what I know about teaching students in a new language. Of course it helps to provide concrete support and in-depth, engaging instruction." In fact, many of the instructional procedures represented in the vocabulary studies described in this chapter also reflect key ideas from effective second-language teaching. These key ideas fit into five principles, and I expand on them in the following segment of text. It is important to examine *why* the techniques in the research studies are likely to be effective, because knowing why provides important criteria for selecting effective vocabulary teaching practices for ongoing classroom use.

Instruction Builds on What Students Already Know. We saw in the vocabulary research that projects that provided support in the student's home language, such as preview/review, translation of words, and making connections to cognates in the home language, were successful in developing vocabulary in English. Understanding students' home languages and how they relate to English provides information for the teacher to help students transfer knowledge that is similar or clarifies misconceptions that may arise because of distinctive features across the languages. Research on second-language learning highlights the importance of an additive as opposed to a subtractive philosophy of language learning, connecting instruction to students' lives, as well as using culturally respectful teaching practices (Au, 2006; Center for

Research on Education, Diversity & Excellence [CREDE], 2002; Peregoy & Boyle, 2001).

Instruction Is Tailored to the Particular Needs of Students Learning English. Scaffolding may include the use of visuals, hands-on activities, a developmental progression of words or sequenced readers, and simplified, student-friendly language. All of the successful studies referenced above used scaffolded techniques of various sorts to support student learning in vocabulary. Research on second-language learning has long highlighted the concept of sheltered instruction and provided examples of how to make instruction comprehensible to students learning English (Baker, Gersten, Haager, & Dingle, 2006; Cheung & Slavin, 2005; Fitzgerald & Graves, 2004; Peregoy & Boyle, 2001; Saunders & Goldenberg, 2001).

Vocabulary Instruction Is Taught in Meaningful Contexts. The research studies that were presented showed that more vocabulary learning took place when words were taught in context and when there were multiple opportunities for application in and out of the classroom. This finding aligns with second-language learning research that supports the use of social interaction strategies such as group work and collaboration, as well as opportunities for guided application of new learning (CREDE, 2002; Baker et al., 2006; Peregoy & Boyle, 2001).

Instruction Is In-Depth and Comprehensive. In the research studies presented, the curriculum went beyond surface-level definitions; it addressed a variety of vocabulary components including the multiple meanings of words, finding synonyms and antonyms, using the spelling-meaning connection, and engaging in higher order thinking tasks. Rich instruction proved more effective for English learners. The idea of complex and interesting curriculum to engage and motivate diverse learners is supported throughout the literature (Au, 2006; CREDE, 2002; Gersten & Jiménez, 1994).

Goals Are Challenging, but Not Impossible.
A consistent thread in the reflections of the vocabulary researchers was the need to implement a cohesive program and make a long-term commitment to its implementation. Several studies addressed the extra attention needed as students in bilingual programs transition to English-only classrooms. The literature in the second-language field tells us that language learning takes time and, while students need high expectations, they also need consistency and support to become academically proficient in a new language (Cummins, 2003; Genesee et al., 2005; Peregoy & Boyle, 2001).

These key instructional principles give teachers an overarching perspective on what to look for when planning research-based vocabulary instruction for English learners. The remainder of this chapter presents concrete examples of teaching practices that put these principles into action.

Providing Research-Based Vocabulary Instruction With English Learners

Effective vocabulary instruction for English learners will reflect the research both in vocabulary learning and in second-language acquisition because students are learning to read and write in English at the same time they are learning to speak the language. Limitations on their vocabulary skills will hold students back from comprehending the grade-level materials they encounter in the classroom. For this reason, vocabulary instruction needs to be thought of not as a separate curriculum area but rather as an integrated part of every instructional activity for English learners. In a recent "Theory into Practice" article, Blachowicz, Fisher, Ogle, and Watts-Tafe (2006). outlined three characteristics of strong vocabulary instruction: (1) the need for language- and word-rich environments, (2) the intentional teaching of selected vocabulary, and (3) the developing of word-learning strategies (see Chapter 2, this volume ["Attentional Vocabulary Instruction: Read-Alouds, Word

Play, and Other Motivating Strategies for Fostering Informal Word Learning," Blachowicz & Fisher, in *What Research Has to Say About Vocabulary Instruction*] for similar work by Blachowicz and Fisher). These characteristics are equally, if not more, important for English learners as they develop oral language and literacy skills simultaneously.

The next section addresses many important topics relating to research-based vocabulary instruction with English learners:

- What words are most important for students to know?
- How can the research guide teachers to select effective vocabulary activities for English learners?
- How can vocabulary learning be integrated into all areas of the curriculum?
- How can teachers modify their instruction for students with various levels of English proficiency to build up all students' vocabularies?
- What materials will support vocabulary learning in the classroom?

What Words Are Most Important for English Learners to Know?

English learners enter elementary classrooms at all levels of English proficiency. Some students may be new to the country and speak little to no English. Others may have lived in the United States for an extended period of time, may have been in school for a number of years, and may be nearing oral proficiency. Scaffolding instruction so that students learn the academic vocabulary and complex language structures of English requires in-depth teacher professional knowledge (Dutro & Moran, 2003). An important first step is for teachers to have information about their students' oral language proficiency in English so they can match their instruction to what students need next.

When possible, teachers should review available language assessment data to better understand their students' oral proficiency levels. A student who has scored at a beginning level is learning individual words and using one- to two-word responses; in contrast, a student at the early advanced level understands more complex stories and speaks using consistent standard English forms (California Department of Education, 1999). The first student will need to develop a basic oral vocabulary while the latter will need to work on the vocabulary of academic study. Once the teacher has a general idea of a student's oral English proficiency, informal measures can be used to assess particular vocabulary needs. Teachers can talk with students, ask questions, listen to their stories and retellings of personal or academic information, and observe interactions with others. Depending on students' reading and writing skills, written assessments can also help teachers understand what words students know.

Several factors come into play when considering what words should be taught to English learners. Students new to the language should focus on essential survival vocabulary—basic communication phrases and labels for common objects and school-related terms. (I offer suggestions for helping students learn a basic oral vocabulary below.)

Many English learners in mainstream classrooms have mastered a basic oral vocabulary, but they still have significant gaps in their knowledge of words common in print. Graves (2006) suggests that teachers need to provide explicit instruction in words that are highly frequent in texts but less common in oral language to ensure that English learners understand and learn to read the most frequent English words.

Once English learners get beyond the beginning level of proficiency, they will have mastered the majority of words in everyday speech. It is at this point that teachers often think that students are "fluent," or can be instructed without special consideration. Unfortunately most English learners do not have the depth of vocabulary knowledge needed to effectively understand the academic language of print without additional support. In discussing what words are most important to be taught, Kamil and Hiebert (2005) propose several guiding factors. Words may be selected because they are high frequency in

print, they are important and useful, they relate to classroom instructional topics, or they foster important conceptual learning. While some vocabulary researchers suggest that teaching the most frequent words is unnecessary and recommend concentrating on the words used by mature language users, other researchers familiar with English learners see the need to include high-frequency words in print in the vocabulary curriculum of their students (Bear, Helman, Templeton, Invernizzi, & Johnston, 2007; Biemiller, 2004; Calderón et al., 2005; Graves, 2006).

In summary, the words that are most important to teach depend first on the English proficiency level of students, and next on the frequency, utility, and instructional potential of the words. The following segments describe some ways to help students develop a basic oral vocabulary when they are beginning to learn English and give some suggestions for the kinds of words to teach students as they become more orally proficient and grow in their ability to read and write in English.

Developing a Basic Oral Vocabulary. When students are beginning to learn a new language, they need clear, comprehensible instruction that is offered in short chunks but is repeated over time. Students can only handle so much input before they tire and need to let the new words sink in. While it is important to provide opportunities for students to use language with others, teachers must be aware that beginners often do not have the words in English to express themselves fluently. Teachers can support English learners by creating simplified questions for students to show what they know, providing them with visuals or manipulatives to use as props, or finding ways for students to share what they know in their home languages.

An essential first step in developing a basic oral vocabulary is to help students learn the labels for common items in and outside of the classroom. Provide time for a "language buddy" to practice naming common words with the focus student using a photo library or other visual materials. A language buddy can be an educational assistant, a classroom volunteer, an older student, or a more-fluent classmate. These tutoring and practice sessions should be short but take place on a daily basis, if possible. In addition to learning the names of common terms, consider supporting beginning English speakers by

- Finding fellow students and community volunteers who can help translate important vocabulary for the student

- Providing student-friendly reference materials such as picture dictionaries, classroom charts and labels, and agendas of the day's schedule

- Embedding language development activities within content area study such as taking the time to clearly define key terms and processes, using visuals and gestures

- Providing breaks for students new to English to process their learning, such as by reviewing the material with others who speak their home language

Selecting Words for Intentional Vocabulary Instruction. There simply isn't enough time in the academic schedule for teachers to spend extended class time on every important and useful word in the English language. Focus words should help students to better understand grade-level material and extend their current knowledge. The kinds of words featured will depend on the following:

- The thematic studies that take place in the classroom—For example, a class that studies electricity will need to work in depth with words in that topic area such as *current* and *charge.*

- Words that describe important conceptual processes at each grade level—For example, words like *construct*, *separate*, *contrast*, and *summarize* represent essential activities that students will need to enact as they participate in classroom activities across the elementary grades.

- The reading texts used in the class—For example, a class listening to a read-aloud about the Wright Brothers will need to understand words such as *aerodynamic*, *invention*, and *biplane.*

- The word-study level of the class—As students develop reading skills, they examine deeper levels of the English orthography. Whether students are learning sound–symbol relationships, vowel patterns or connections between spelling and meaning, selecting vocabulary words that support their studies reinforces and extends this learning. In contrast to native speakers, English learners need explicit instruction in the meaning of some of the words that are used in their word-study lessons and need opportunities to extend their repertoire of available words that represent specific orthographic features. Table 9.1 outlines the kinds of words studied at various levels of orthographic development (cf. Bear, Invernizzi, Templeton, & Johnston, 2008; Henderson, 1981) and example vocabulary words that support students' learning.

Words selected for intentional focus in the classroom must be connected with other classroom learning and should be useful and relevant enough to merit the allocation of precious instructional time.

How Can the Research Guide Teachers to Select Effective Vocabulary Activities for English Learners? Earlier in this chapter, I presented key ideas gleaned from the vocabulary research with English learners. The research literature suggested that techniques found to be effective in vocabulary instruction for native speakers would likely be effective with English learners as well, but that tailoring instruction to students' multilingual capabilities is important. Effective procedures include scaffolding, presenting words in meaningful contexts, motivating students and connecting to their background knowledge and languages, including opportunities for discourse, and focusing on strategies for word learning. A number of vocabulary activities fit with one or more of these guiding ideas.

Table 9.1
Levels of Orthograhic Development and Word-Study Focus

Level of orthographic development	Word-study focus and sample words	Focus for English learners
Emergent: Students begin to learn about print, develop phonological awareness and make initial sound-symbol connections.	ABCs (*alligator, zebra*) rhyming words (*snug, bug, rug*) beginning sounds (/b/ for *ball, bounce,* and *bottle*)	Learn words that are common in alphabet books. Learn simple rhymes with natural language patterns.
Alphabetic: Students study letter-sound correspondences and short-vowel word families.	Less-common short-vowel words (*peg, mug, jab*) Words with blends (*clip, strand*) Words with digraphs (*chat, dash*)	Make sure that words used in phonics studies are comprehended.
Within-word pattern: Students study more complex vowel patterns. They begin to examine multiple meaning words and homophones.	Homophones (*meat, meet*) Words with multiple meanings (*lean, safe*) Idioms (*"lend an ear"*)	Continue to clarify unfamiliar vocabulary in reading materials and word study. Explicit focus on how spelling influences word meaning.
Syllables and affixes: Students study multisyllable words; base words and affixes; and interrelate spelling, meaning, and grammatical use.	Inflected endings (*glances, glanced, glancing*) Compound words (*backfire, eyewitness*) Affixes (**pre**paid, power**ful**) Two-syllable homophones and homographs (bury/berry, **re**cord/re**cord**)	Build vocabulary interest by investigating spelling-meaning connections. Look for cognates in grammatical affixes across languages (e.g., **pre**suppose/**pre**suponer, eat**ing**/com**iendo**).
Derivational relations: Students study morphology and word etymology, especially Latin and Greek roots, related words across languages and sound alternations across derivations.	Latin roots (*rupt* = to break: *disrupt, rupture, interrupt*) Greek roots (*bio* = life: *biology, biopsy, biography*) Cognates (*transparency/transparencia*) Sound changes in related words (*revise/revision*)	Use cognates to access academic vocabulary. Teach students to analyze word parts to delve into meaning.

In this section, I share several example instructional ideas for students at the early grades, the transitional grades, and the upper grades of the elementary school that align with the research base on vocabulary instruction with English learners. The research has also told us that effective interventions take place over time with opportunities to practice and review. Any of the strategies selected should be implemented intentionally and consistently.

The Early Grades. Students in kindergarten, first grade, and early second grade are learning about print and interacting with simple beginning reading materials (Bear & Helman, 2004). While it is important to make sure students understand the words in the texts they are reading, these materials may not be a rich source of words to extend students' academic vocabularies. Read-aloud materials, however, provide fertile ground to engage students in inquiring about, defining, practicing, and discussing interesting and useful words. Interactive oral reading has been supported in the vocabulary research literature relating to both native speakers and English learners (Biemiller, 2004; Calderón et al., 2005; Nagy & Scott, 2000). Graves (2006) outlines the characteristics of interactive oral reading and describes four research-based instructional programs in use. Classroom teachers use this procedure as they share an interesting book with students, focusing explicitly on a few select words, expanding on the text and asking questions, eliciting students' background knowledge about the words, and providing clarifying examples. With English learners, interactive oral reading may also involve translating the focus words into students' home languages and making the content more comprehensible through visuals and demonstrations. For instance, an oral reading of *The Wolf's Chicken Stew* (Kasza, 1987) invites a focus on the word *prey*. The teacher might share that an animal's prey is what it hunts and eats; probe students' understanding of which animals are prey for others; and give translations of the word, such as *presa* in Spanish. The teacher might help students to act out an animal hunting for food or model an oral language pattern such as "A (*animal*) is prey for a (*animal*)" for students to create their own statements. If students bring up the meaning of the homophone *pray*, the teacher is presented with a wonderful opportunity to talk about how words that sound the same sometimes have different meanings. Depending on the literacy level of the students, the spelling of both words can be compared and discussed.

Another idea for vocabulary instruction with emergent and beginning readers who are learning English is concept sorts (Bear et al., 2007). Concept sorts involve taking a set of pictures or small objects and having students divide them into related groups. For instance, a set of animal pictures can be sorted by those with hair or without hair; those that swim, walk, or fly; big animals or small animals; or any other number of features. Students do not need to know the English vocabulary to be able to sort their pictures, but working with the visuals provides a rich opportunity for them to express the English words they know and ask language mentors for the labels they do not. When teachers listen to students describe their sorts, teachers have the opportunity to assess each student's vocabulary needs. Concept sorts encourage participation and sharing, build on student background knowledge, and provide scaffolding in the form of visual support. They can be used with students learning English at the upper grades as well, and the thematic topics can be adjusted to grade-level content.

The Transitional Grades. As students become better readers, their reading texts at the second- and third-grade level contain more challenging words. The vocabulary activities suggested for early grade students are still effective at this level, but a new opportunity now arises to help students learn vocabulary through their own reading materials. For transitional readers—no longer word-by-word beginning readers, but still not yet completely independent—I discuss two instructional activities that reflect effective principles from the vocabulary research: building vocabulary within book discussion groups and word study examining early spelling–meaning connections.

When students read books in small groups or book clubs (cf. McMahon & Raphael, 1997), words can be examined in meaningful and interesting contexts. After students read a section of their book, they meet to share thoughts and questions about the content and to address related class assignments. As part of the book club or reading group, teachers can ask students to keep track of words that they think are tricky or assign an individual student to lead the group in focusing on specific vocabulary words. For instance, a student reading *The Polar Express* (Van Allsburg, 1985) may draw attention to the interesting words *nougat*, *barren*, and *Great Polar Ice Cap*. Teachers can also add important conceptual words to the group's discussion to ensure that all students have the language to engage with the book's theme.

As described in Table 9.1, students at the transitional stage of reading are working with word-pattern spellings, such as those of long vowel words. This is an excellent time to provide focused instruction on the different meanings and spellings of homophones such as *meat/meet* or *tide/tied*. In word study-groups, students can match homophone pairs and share the words' distinct meanings by using them in sentences or illustrating them, while at the same time investigating and sorting the words by vowel patterns. For instance, homophones could be sorted by spelling pattern as in

- Vowel-consonant -*e* as in *male*, *bare*, and *tide* as compared with vowel-vowel-consonant as in *mail*, *bear*, and *tied*
- Spelling patterns for a specific long vowel, such as *ea* as in *cheap*, *dear*, *jeans*, *meat*, and *heal*, compared with *ee* as in *wee*, *deer*, *meet*, *heel* or the spelling of *genes* or *we*

For additional visual support, homophone pairs can be noted on charts and lists in the classroom and in students' personal picture dictionaries. These lists will aid students as they expand their writing vocabulary. It is hoped that students' beginning explorations of the spelling–meaning connection will infuse the classroom with a contagious excitement about word learning that may expand into studying synonyms, antonyms, and idioms at this stage as well.

Upper Elementary Grades. As English learners become intermediate readers, the academic vocabulary demands of their texts will likely be the greatest obstacles to their proficient reading. A teacher's scaffolding of important content area vocabulary is essential to comprehension. In their book on scaffolded reading experiences, Fitzgerald and Graves (2004) outline in detail procedures for supporting English learners before, during, and after text reading. The upper grades are also an important time to give students tools to take words apart by their meaningful chunks—morphemic analysis—and to provide students with explicit support in connecting cognates in their home language to English words, as described below.

Provide opportunities for students to identify and work with base words, word roots, and affixes. Start with simple prefixes or suffixes such as *un-*, *re-*, or *-ful*. Discuss what the word part means and help students create new words with it. For example, the suffix *-ful* means "an amount that fills." Guide students to create words using this suffix such as *hopeful*, *painful*, or *mouthful*, and discuss how the suffix changes the meaning of the word. Continue introducing and analyzing common affixes and helping students to build as many words as they can come up with. Have students work together to brainstorm, keep ongoing lists in their notebooks, and post charts in the classroom. Provide simple dictionaries and reference books that give students access to the meanings of word parts. After students are successful at coming up with sample words, guide them to use their skills to take apart words. For example, show students the word *replace*. Can they find two meaningful parts in that word? (*re-* and *place*). What can they predict about the meaning of the word? What about the word *replacement*? How does adding *-ment* to the end change the word's meaning? Helping students to build and take apart words containing multiple morphemes is an excellent strategy to extend word learning in their independent reading.

Several of the research studies noted in this chapter support explicit instruction with Spanish speakers on identifying cognates. For example, students can be asked to review a section of their content area reading text and note words that they think have cognates. A passage on nutrition, for example, may spark associations with the following cognates for Spanish speakers: *calorie/ caloria*, *carbohydrate/carbohidrato*, *nutrient/ nutriente*, and *vitamin/vitamina*. Discussions of these cognate pairs help students apply knowledge in their home language to the work of comprehending English texts. Keep track of cognates from important content material on charts in the classroom or in the students' notebooks. Connect cognate study to learning about the Latin and Greek roots of words. For example, students with Latinate home languages such as Spanish will be able to contribute information about vocabulary words such as *arboretum* by connecting the Spanish word *·rbol,* related to the Latin word *arbor*. Extensive lists of cognates exist in published sources such as NTC's *Dictionary of Spanish Cognates* (Nash, 1997). These reference materials are invaluable for helping students to apply the important background knowledge they have to their academic reading in English. (See also Chapter 5, this volume ["The Nature, Learning, and Instruction of General Academic Vocabulary," Hiebert & Lubliner, in *What Research Has to Say About Vocabulary Instruction*], for further discussion of using cognates in vocabulary instruction.)

How Can Vocabulary Learning Be Integrated Into All Areas of the Curriculum?

An effective vocabulary program extends beyond the instructional time in which a set of words is explicitly taught. An atmosphere of interest and engagement with words, a "word consciousness," must be cultivated so that students are motivated to learn words outside of directed lessons (Graves, 2006; Scott & Nagy, 2004). The tone of a classroom, the ways of interacting within its community of learners, and the way the physical environment supports an interest in learning about words are all key aspects of developing language and vocabulary. The following is a list of suggestions for encouraging English learners to reflect upon, engage with, and appreciate words throughout the curriculum and the school day.

Focus on Meaning. Do students comprehend the content of the instruction, whether that be a read-aloud story, a textbook chapter, or the words in their spelling program? How can you tell? Check for understanding in numerous ways throughout the day. Don't ever abandon meaning to simply teach a skill. Students can easily get into the habit of going through the motions—for example reading a passage quickly without understanding it—if they don't think that comprehension is being valued. Provide ways for students to let you know if they don't understand what they are hearing or reading without feeling singled out. Once you get to know the language proficiency levels of your students, take the time to preteach and discuss words that you suspect will be critical to their understanding.

Create Safe Environments for Students to Talk and Use Their Growing English. As students interact, they cement their vocabulary and other language capabilities. Some students are not as verbal as others. Encourage all students to add their voices in class whether through partner sharing, small-group interactions, games, creative dramatics, or dictating or reading their personal stories. Listen to what students say to informally assess their vocabulary needs in specific content areas.

Provide a Word-Rich Physical Environment for Students to Learn New Vocabulary. Label important objects in the classroom such as tools used in science studies. Post charts with important words and directions for student reference. Display content area words with matching visuals in word banks. Supply easy reference materials such as picture dictionaries, rhyming dictionaries, cognate lists, bilingual dictionaries, and thematically organized encyclopedias so that students have access to words, meanings and spellings. Organize classroom library materials so that students can easily access thematic books and literary genres.

Model an Excitement and Curiosity About Words. Think out loud about interesting or unknown words. Show students how you use reference materials to find out more about a word. Make connections to how words are used across curricular areas. Have students look for examples of the words they are studying outside the classroom. Play games and make simple jokes involving word plays. Help English learners understand idioms and the multiple meanings of words that inspire this humor. Notice and appreciate when students use delightful vocabulary in their speech or writing.

How Can Teachers Modify Their Instruction for Students With Various Levels of English Proficiency to Build Up All Students' Vocabularies?

English learners enter elementary school classrooms with a wide range of oral proficiency in English. What is comprehensible to an early advanced student of English will likely be beyond the understanding of a beginning level English learner. How then might teachers accommodate their vocabulary instruction to students of various levels—challenging all but not overwhelming any? Key ideas of effective vocabulary instruction discussed throughout this chapter include meaningful contexts, in-depth instruction, student participation and discourse, scaffolding content, and teaching word-learning strategies. These ideas once again serve as useful guidelines to assist teachers in differentiating vocabulary instruction for English learners.

Begin at the Beginning. Newcomers or other students at the beginning level of proficiency in English need particular instruction focusing on basic vocabulary and survival English. These students will profit from shorter lessons focusing on fewer words at a time with plenty of repetition and review. Efforts should be made to preview, review, and possibly translate key vocabulary from content area lessons for beginning speakers. When possible, partner newcomers with a language buddy who can discuss the content in the student's home language. In other words, provide as many life rings as possible so the student doesn't sink.

Become a Sheltered-Instruction Teacher. The more you scaffold your teaching, the more likely your instruction will be understandable to students at a variety of oral proficiency levels. Sheltered strategies include speaking with clear, easy-to-understand language and using visuals, manipulatives, or physical actions to make your content more comprehensible. Sheltered instruction also involves organizing the content in thematic or other meaningful ways, designing group work, and creating opportunities for social interaction among students (Echevarria, Vogt, & Short, 2000; Genesee et al., 2005; Peregoy & Boyle, 2001). Consider making a list of sheltered strategies and keeping track of how many you will use as you plan and implement vocabulary and literacy lessons. Sheltered instruction supports all students' learning, and it is an absolutely essential practice to provide English learners with access to the curriculum.

Foster a Community of Language Learners. An excellent way to provide differentiated vocabulary instruction is to enlist the resources of all members of your classroom and school community. Create an atmosphere in class in which students feel included and expected to excel. Make the classroom a safe place to experiment and grow with language without fear of being laughed at. Help all students become mentors—those who speak more English serve as supports to beginning speakers and all students' home languages become resources to share with the group. As the classroom leader, show students how to support the learning of their peers without doing their work for them. Demonstrate that you value their role as co-teachers. When you are not familiar with the home languages of your students, bring in family members or community members to talk about their languages and cultures. Ask community members to share stories and vocabulary related to current units of study in the classroom. Take the concept of word consciousness and transform it into "language consciousness"—an interest and motivation to learn about words in many languages and get to know the people who speak them.

Be Aware of Overload. An important aspect of delivering effective instruction is knowing how much is enough. Differentiating vocabulary instruction for English learners may not only mean providing more scaffolding, it may also mean controlling the number of words or the length of time of each lesson for specific students. While you teach, notice when English learners seem to fill up with new words or content. For instance, beginning English speakers may do well to focus on about three new words at a time, whereas intermediate speakers may be fine with 5–7, and advanced speakers with 7–10 (Helman & Burns, in press). If you can provide small-group instruction for students at similar proficiency levels, you can adjust the length of lessons accordingly. If you are presenting lessons with heterogeneous groups of English learners, find ways to accommodate students' language levels in your expectations, perhaps giving beginners a reduced list of focus vocabulary words. Provide many opportunities within the lesson for students to process the information with peers or apply their learning independently.

Reach for the Stars, but Prioritize. The research tells us that high expectations and in-depth content instruction are critical to the academic success of linguistically diverse students (Au, 2006; CREDE, 2002; Echevarria, Short, & Powers, 2006; Genesee et al., 2005). In your classroom, work diligently to help all students meet high standards, and positively communicate your vision of their coming success. At the same time you hold high aspirations for English-learning students, know that not all standards are "created equal." Assess your students informally to understand their language and literacy strengths and compare these with your grade-level goals. What skills and strategies will give students the most power to be successful in many aspects of their academic work? A priority area could be a specific reading skill such as more automatic recognition of high frequency words, knowledge of key vocabulary words in a math or science unit, or learning how to extract important information from nonfiction texts. Discuss your priorities with colleagues, students, and their family members and see what they have to add. Find ways for students to monitor and demonstrate progress, such as through graphs, portfolios, and personal checklists. Share accomplishments in the classroom and in communications with families. Help students know that you believe in them, and that you will do whatever you can to help them succeed.

What Materials Will Support Vocabulary Learning in the Classroom?

A word-rich physical environment can heighten vocabulary learning for students and serve as an extra pair of hands for the teacher. Print in the form of labels, word cards, posters and charts, reference books, and so on are often so well-used in the classroom that they wear out and need to be periodically replaced. The following is a suggested shopping list of possible print materials that your English learners will find extremely helpful. The particular materials you need vary depending on the developmental level and English proficiency of your students:

- Desktop reference materials for students such as picture alphabets and letter–sound charts
- Visual reference materials such as illustrated encyclopedias and picture dictionaries
- Small picture cards to use in concept sorts (see Bear et al., 2007, for examples)
- Pocket charts and photograph libraries to display and label items relating to thematic studies and new vocabulary words
- Illustrated word books that show photographs and labels around thematic topics (see *My Big Animal Book*, Priddy, 2002, as an example)
- Charts or posters illustrating and labeling thematic topics such as parts of the body or the solar system
- Manipulatives for storytelling such as flannel board pieces, props, or small plastic objects
- Puzzles with pieces that connect a picture and the object's name
- Bilingual puzzles connecting words in students' home languages and English
- Picture books from students' home languages so students can identify vocabulary words
- Longer texts in students' home languages for their independent reading

- Magazines with interesting pictures to prompt storytelling
- Nonfiction books on the topics the class is studying that are easier to read and contain more visuals than typical materials for that grade level
- Picture books that expand students' understanding of words, such as *Many Luscious Lollipops* (Heller, 1998)
- Cognate dictionaries for your students' home languages and English
- Bilingual dictionaries for the languages your students speak
- Cards, posters, or books with Latin and Greek roots and their meanings
- References for word derivations and etymologies such as *The Concise Oxford Dictionary of English Etymology* (Hoad, 2003)
- Lists of useful website addresses for research or word study (for home or school use)
- Technology support such as a projector to display the computer screen
- Computer programs for word learning and matching
- Composition books for students to use as word study or vocabulary notebooks to record their word lists of all kinds

The items listed above serve both as reference materials for students and as discussion starters. Students will use them to help explain things for which they don't yet have the words and, as a teacher, you will find them indispensable for clarifying what you are communicating to students.

Conclusions

Developing a broad and deep vocabulary repertoire in English is critical to the academic success of English learners in U.S. schools. While there is extensive research on effective vocabulary instruction for native speakers of English,

the research base with English learners is much smaller. Many instructional strategies used with native speakers are likely to be effective with English learners as well, but will need to be adapted to accommodate students' specific strengths and background knowledge.

In the vocabulary research reviewed in this chapter, effective programs used instructional procedures such as choosing useful and interesting words presented in meaningful contexts, providing in-depth instruction over time with repetition and application tasks outside of the classroom, scaffolding instruction through sheltered techniques, building on students' background languages and finding cognates, encouraging participation and interactions with fellow students, and teaching strategies for word learning like structural analysis. These key procedures help teachers select and plan effective vocabulary instruction in their own classrooms.

The chapter answered some specific questions about how to help English learners acquire basic and academic vocabulary words both in and out of their literacy instruction, such as how to select important words for vocabulary study, depending on students' levels of English proficiency. I also provided example activities at the early, transitional, and upper elementary grades that reflected key ideas from the research base. I encouraged teachers to integrate vocabulary learning into all areas of the curriculum focusing on meaning, providing a safe environment for students to talk, providing a word-rich environment, and modeling an excitement and curiosity about interesting words.

In the final sections, I gave examples of how teachers can modify their instruction for students at various English proficiency levels by following research-based instructional principles. Teachers provide extra support to beginning English learners by adjusting the quantity and focusing on priority vocabulary words. Sheltered instructional techniques are used to make the instruction more comprehensible. A community of word learners is fostered that relies on all students' participation and high expectations. I ended with a suggested list of materials teachers might obtain to support oral and written vocabulary teaching in their elementary-grade classrooms.

As English learners become a larger percentage of students in elementary classrooms across the country, it is critical to build on the small research base relating to what vocabulary instruction works best for them. The field needs research that explores the specifics of effective vocabulary instruction as it relates to students at each level of reading and oral proficiency development. For instance, at what reading and language proficiency level is instruction in cognates most effective? How can early grade teachers best support the academic vocabulary learning needs that students will confront in the upper elementary grades? How can teachers at many grade levels, not just the early grades, learn how to best work with students who enter class with limited formal schooling and beginning-level skills in English?

This chapter has outlined many issues in vocabulary instruction with elementary-age English learners. It provides teachers with ideas for planning classroom instructional programs that incorporate research-based principles of effective vocabulary instruction. I encourage you to enjoy the journey as you lead students to learning about words and languages through systematic, meaningful, research-based vocabulary instruction in your teaching.

References

Au, K.H. (2006). *Multicultural issues and literacy achievement*. Mahwah, NJ: Erlbaum.

August, D., & Hakuta, K. (1997). *Improving schooling for language-minority children: A research agenda*. Washington, DC: National Academy Press.

August, D., & Shanahan, T. (Eds.). (2006). *Developing literacy in second-language learners: Report of the National Literacy Panel on Language Minority Children and Youth*. Mahwah, NJ: Erlbaum.

Baker, S.K., Gersten, R., Haager, D., & Dingle, M. (2006). Teaching practice and the reading growth of first-grade English learners: Validation of an observation instrument. *The Elementary School Journal, 107*(2), 199–219.

Bear, D.R., & Helman, L. (2004). Word study for vocabulary development in the early stages of literacy learning: Ecological perspectives and learning English. In J.F. Baumann & E.J. Kame'enui (Eds.), *Vocabulary instruction: Research to practice* (pp. 139–158). New York: Guilford.

Bear, D.R., Helman, L., Templeton, S., Invernizzi, M., & Johnston, F. (2007). *Words their way with English learners: Word study for phonics, vocabulary, and spelling instruction*. Upper Saddle River, NJ: Pearson Prentice Hall.

Bear, D.R., Invernizzi, M., Templeton, S., & Johnston, F. (2008). *Words their way: Word study for phonics, vocabulary, and spelling instruction* (4th ed.). Upper Saddle River, NJ: Prentice Hall.

Beck, I.L., & McKeown, M.G. (2007). Increasing young low-income children's oral vocabulary repertoires through rich and focused instruction. *The Elementary School Journal, 107*(3), 251–271.

Beck, I.L., Perfetti, C.A., & McKeown, M.G. (1982). The effects of long-term vocabulary instruction on lexical access and reading comprehension. *Journal of Educational Psychology, 74*(4), 506–521.

Biemiller, A. (2004). Teaching vocabulary in the primary grades: Vocabulary instruction needed. In J.F. Baumann & E.J. Kame'enui (Eds.), *Vocabulary instruction: Research to practice* (pp. 28–40). New York: Guilford.

Biemiller, A., & Boote, C. (2006). An effective method for building meaning vocabulary in primary grades. *Journal of Educational Psychology, 98*(1), 44–62.

Blachowicz, C.L.Z., Fisher, P.J., Ogle, D., & Watts-Taffe, S.M. (2006). Vocabulary: Questions from the classroom. *Reading Research Quarterly, 41*(4), 524–539.

Calderûn, M., August, D., Slavin, R.E., Duran, D., Madden, N., & Cheung, A. (2005). Bringing words to life in classrooms with English-language learners. In E.H. Hiebert & M.L. Kamil (Eds.), *Teaching and learning vocabulary: Bringing research to practice* (pp. 115–136). Mahwah, NJ: Erlbaum.

California Department of Education. (1999). Content standards: English language development, English version. Retrieved April 15, 2007, from www.cde.ca.gov/be/st/ss

Carlo, M.S., August, D., McLaughlin, B., Snow, C.E., Dressler, C., Lippman, D.N., et al. (2004). Closing the gap: Addressing the vocabulary needs of English-language learners in bilingual and mainstream classrooms. *Reading Research Quarterly, 39*(2), 188–215.

Center for Research on Education, Diversity & Excellence (CREDE). (2002). *Research evidence: Five standards for effective pedagogy and student outcomes* (Technical Report No. G1). Santa Cruz: University of California.

Cheung, A., & Slavin, R.E. (2005). Effective reading programs for English language learners and other language-minority students. *Bilingual Research Journal, 29*(2), 241–267.

Cummins, J. (2003). Reading and the bilingual student: Fact and friction. In G.G. Garcìa (Ed.), *English learners: Reaching the highest level of English literacy* (pp. 2–33). Newark, DE: International Reading Association.

Cunningham, A.E., & Stanovich, K.E. (1997). Early reading acquisition and its relationship to reading experience and ability 10 years later. *Developmental Psychology, 33*(6), 934–935.

Dutro, S., & Moran, C. (2003). Rethinking English language instruction: An architectural approach. In G.G. Garcìa (Ed.), *English learners: Reaching the highest level of English literacy* (pp. 227–258). Newark, DE: International Reading Association.

Dufra, M., & Voeten, M.J.M. (1999). Native language literacy and phonological memory as prerequisites for learning English as a foreign language. *Applied Psycholinguistics, 20*(3), 329–348.

Echevarria, J., Short, D., & Powers, K. (2006). School reform and standards-based education: A model for English-language learners. *The Journal of Educational Research, 99*(4), 195–210.

Echevarria, J., Vogt, M.E., & Short, D.J. (2000). *Making content comprehensible for English language learners: The SIOP model*. Boston: Allyn & Bacon.

Fitzgerald, J., & Graves, M.F. (2004). *Scaffolding reading experiences for English-language learners*. Norwood, MA: Christopher-Gordon.

Garcìa, G.E. (1991). Factors influencing the English reading test performance of Spanish-speaking Hispanic children. *Reading Research Quarterly, 26*(4), 371–392.

Genesee, F., Lindholm-Leary, K., Saunders, W., & Christian, D. (2005). English language learners in U.S. schools: An overview of research findings. *Journal of Education for Students Placed at Risk, 10*(4), 363–385.

Gersten, R., & Jimènez, R.T. (1994). A delicate balance: Enhancing literature instruction for students of English as a second language. *The Reading Teacher, 47*(6), 438–449.

Graves, M.F. (2006). *The vocabulary book*. New York: Teachers College Press.

Helman, L.A., & Burns, M.S. (in press). What does oral language have to do with it? Helping young English-language learners acquire a sight word vocabulary. *The Reading Teacher, 62*(1).

Henderson, E.H. (1981). *Learning to read and spell: The child's knowledge of words*. DeKalb, IL: Northern Illinois Press.

Hoad, T.F. (2003). *The concise Oxford dictionary of English etymology*. Oxford: Oxford University Press.

Jimènez, R.T., Garcìa, G.E., & Pearson, P.D. (1996). The reading strategies of bilingual Latino/a students who are successful English readers: Opportunities and obstacles. *Reading Research Quarterly, 31*(1), 90–112.

Kamil, M.L., & Hiebert, E.H. (2005). Teaching and learning vocabulary: Perspectives and persistent issues. In E.H. Hiebert & M.L. Kamil (Eds.), *Teaching and learning vocabulary: Bringing research to practice* (pp. 1–23). Mahwah, NJ: Erlbaum.

McGregor, K.K. (2004). Developmental dependencies between lexical semantics and reading. In C.A. Stone, E.R. Silliman, B.J. Ehren, & K. Apel (Eds.), *Handbook of language and literacy: Development and disorders* (pp. 302–317). New York: Guilford.

McMahon, S.I., & Raphael, T. (1997). *The book club connection: Literacy learning and classroom talk*. New York: Teachers College Press.

Nagy, W.E. (1997). On the role of context in first- and second-language vocabulary learning. In N. Schmitt & M. McCarthy (Eds.), *Vocabulary: Description, acquisition and pedagogy* (pp. 64–83). Cambridge: Cambridge University Press.

Nagy, W.E., Garcìa, G.E., Durgunoglu, A.Y., & Hancin-Bhatt, B. (1993). Spanish-English bilingual students' use of cognates in English reading. *Journal of Reading Behavior, 25*(3), 241–259.

Nagy, W.E., & Scott, J.A. (2000). Vocabulary processes. In M.L. Kamil, P.B. Mosenthal, P.D. Pearson, & R. Barr (Eds.), *Handbook of reading research* (Vol. 3, pp. 269–284). Mahwah, NJ: Erlbaum.

Nash, R. (1997). *NTC's dictionary of Spanish cognates thematically organized*. Lincolnwood, IL: NTC Publishing Group.

National Center for Education Statistics. (2005). *Reading assessment*. Retrieved April 19, 2007, from nces.ed.gov/nationsreportcard/itemmaps/?year=2005&grade=4&subj=Reading.

National Center for Education Statistics. (2006). *The condition of education 2006*. NCES 2006-071. Washington, DC: U.S. Government Printing Office. Retrieved April 19, 2007, from nces.ed.gov/pubsearch/pubsinfo.asp?pubid=2006071.

National Institute of Child Health and Human Development. (2000). *Report of the National Reading Panel. Teaching children to read: An evidence-based assessment of the scientific research literature on reading and its implications for reading instruction* (NIH Publication No. 00-4769). Washington, DC: U.S. Government Printing Office.

Peregoy, S.F., & Boyle, O.F. (2001). *Reading, writing, and learning in ESL: A resource book for K–12 teachers*. New York: Longman.

Pèrez, E. (1981). Oral language competence improves reading skills of Mexican American third graders. *The Reading Teacher, 35*(1), 24–27.

Rayner, K., Foorman, B.R., Perfetti, C.A., Pesetsky, D., & Seidenberg, M.S. (2001). How psychological science informs the teaching of reading. *Psychological Science in the Public Interest, 2*(2), 31–74.

Roberts, T.A. (2008). Home storybook reading in primary or second language with preschool children: Evidence of equal effectiveness for second-language vocabulary acquisition. *Reading Research Quarterly, 42*(2), 103–130.

Saunders, W., & Goldenberg, C. (2001). Strengthening the transition in transitional bilingual education. In D. Christian & F. Genesee (Eds.), *Bilingual education* (pp. 41–56). Alexandria, VA: Teachers of English to Speakers of Other Languages.

Scott, J.A., & Nagy, W.E. (2004). *Developing word consciousness*. In J.F. Baumann & E.J. Kame'enui (Eds.), *Vocabulary instruction: Research to practice* (pp. 201–217). New York: Guilford.

Shanahan, T., & Beck, I.L. (2006). Effective literacy teaching for English-language learners. In D. August & T. Shanahan (Eds.), *Developing literacy in second-language learners: Report of the National Literacy Panel on Language Minority Children and Youth* (pp. 415–488). Mahwah, NJ: Erlbaum.

Snow, C.E., Burns, M.S., & Griffin, P. (Eds.). (1998). *Preventing reading difficulties in young children*. Washington, DC: National Academy Press.

Vaughn-Shavuo, F. (1990). *Using story grammar and language experience for improving recall and comprehension in the teaching of ESL to Spanish-dominant first-graders*. Unpublished doctoral dissertation, Hofstra University, New York.

Verhoeven, L.T. (1990). Acquisition of reading in a second language. *Reading Research Quarterly, 25*(2), 90–114.

Literature Cited

Heller, R. (1998). *Many luscious lollipops: A book about adjectives*. New York: Putnam.

Kasza, K. (1987). *The wolf's chicken stew*. New York: Putnam.

Priddy, R. (2002). *My big animal book*. New York: St. Martin's.

Van Allsburg, C. (1985). *The polar express*. Boston: Houghton Mifflin.

Questions for Reflection

• Think about a time you tried to learn words in a new language, perhaps when you visited another country. What techniques did you find helpful for remembering new vocabulary? What, if any, of these techniques might be applicable to support English learners' vocabulary development in your classroom?

• Find a paragraph of text in Spanish, either from the Internet or a book or periodical. Read through the words looking for cognates. When you see a possible cognate write it down along with your prediction about its meaning. Discuss your list of possible cognates with a partner.

• Take a reading or writing lesson plan from a teacher's manual at your students' grade level. Highlight vocabulary words that you think would be challenging for students learning English. Now list four ways that you could scaffold the lesson to make it more comprehensible to your students.

• Consider the word-study or spelling program used at your students' grade level. Make a list of words that English learners may find difficult to understand. How could you supplement the word study with rich instruction or print materials to support your students' learning?

Teaching Vocabulary Through Text and Experience in Content Areas

Marco A. Bravo and Gina N. Cervetti

ontent area vocabulary presents both a set of challenges and possibilities for word learning. On the one hand, content areas expose students to a large corpus of challenging and often abstract words, many of which require the use of other equally challenging words to define and exemplify them. Yet content areas also present students with multiple, multimodal, thematically related, and contextualized experiences with target words, all of which can increase student opportunities to build active control of generative academic language.

This chapter illustrates the importance of vocabulary teaching and learning in content areas, outlines the challenges of vocabulary learning in these contexts, and suggests possibilities for rich vocabulary teaching in the content areas.

Importance of Vocabulary in Content Areas

With increased attention to integration of literacy with content area instruction (Hapgood, Magnusson, & Palincsar, 2004; Hopkins, 2007; Hilve, 2006), vocabulary teaching and learning in these contexts has gained considerable visibility. In part, interest in the role of vocabulary learning in content area instruction stems from the understanding that word knowledge is essential to reading for comprehension of content area texts (Anderson & Freebody, 1981; Nagy, 1988) just as appropriate vocabulary use is essential to high-quality content area writing (Jones &

Thomas, 2006; Rothstein, Rothstein, & Lauber, 2006). The link between word knowledge and comprehension of content area text and quality writing makes common sense and is well established by research (Beck, Perfetti, & McKeown, 1982; Blachowicz & Fisher, 2000). For example, Carney, Anderson, Blackburn, and Blessing (1984) found that preteaching social studies vocabulary to fifth-grade students resulted in significantly improved reading comprehension of passages that contained the target words. Similarly Amaral, Garrison, and Klentschy (2002) found an increase in the quantity and quality of writing produced by elementary grade students in science when the vocabulary of science was a focus of instruction.

Moreover learning the language of the content area is as important as learning the content itself; one can argue that words are, in fact, the surface level instantiations of the deeper underlying concepts and that, as such, they provide the connections to the everyday discourse that makes the concepts transparent. Gaining control over disciplinary vocabulary is critical for conceptual understanding; knowing disciplinary terms is fundamental to the comprehension of content area concepts. To deal effectively with the content of content area textbooks, it is critical to understand the terminology of the discipline. Readence, Bean, and Baldwin (1985) suggest that students are often "outsiders" to subjects like math, science, and social studies and that by demystifying the vocabulary of these disciplines, we can help students become "insiders" (p. 149) with the concepts of the

Reprinted from Bravo, M.A., & Cervetti, G.N. (2008). Teaching vocabulary through text and experience in content areas. In A.E. Farstrup & S.J. Samuels (Eds.), *What research has to say about vocabulary instruction* (pp. 130–149). Newark, DE: International Reading Association.

domain. Armbruster (1992) notes that, in content area instruction, new words are typically closely tied to the major purpose of the lesson, which is typically the acquisition of new knowledge; in fact it would be surprising if the words were not related to the primary goal of knowledge acquisition. While challenging terms in literature are often peripherally related to important themes, challenging content area words are more often labels that describe, or stand for, the key content area concepts (Armbruster, 1992; Cervetti, Pearson, Bravo, & Barber, 2006). Collectively concepts compose areas of study within content matter (Harmon, Hedrick, & Wood, 2005). Concepts such as *polygon*, *convex*, *equilateral*, and *vertex*, for example, make up a section of the study of geometry in math. These concepts build upon each other to construct the conceptual knowledge of the content area. Not knowing concepts or having passive understanding of concepts can leave gaps in areas of study and can negatively affect future learning in that discipline (Blachowicz & Obrochta, 2005). For example, not understanding the term *square* will make understanding terms like *perimeter* and *area* much more difficult. While this relationship between vocabulary and comprehension is well established by research, precious little vocabulary instruction uses conceptual relatedness as a basis for content area vocabulary instruction particularly across content areas (Ryder & Graves, 1998).

Acquiring technical terminology of content areas is also tied to successful functioning in the domain (Schleppegrell, 2007; Spencer & Guillaume, 2006; Vacca & Vacca, 2002); in other words, it is hard to engage in key cognitive activities unless one knows enough of the key vocabulary to transform what could be empty processes into meaningful participatory structures. Lemke (1990) suggested that to do science it is essential to know the language of science. In science, precision with specialized language is essential for understanding and supports students' ability to participate in disciplinary inquiry and to communicate the results of the inquiry. For example, the use of the term *observe* instead of *see* is critical to the practice of science. While the distinction between this pair of words may be unimportant in everyday conversation, in science a term like *observe* invokes other elements not present in the everyday term *see*, including looking at something with attention to detail, extending the examination for a prolonged period of time, and using all of one's senses to imbue the activity with meaning. Not knowing the terminology of the content compromises students' ability to inquire in the discipline and makes students "outsiders" to the discipline (Readence et al., 1985).

Challenges of Content Area Vocabulary

Some of the challenges associated with content area vocabulary learning include the fact that disciplinary words are typically numerous (Schell, 1982), often abstract (Nagy, Anderson, & Herman, 1987), frequently carry more than one meaning (Kopriva & Saez, 1997), and are likely to be new labels for unknown ideas even when their form is recognizable (Armbruster, 1992). These features combine to create a lexical overload for students in content areas that can only be overcome by demystifying the meanings and interrelationships of key vocabulary (Beck & McKeown, 1985).

Copious Vocabulary

One common vocabulary feature across disciplines is the sheer number of complex terms students are exposed to. According to Armstrong and Collier (1990), an introductory biology textbook averages 738 pages and presents over 3,500 new terms, which is around 45%–50% more new words than are presented in a semester of foreign language instruction. Similarly, math texts have been found to include "more concepts per word, per sentence, and per paragraph than any other [subject] area" (Schell, 1982, p. 544). Harmon, Hedrick, and Fox (2000) examined the nature and representation of vocabulary instruction in the teachers' editions of social studies textbooks for grades 4–8 and also found a heavy vocabulary demand. Encountering this number of words independently within one content area would be difficult, but because students will experience all content areas, this multiplies the dilemma (Harmon et al., 2005).

Abstractness of Content Area Vocabulary

An additional challenge of teaching and learning content area vocabulary stems from the fact that many important words in subject matter domains are abstract (Vacca & Vacca, 2002), making them more difficult to acquire (Schwanenflugel & Noyes, 1996). Levels of concreteness or abstractness have been found to influence how well students learn target words (Gentner, 1982; Nagy et al., 1987; Schwanenflugel, Stahl, & McFalls, 1997). For example, Schwanenflugel et al. (1997) in their study of fourth-grade students examined whether vocabulary knowledge changed as a function of story reading and found that for partially known words, word concreteness (defined by degree of imageability) was positively related to students' learning of targeted words. The researchers attributed easier access to concrete words to three related factors: (1) the "imageability" (p. 541) of the words, (2) the capacity of "imageable" (p. 541) words to allow students to use all, or at least some, of the five senses to make sense of the concept, and (3) the stronger likelihood that more concrete words will, in general, permit greater student reliance on prior knowledge to access target concepts. Nagy et al. (1987) also found that degree of abstractness influenced word learning; for complex, abstract words, there was little evidence of incidental word learning, indicating that for such words students could make only very generic distinctions among their meanings.

Multiple-Meaning Words

Many unfamiliar and challenging disciplinary words carry more than one meaning, which opens the possibility, perhaps the likelihood, that comprehension will be complicated (Kopriva & Saez, 1997). A word like *operation*, for example, can reference what takes place in a hospital or a mathematical process in which particular rules are applied. Words that have one meaning

in everyday language and a more specialized meaning in content area learning are especially vulnerable to misunderstanding and semantic "interference." Multiple meaning words abound in the English language. Johnson, Moe, and Baumann (1983) found that among the identified 9,000 critical vocabulary words for elementary-grade students, 70% had more than one meaning. These words are not limited to written language: teachers' talk also includes words with multiple meanings. Lazar, Warr-Leeper, Nicholson, and Johnson (1989) found that 36% of teacher utterances from kindergarten to grade 8 contained at least one word that had a multiple meaning.

The interference potential of multiple-meaning words (Marzano, 2004) can be particularly challenging to the growing population of English learners (Carlo, August, & Snow, 2005; Graves, 2006). Consider the shades of meaning in the terms *expression* in math, *current* in science, and *capital* in social studies. All of these terms have an everyday meaning familiar to students, along with a specialized meaning in their respective fields that is less likely to be known by students. Complicating the issue a bit more, the same multiple-meaning words can be found across content areas where within each domain a different specialized meaning is intended. The term *solution* in science, for example, can mean when one thing is dissolved in another. In mathematics, the term refers to the answer and steps taken to solve a problem; in social studies, the intended meaning can be the act of ending a dispute or the payment of a debt. As students move through instruction across content areas, an extra level of analysis is necessary to choose the intended meaning in the respective subject matter. Other terms that fall into this category include *property*, *add*, and *climate*.

New Labels for Unknown Words

Armbruster (1992) suggested that a primary difference between vocabulary encountered in content areas and those encountered in literature-focused instruction is the degree of conceptual familiarity. They note that, while learning vocabulary in narrative-dominant reading lessons often involves learning new labels for known concepts (i.e., *stunning* for *beautiful*), content area vocabulary learning is more challenging because the vocabulary in these contexts is less often associated with a familiar concept. The technical vocabulary that students encounter in content areas is likely to be new labels for new ideas (Armbruster, 1992); consequently, as students are learning new words, they are also learning new and challenging concepts (Graves & Prenn, 1986).

Graves (2000), in his typology of vocabulary learning tasks, found that this process was mediated by whether students are learning to read known words, learning new words that represent known concepts, or learning new words representing new concepts. Learning to read known words includes words students possess in their listening or speaking vocabulary but not in their reading or writing vocabularies. Words for which a concept already exists in the students' lexicon are exemplified by the situation when students already have a concept but are confronted with an unfamiliar synonym. These synonyms often invoke a nuanced meaning that is different from the original word, but students will likely have some background knowledge that they can leverage to make sense of the target concept (Bravo, Hiebert, & Pearson, 2006). Some examples of this type include the word pairs *equivalent/same* and *solution/answer*. The final category, which best describes the bulk of content area vocabulary, includes words where both the label and the concept are foreign to students. For example, students' first encounters with terms such as *polygon* and *isosceles* are likely to take place in a math class and both the label and concept are likely to be unfamiliar.

These differing vocabulary-learning tasks bear different instructional implications (Hiebert, 2005). Teaching new labels for known concepts can require different levels of instructional involvement than teaching unknown labels for challenging concepts. Instruction for these tasks can range from pronouncing a word for students—a word that they already possess in their listening vocabularies—as they read so that they make an association between the word they know and the target word, to having in-depth and extended discussions coupled with contextual definitions to illustrate new words and concepts.

Vocabulary Learning Possibilities in Content Areas

The challenges notwithstanding, several key factors make content areas a potentially rich and interesting context for vocabulary development. A saving grace of content area writing is that novel words, because they are conceptually central to the topic under study, are likely to be repeated in text designed to explain the topic. Hence students are likely to encounter multiple instances of the word in varied contexts, and both multiple and varied exposures are important to acquiring new vocabulary. Conceptually core words in content areas are also likely to be thematically related, making for a rich contextualized word-learning experience. Moreover content areas lend themselves to the use of multiple modalities (written, oral, and experiential language contexts) to acquire vocabulary knowledge. All of these conditions conspire to present students with an optimal word-learning experience.

Multiple and Varied Exposures

Existing research not only suggests that vocabulary learning is dependent on multiple exposures to target words (Beck et al., 1982; Nagy, 1988; Stahl & Fairbanks, 1986), but also that it is related to the nature of the exposures (Graves & Prenn, 1986). Approaches that provide meaningful information about words—both definitional and contextual information—appear to be more powerful than approaches that focus on only one kind of information (Nagy & Scott, 2000).

Research suggests that definitional information is important, but insufficient for word learning. Several studies compare some version of definitional instruction in which students memorized, looked up in dictionaries, or discussed the definitions of a set of words with approaches that provide more contextual and semantic information about the words (e.g., Anders, Bos, & Filip, 1984; Stahl, 1983; Stahl & Kapinus, 1991). Taken together, this research suggests that approaches that provide more information about the words, particularly about the relationships among words, result in increased word learning and often in stronger comprehension of texts that use the target words. For example, Stahl (1983) compared two approaches to teaching text-based words to fifth-grade students: a definitional approach, in which students looked words up in a dictionary and discussed the words, and a mixed approach, in which students were given words and definitions, discussed the definitions, and generated sentences with the words. Both of these groups performed better on posttest measures of vocabulary learning than a group that received no special instruction on measures of vocabulary and comprehension. The mixed approach group scored higher on the vocabulary measures (but not the comprehension measure) than the definitional group.

Bos and Anders (1990) studied the science vocabulary learning of learning-disabled junior high school students using three semantic mapping and semantic feature analysis approaches and a definitional approach. Students in the semantic mapping and semantic feature analysis groups outperformed the students in the definitional group on measures of vocabulary learning and comprehension. Bos, Anders, Filip, and Jaffe (1989) compared two approaches to prereading vocabulary instruction in social studies among learning-disabled high school students: a dictionary method of vocabulary instruction, in which students used a dictionary to write definitions of words then wrote sentenceswith the words, and an approach using semantic feature analysis. Students who received instruction using semantic feature analysis performed significantly better on a comprehension measure after reading. (See Chapter 3, this volume ["Instruction on Individual Words: One Size Does Not Fit All," Graves, *What Research Has to Say About Vocabulary Instruction*] for more detail on semantic mapping and semantic feature analysis.)

There are several possible limitations to approaches that rely on definitions alone: Definitions do not provide enough information to support students in acquiring more than partial understanding; definitions do not provide very much information about context of use, limiting students' ability to recognize and use the words in various contexts; and definitional approaches teach words as isolated units, even though deep, flexible word knowledge involves a process of integrating new words into semantic networks with a range of known words. In content areas in particular, simple definitions often will not suffice (Armbruster, 1992). Even so, context in and of itself does not fare much better as a solo word-learning strategy. For example, Brett, Rothlein, and Hurley (1996) found that fourth graders who listened to stories and were provided with an explanation of the meaning of unfamiliar words were more likely to learn the words than students who listened to the words read in the context of the stories without explanation of their meaning. Biemiller and Boote (2006) found that grade K–2 students who encountered words through repeated readings of fictional stories learned about 12% of words' meanings. When repeated readings were accompanied by explanations of the word meanings, students learned about 22% of the words. Notably children with smaller vocabularies benefited more from explanations of words (during encounters in text) than children with larger vocabularies. We, the authors, would like to point out that part of the advantage of direct explanation may be that it draws attention to words that might otherwise be overlooked by young readers: It can be difficult for these readers to attend to individual words while reading or listening to connected text.

In addition to providing multiple encounters with conceptually core vocabulary, content areas also typically supply students with exposures in varied contexts, the kinds of exposures that are meaningful and in context, critical for in-depth understanding of target words. Due to the central role content area vocabulary plays in content area learning, important terms tend to appear often in the texts and talk surrounding instruction (Spencer & Guillaume, 2006). Hiebert (2005) has found, for example, that conceptually important words are repeated often in nonfiction science books for young readers. Since word meanings are accumulated gradually (Nagy & Scott, 2000), getting more than one shot at deciphering the meaning of terms can lead to more sophisticated understandings of target words. McKeown, Beck, Omanson, and Pople (1985), for example, found that more than 10 encounters with target words, reliably predicted fourth-grade students' increased reading comprehension.

Each subsequent encounter with target words, especially when that encounter is different from a previous encounter, serves as an opportunity to accumulate information about that word. This can include understanding the appropriate contextual usage of a term, the word's grammatical form, and nuanced conceptual meanings (Nation, 1990). For example, in an initial encounter with the science term *adaptation* in the sentence "These plants and animals have many adaptations," students may understand that the term is in noun form and understand that it is something that a plant or animal possesses. In later encounters, as in the sentence "Those plants and animals adapted to their environment by way of certain behaviors and structures that develop over time," students gain access to additional information about the term, including the fact that the term can also be used in verb form and that the term refers to certain actions and body parts that plants and animals need in their environment and that it takes time to develop those behaviors and structures.

Content areas, by their very nature, lend themselves to these two key conditions—varied contexts and rich explanations—necessary to develop in-depth and enduring understanding of vocabulary. Given that word learning is multifaceted, that content area vocabulary is often abstract, and that both the labels and the ideas are likely to be new, multiple exposures are vital to content vocabulary learning. In addition, the treatment of important and challenging words in content areas often has a more conceptual focus that provides both definitional and contextual information. Definitional and contextual information provide the type of meaningful information needed to access key content area concepts and subsequently assist in building the conceptual knowledge in the domain.

Teaching Words as Thematically Related Concepts

Teaching words as related concepts appears to add value to vocabulary instruction. Semantic mapping, broadly defined as any approach that makes explicit the relationships among sets of words, has been shown to have positive effects beyond definitional and contextual vocabulary instruction alone. Margosein, Pascarella, and Pflaum (1982) compared two approaches to vocabulary learning among seventh- and eighth-grade students: (1) a semantic mapping approach that tied new words to known words through discussion of the similarities and differences between the new and related, familiar words and (2) a context approach that presented each target word in three-sentence passages where the target word was used in each sentence and defined. The semantic mapping intervention produced significantly higher scores than the context group on weekly vocabulary tests, treatment tests, and the Gates-MacGinitie vocabulary subtest. The results of two other subtests of the Gates-MacGinitie (comprehension and definition tests) likewise showed slightly higher scores for the semantic mapping intervention.

While the Margosein et al. (1982) study did not focus on content area vocabulary, the implications for vocabulary instruction in content areas were apparent. Smith (1990) and Armbruster (1992) noted that viewing vocabulary instruction as a study of relationships is particularly relevant in content area reading. In science, social studies, and mathematics, words index important concepts and those concepts are organized in thematically related networks. Terms like *community*, *culture*, *custom*, and *tradition* are introduced in social studies texts not separate from, but in relation to, each other. These terms are linked to other areas of study within the discipline, which together construct the overall conceptual flow of the content area. The nature of this organization of concepts highlights the association between terms. Recognizing how terms are related to one another suggests high degrees of word knowledge (Stahl, 1999) since students have to situate the term's particular meaning in the context of the meanings of other terms.

This web of concepts affords students a rich context from which they can learn the new technical terminology offered by content areas. Yet, students must be challenged to consider the semantic relationship among the core set of words. Under this approach, a term like *organism* would be semantically introduced as referencing such living things as plants and animals. An example of such is an *isopod*, an animal characterized by its seven pairs of legs, flattened body, and existence in forest floor *habitats*, which is the place where it gets what it needs to *survive*, including *shelter*, *food*, *protection*, *moisture*, and so forth. These italicized words tied semantically together assemble a structure of knowledge within the life science domain.

Exploiting the inherent organization of content area concepts can facilitate vocabulary learning and subsequently content area learning. Assisting students in recognizing and understanding the thematic relationship between core vocabulary within the discipline helps build established levels of word knowledge (Johnson & Pearson, 1984) while helping students construct a knowledge base of the domain as an organized network of related information, assuring more in-depth understanding of important concepts (Glynn & Muth, 1994).

Multimodal Experiences With Content Area Vocabulary

Experiences with vocabulary in modalities other than reading and writing also advance word learning (Carlisle, Fleming, & Gudbrandsen, 2000; Stahl & Clark, 1987; Stahl & Kapinus, 1991). In particular, discussion and experience seem to support word learning because they demand a high level of involvement, or deep processing, of information about the words and because they call on both contextual and definitional understanding. Stahl and Kapinus (1991) found that students who participated in a possible sentences intervention made greater growth in vocabulary than students in semantic mapping and no-treatment interventions. In

possible sentences, the teacher chooses words (usually key concepts) that are used to generate sentences. Students discuss whether the sentences are true or not based on their reading and, if not, how they could be modified to be made true. Stahl and Kapinus suggest that the power of the possible sentences strategy lies in its ability to draw upon students' prior knowledge of the topic and requires that students think about and discuss relations between word concepts rather than treating each word as a separate entity. They also suggest that, because possible sentences involves interactions among students, it encourages active processing of information. In addition, Stahl and Vancil (1986) compared word learning among sixth graders in three conditions: (1) discussion of words, (2) mapping of words, and (3) full semantic mapping involving the physical map and discussion. The discussion group and full semantic mapping group outperformed the word mapping group on a posttest of vocabulary learning. In a related study, Stahl and Clark (1987) studied the learning of science vocabulary with fourth- and fifth-grade students in an instructional intervention involving semantic mapping and discussion. Students who were told they would participate in discussion and those who were called on to participate performed significantly better on a test of vocabulary learning than students in the same classes who did not participate in the discussions.

Similarly Carlisle, Fleming, and Gudbrandsen (2000) found that involvement in discussions and firsthand experiences in fourth- and eighth-grade science led to word learning particularly for students who had partial knowledge of the words. These gains were attributed to students' ability to connect with words through varied sensory representations that allowed students to use multiple codes for understanding target words. Students not only made growth on their recognition of the meaning of the topical words but also on the quality of the explanation of word meanings during open-ended interviews (e.g., what does the word _____ mean?).

Beck, McKeown, and Kucan (2002) concluded that students who engage with words by hearing them, using them, manipulating them semantically, and playing with them are more likely to learn and retain new vocabulary. Opportunities for students to learn and encounter difficult words through reading, writing, talk, and experience are widely available in content area learning.

Research Implications: Some Principles for Content Area Vocabulary Instruction

Informed by the research reviewed, we offer several suggestions for helping students gain word knowledge in content areas. We have organized our suggestions into four "lessons" for solid vocabulary instruction.

Word Selection Is Key to Shaping Vocabulary Instruction

The initial challenge when confronting a large corpus of content area vocabulary is to identify words to target for instruction. We recommend selecting words that are high-utility, necessary for understanding the domain, and connected with one other conceptually.

Select Words That Are High-Utility in the Discipline. Beck et al.'s (2002) classification of terms provides some guidance for the selection of high-utility terms. Beck et al. classified terms into three tiers: Tier 1 words are those that are highly frequent in everyday talk (e.g., *pencil*, *paper*); tier 2 words, which occur with regularity across domains and are used by adults in literate discourse, are essentially uncommon labels for common ideas (predict rather than guess; habitat rather than home); tier 3 words (e.g., *trapezoid*, *stoma)* are the highly specialized, rare words that often occur solely within content areas. Beck and her colleagues suggested targeting tier 2 words for instruction because they are high-utility words and appear frequently in a variety of academic contexts. Tier 2 words in content areas might be thought of as those that are high-utility and ubiquitous within the discipline and across subfields of the discipline even if they are not necessarily part of the lexicon of everyday adult speech. In science, for example, terms associated with science inquiry, such as *hypothesis*, *evidence*, and *model*, occur often across life, earth, and physical science. Similarly *mean*, *expression*, and *product* occur regularly in arithmetic, algebra, and geometry. In social studies, words such as *demand*, *region*, *culture*, and *modify* have utility in geography, history, and civics studies. These "intradisciplinary" words may not be used by adults outside of the domain, yet they appear in textbooks and in tests and will be encountered by students throughout their school careers and, therefore, deserve explicit attention. They support students' ability to participate in the discourse of science (Cervetti & Bravo, 2005), discussions in social studies (Hess, 2004), or problem solving in math (Schleppegrell, 2007).

Select Words That Are Necessary for Understanding the Concepts and Processes of the Domain. While tier 2 terms are critical, more specialized tier 3 words are equally, if not more, important to content area understanding. These terms are often unique to a content area and necessary for understanding of the subject matter concepts. Select words for study that represent the most important concepts or processes. Words like *decomposition*, *habitat*, and *adaptation* in a second-grade earth science unit are specialized terms that index some of the most important concepts in the domain. Renewed interest in generating word lists for subject areas may be one way to identify terms that are conceptually core (Marzano, Kendall, & Paynter, 2005). Also, Ryder and Graves (1998) found it helpful to allow students (with teacher guidance) to be involved in determining which terms are essential to describe and talk about the learning goals. While conceptually core vocabulary may appear frequently within a domain of study (Spencer & Guillaume, 2006), they are not likely to travel across subject matter domains. Hence instruction around these terms must be focused, direct, and true to each term's role in subject matter learning (Ryder & Graves, 1998).

Select Words That Together Represent Important Related Concepts in the Domain.

Learning the vocabulary of a discipline should be thought of as learning about the interconnectedness of ideas and concepts indexed by words. Select words that help students develop rich networks of related word and concepts and those words that assist them in discussing and participating in disciplinary inquiry. One way to do this is to create a map of important concepts for instruction and then to associate one or more words with each concept. For example, in the domain of science the words *transmit*, *reflect*, and *absorb* can be mapped in relation to one another as different ways that light interacts with materials.

Provide Many Opportunities to Learn Target Words

Knowing a word is not an all or nothing phenomenon (Anderson & Freebody, 1981; Nagy & Scott, 2000). Vocabulary knowledge is multifaceted and students come to content areas with varying degrees of vocabulary knowledge (Ryder & Graves, 1998). Vocabulary knowledge can include at least three levels of word knowledge: unknown, acquainted, and established (Beck, McKeown, & McCaslin, 1983). When a term is unknown, the student has never heard nor seen the word. For example, a term like *habitat* may be at the unknown level for kindergarten students.

For some purposes, such as reading a story, an acquaintance level of vocabulary understanding in which a student can decode the word and provide a basic definition may suffice. Content area texts, which usually involve informational texts, are much more dependent on specific terms that are crucial for content area understanding (Blachowicz, Fisher, Ogle, & Watts-Taffe, 2006). Harmon et al. (2005) pointed out that, while partial knowledge of unfamiliar words may be sufficient to support comprehension in the reading of a narrative text, content area reading often demands a higher level of word knowledge because the words are labels for important concepts. Harmon and colleagues further noted that not knowing the precise definition of terms in content areas has the potential to create much more frustration for students than when encountering unclear meanings in narrative texts.

To support students, develop word knowledge at a depth of understanding that is appropriate to content area instruction and provide opportunities for students to encounter important words often and in contexts that provide varied and meaningful information about the words, including definitional, contextual, and relational information. Create a classroom environment where the selected words are present in print and in talk and where the opportunities to use domain-appropriate language in place of everyday language are common. Use texts, charts, concept walls, discussions, and writing experiences to create an environment that is rich in the language of the domain.

Introduce Target Words in Relation to Other Related Words and Connect Known to Unknown Words

Approaches that connect new words to known words treat word learning in content areas as the building of conceptual understanding. Using semantic maps and related word mapping approaches can help students recognize the relationships among words/concepts. Semantic feature analysis (Johnson & Pearson, 1984) uses a table to represent the similarities and differences between examples of the same category, such as the similarities and differences between different forms of government.

It is also important to distinguish between new content area words and other words with which they might be confused including synonyms in everyday language and words with the same orthography but different meanings.

Involve Students in Domain-Appropriate Experiences

Students learn new words when they are engaged with words in ways that involve them personally in constructing meanings (Vogel, 2003). In many ways, content areas are ideal contexts for this kind of engagement with words. Using experiences in the domain as opportunities for vocabulary learning can support flexible and expressive control over important content words. Science, for example, provides natural opportunities for authentic, repeated, and varied encounters with new words and concepts—and ways of using them to talk, explain, and argue—during firsthand experiences, through texts, and in discussions and written activities. All of these contexts provide students opportunities to encounter words, to make personal meaning with the words, to tie word knowledge to experience, and to practice using the words in appropriate ways. In any content area domain, it is appropriate to encourage students to describe and discuss their inquiry and problem-solving experiences using the words of the discipline. The discourse of disciplines includes a particular and specialized vocabulary, but it is more than specialized words—it also includes ways of using these words in arranging arguments and leveraging evidence for explanations and conclusions. Binding the use of words to experiences provides opportunities for students to practice using these words in the interest of important practices in the domain.

Conclusions

In this chapter, we have championed vocabulary in content area learning, including the need for students to control content area vocabulary to promote literacy in content area learning. We have also illustrated some of the challenges of content area vocabulary learning. The fact that content area vocabulary terms are numerous, abstract, polysemous, and conceptually unfamiliar can potentially derail content area learning. Yet, the research also demonstrates that content area instruction also offers opportunities for rich and powerful word-learning experiences. In the content areas, students are likely to have multiple, meaningful, and multimodal experiences with vocabulary, all of which are needed to build enduring understanding of challenging subject matter vocabulary.

Explicit instructional measures are surely needed to reap the benefits of such favorable word-learning conditions. This includes being judicious with the number of words targeted for instruction and choosing words with clear criteria in mind—utility, domain centrality, and semantic relatedness. Vocabulary instruction must also actively involve students in uncovering nuanced and deep meanings of target words through domain-appropriate experiences. Recognizing the importance and navigating the challenges of content area vocabulary can help to demystify word learning for students who can otherwise be overwhelmed by the demands of reading in subject matter domains.

References

Amaral, O.M., Garrison, L., & Klentschy, M. (2002). Helping English learners increase achievement through inquiry-based science instruction. *Bilingual Research Journal*, 26(2), 213–239.

Anders, P.L., Bos, C.S., & Filip, D. (1984). The effect of semantic feature analysis on the reading comprehension of learning-disabled students. *Changing perspectives in research on reading/language processing and instruction* (33rd yearbook of the National Reading Conference, pp. 162–166). Rochester, NY: National Reading Conference.

Anderson, R.C., & Freebody, P. (1981). Vocabulary knowledge. In J. Guthrie (Ed.), *Comprehension and teaching: Research reviews*. Newark, DE: International Reading Association.

Armbruster, B.B. (1992). Vocabulary in content area lessons. *The Reading Teacher*, 45(7), 550–551.

Armstrong, J.E., & Collier, G.E. (1990). *Science in biology: An introduction*. Prospect Heights, IL: Waveland Press.

Beck, I.L., & McKeown, M.G. (1985). Teaching vocabulary: Making the instruction fit the goal. *Educational Perspectives*, 23(1), 11–15.

Beck, I.L., McKeown, M.G., & Kucan, L. (2002). *Bringing words to life: Robust vocabulary instruction*. New York: Guilford.

Beck, I.L., McKeown, M.G., & McCaslin, E.S. (1983). Vocabulary development: All contexts are not created equal. *The Elementary School Journal*, 83(3), 177–181.

Beck, I.L., Perfetti, C.A., & McKeown, M.G. (1982). The effects of long-term vocabulary instruction on lexical access and reading comprehension. *Journal of Educational Psychology*, 74(4), 506–521.

Biemiller, A., & Boote, C. (2006). An effective method for building vocabulary in primary grades. *Journal of Educational Psychology*, 98(1), 44–62.

Blachowicz, C.L.Z., & Fisher, P. (2000). Vocabulary instruction. In M.L. Kamil, P.B. Mosenthal, P.D. Pearson, & R. Barr (Eds.), *Handbook of reading research* (Vol. 3, pp. 503–523). Mahwah, NJ: Erlbaum.

Blachowicz, C.L.Z., Fisher, P., Ogle, D., & Watts-Taffe, S.M. (2006). Vocabulary: Questions from the classroom. *Reading Research Quarterly, 41*(4), 524–539.

Blachowicz, C.L.Z., & Obrochta, C. (2005). Vocabulary visits: Virtual field trips for content vocabulary development. *The Reading Teacher, 59*(3), 262–268.

Bos, C.S., & Anders, P.L. (1990). Toward an interactive model: Teaching text-based concepts to learning disabled students. In H.L. Swanson & B. Keogh (Eds.), *Learning disabilities: Theoretical and research issues* (pp. 247–262). Hillsdale, NJ: Erlbaum.

Bos, C.S., Anders, P.L., Filip, D., & Jaffe, L.E. (1989). The effects of an interactive instructional strategy for enhancing learning disabled students' reading comprehension and content area learning. *Journal of Learning Disabilities, 22*(6), 384–390.

Bravo, M.A., Hiebert, E.H., & Pearson, P.D. (2006). Tapping the linguistic resources of Spanish–English bilinguals: The role of cognates in science. In R.K. Wagner, A. Muse, & K. Tannenbaum (Eds.), *Vocabulary development and its implications for reading comprehension* (pp. 140–156). New York: Guilford.

Brett, A., Rothlein, L., & Hurley, M. (1996). Vocabulary acquisition from listening to stories and explanations of target words. *The Elementary School Journal, 96*(4), 415–422.

Carlisle, J.F., Fleming, J.E., & Gudbrandsen, B. (2000). Incidental word learning in science classes. *Contemporary Educational Psychology, 25*(2), 184–211.

Carlo, M.S., August, D., & Snow, C.E. (2005). Sustained vocabulary-learning strategies for English-language learners. In E.H. Hiebert & M.L. Kamil (Eds.), *Teaching and learning vocabulary: Bringing research to practice* (pp. 137–153). Mahwah, NJ: Erlbaum.

Carney, J.J., Anderson, D., Blackburn, C., & Blessing, D. (1984). Preteaching vocabulary and the comprehension of social studies materials by elementary school children. *Special Education, 48*(3), 195–197.

Cervetti, G.N., & Bravo, M.A. (2005, May). *Designing and implementing literacy and science activities through discourse.* Paper presented at the 50th annual meeting of the International Reading Association, San Antonio, TX.

Cervetti, G.N., Pearson, P.D., Bravo, M.A., & Barber, J. (2006). Reading and writing in the service of inquiry-based science. In R. Douglas, M.P. Klentschy, & K. Worth (Eds.), *Linking science and literacy in the K–8 classroom* (pp. 221–244). Arlington, VA: National Science Teachers Association.

Gentner, D. (1982). Why nouns are learned before verbs: Linguistic relativity versus natural partitioning. In S.A. Kuczaj (Ed.), *Language development: Language, thought, and culture* (Vol. 2, pp. 301–334). Hillsdale, NJ: Erlbaum.

Glynn, S., & Muth, K.D. (1994). Reading and writing to learn science: Achieving scientific literacy. *Journal of Research in Science Teaching, 31*(9), 1057–1073.

Graves, M.F. (2000). A vocabulary program to complement and bolster a middle-grade comprehension program. In B.M. Taylor, M.F. Graves, & P.W. van den Broek (Eds.), *Reading for meaning: Fostering comprehension in the middle grades* (pp. 116–135). New York: Teachers College Press; Newark, DE: International Reading Association.

Graves, M.F. (2006). *The vocabulary book: Learning and instruction.* New York: Teachers College Press.

Graves, M.F., & Prenn, M.C. (1986). Costs and benefits of various methods of teaching vocabulary. *Journal of Reading, 29*(7), 596–602.

Hapgood, S., Magnusson, S.J., & Palincsar, A.S. (2004). Teacher, text and experience: A case of young children's scientific inquiry. *Journal of the Learning Sciences, 13*(4), 455–505.

Harmon, J.M., Hedrick, W.B., & Fox, E.A. (2000). A content analysis of vocabulary instruction in social studies textbooks for grades 4–8. *The Elementary School Journal, 100*(3), 253–271.

Harmon, J.M., Hedrick, W.B., & Wood, K.D. (2005). Research on vocabulary instruction in the content areas: Implications for struggling readers. *Reading & Writing Quarterly, 21*(3), 261–280.

Hess, D.E. (2004). Discussion in social studies: Is it worth the trouble? *Special Education, 68*(2), 151–168.

Hiebert, E.H. (2005). In pursuit of an effective, efficient vocabulary curriculum for the elementary grades. In E.H. Hiebert & M.L. Kamil (Eds.), *The teaching and learning of vocabulary: Bringing scientific research to practice* (pp. 243–263). Mahwah, NJ: Erlbaum.

Hilve, F. (2006). Creative writing in the social studies classroom: Promoting literacy and content learning. *Special Education, 70*(4), 183–186.

Hopkins, M.H. (2007). Adapting a model for literacy learning to the learning of mathematics. *Reading & Writing Quarterly, 23*(2), 121–138.

Johnson, D.D., Moe, A.J., & Baumann, J.F. (1983). *The Ginn word book for teachers: A basic lexicon.* Boston: Ginn.

Johnson, D.D., & Pearson, P.D. (1984). *Teaching reading vocabulary.* New York: Holt/ Rinehart and Winston.

Jones, R.C., & Thomas, T.G. (2006). Leave no discipline behind. *The Reading Teacher, 60*(1), 58–64.

Kopriva, R., & Saez, S. (1997). *Guide to scoring LEP student responses to open-ended mathematics items.* Washington, DC: Council of Chief State School Officers.

Lazar, R.T., Warr-Leeper, G.A., Nicholson, C.B., & Johnson, S. (1989). Elementary school teachers' use of multiple meaning expressions. *Language, Speech, and Hearing Services in Schools, 20*(4), 420–429.

Lemke, J.L. (1990). *Talking science: Language, learning, and values.* Norwood, NJ: Ablex.

Margosein, C.M., Pascarella, E.T., & Pflaum, S.W. (1982). The effects of instruction using semantic mapping on vocabulary and comprehension. *The Journal of Early Adolescence, 2*(2), 185–194.

Marzano, R.J. (2004). The developing vision of vocabulary instruction. In J.F. Bauman & E.J. Kame'enui (Eds.), *Research and theory in vocabulary development* (pp. 100–117). New York: Guilford.

Marzano, R.J., Kendall, J.S., & Paynter, D.E. (2005). A list of essential words by grade level. In D.E. Paynter, E. Bodrova, & J.K. Doty (Eds.), *For the love of words: Vocabulary instruction that works, grades K–6* (pp. 127–202). San Francisco: Jossey-Bass.

McKeown, M.G., Beck, I.L., Omanson, R.C., & Pople, M.T. (1985). Some effects of the nature and frequency of vocabulary instruction on the knowledge and use of words. *Reading Research Quarterly, 20*(5), 522–535.

Nagy, W.E., & Scott, J.A. (2000). Vocabulary processing. In M.L. Kamil, P.B. Mosenthal, P.D. Pearson, & R. Barr (Eds.), *Handbook of reading research* (Vol. 3, pp. 269–284). Mahwah, NJ: Erlbaum.

Nagy, W.E. (1988). *Teaching vocabulary to improve reading comprehension*. Newark, DE: International Reading Association.

Nagy, W.E., Anderson, R.C., & Herman, P.A. (1987). Learning word meanings from context during normal reading. *American Educational Research Journal, 24*(2), 237–270.

Nation, I.S.P. (1990). *Teaching and learning vocabulary*. Boston: Heinle & Heinle.

Readence, J.E., Bean, T.W., & Baldwin, R.S. (1985). *Content area reading: An integrated approach* (2nd ed.). Dubuque, IA: Kendall/Hunt.

Rothstein, A.S., Rothstein, E., & Lauber, G. (2006). *Writing as learning: A content based approach*. Thousand Oaks, CA: Corwin.

Ryder, R.J., & Graves, M.F. (1998). *Reading and learning in content areas* (2nd ed.). New York: Merrill.

Schell, V.J. (1982). Learning partners: Reading and mathematics. *The Reading Teacher, 35*(5), 544–548.

Schleppegrell, M.J. (2007). The linguistic challenges of mathematics teaching and learning: A research review. *Reading & Writing Quarterly, 23*(2), 139–159.

Schwanenflugel, P.J., & Noyes, C.R. (1996). Context availability and the development of word reading skill. *Journal of Literacy Research, 28*(1), 35–54.

Schwanenflugel, P.J., Stahl, S.A., & McFalls, L. (1997). Partial word knowledge and vocabulary growth during reading comprehension. *Journal of Literacy Research, 29*(4), 531–553.

Smith, C.B. (1990). Vocabulary development in content area reading. *The Reading Teacher, 43*(7), 508–509.

Spencer, B.H., & Guillaume, A.M. (2006). Integrating curriculum through the learning cycle: Content based reading and vocabulary instruction. *The Reading Teacher, 60*(3), 206–219.

Stahl, S.A. (1983). Differential word knowledge and reading comprehension. *Journal of Reading Behavior, 15*(4), 33–50.

Stahl, S.A. (1999). *Vocabulary development*. Cambridge, MA: Brookline Books.

Stahl, S.A., & Clark, C.H. (1987). The effects of participatory expectations in classroom discussion on the learning of science vocabulary. *American Educational Research Journal, 24*(4), 541–555.

Stahl, S.A., & Fairbanks, M.M. (1986). The effects of vocabulary instruction: A model-based meta-analysis. *Review of Educational Research, 56*(1), 72–110.

Stahl, S.A., & Kapinus, B.A. (1991). Possible sentences: Predicting word meanings to teach content area vocabulary. *The Reading Teacher, 45*(1), 36–43.

Stahl, S.A., & Vancil, S.J. (1986). Discussion is what makes semantic maps work in vocabulary instruction. *The Reading Teacher, 40*(1), 62–69.

Vacca, R.T., & Vacca, J.L. (2002). *Content area reading: Literacy and learning across the curriculum*. Boston: Allyn & Bacon.

Vogel, E. (2003). Using informational text to build children's knowledge of the world around them. In N.K. Duke & V.S. Bennett-Armistead (Eds.), *Reading and writing informational text in the primary grades: Research-based practices* (pp. 157–198). New York: Scholastic.

Questions for Reflection

- What does research tell us about selecting content area vocabulary for instruction?

- What challenges do students confront in learning content area vocabulary?

- What possibilities are presented in content areas for rich vocabulary learning?

"Bumping Into Spicy, Tasty Words That Catch Your Tongue": A Formative Experiment on Vocabulary Instruction

James F. Baumann, Donna Ware, and Elizabeth Carr Edwards

"If we're reading and we bump into something [a word] that we don't understand...then if you just look up at the [instructional] charts, the context clues, then you can kind of like...get an idea of what it means."

—Paula (all student names are pseudonyms)

"If you're writing and you want...to go into your thesaurus and find another, um, spicy word, tasty [word].... You can just go in there and look and then you can find another word that is a lot better."

—Donald

"Reading means words, words that catch your tongue, and words that don't mean what they sound."

—Gary

These are statements from fifth-grade students near the end of our yearlong inquiry into vocabulary instruction. The purpose of our study was to explore the impact of a comprehensive vocabulary instructional program on students' word knowledge and appreciation. In this article, we describe the vocabulary program and the outcomes of our study that led students to report that they learned how to "bump into spicy, tasty words that caught their tongues."

Background

Our study was grounded on current research on vocabulary development and instruction (Baumann, Kame'enui, & Ash, 2003; Blachowicz & Fisher, 2000; Nagy & Scott, 2000). It was informed particularly by two prior studies in which we explored whether students could be taught to use structural analysis (examining the meaningful parts of words like root words, prefixes, and suffixes) and contextual analysis (scrutinizing surrounding text for cues to word meaning) to learn novel words (Baumann et al., 2002; Baumann, Edwards, Boland, Olejnik, & Kame'enui, 2003). Results of these studies demonstrated that, in general, students could be taught successfully to use these strategies.

It was useful to learn that students could be taught to use structural and contextual analysis, but we realized that there were additional ways to teach vocabulary. Kamil and Hiebert (2005) asserted that "educators need to design classroom experiences that are multifaceted, if students are to acquire new words" (p. 7); however, our examination of the literature revealed no studies that

Reprinted from Baumann, J.F., Ware, D., & Edwards, E.C. (2007). Bumping into spicy, tasty words that catch your tongue: A formative experiment in vocabulary instruction. *The Reading Teacher, 61*(2), 108–122. doi: 10.1598/RT.61.2.1

explored multifaceted vocabulary instruction. In addition, most research was limited in its ability to generalize to classroom contexts—a conclusion expressed by the National Reading Panel (National Institute of Child Health and Human Development, 2000):

> The Panel knows a great deal about the ways in which vocabulary increases under highly controlled conditions, but the Panel knows much less about the ways in which such growth can be fostered in instructional contexts. There is a great need for the conduct of research on these topics in authentic school contexts, with real teachers, under real conditions. (p. 4-27)

To address the need for multifaceted vocabulary research, we explored the effects of a comprehensive vocabulary instruction program outlined by Graves (2000, 2006). Graves's program consists of four components known to be effective for promoting vocabulary: "(1) providing rich and varied language experiences; (2) teaching individual words; (3) teaching word-learning strategies; and (4) fostering word consciousness" (Graves, 2006, p. 5).

To address the need for more generalizable research, we selected a formative experiment (Reinking & Bradley, 2004) research framework. A formative experiment is intended for inquiries exploring the effects of long-term instructional interventions in natural educational settings. Unlike traditional experiments, formative experiments often do not include a control group, and they permit modifications to interventions as a study unfolds in order to better achieve the instructional goal (see examples of formative experiments by Duffy, 2001; Jiménez, 1997; Reinking & Watkins, 2000). Our research question was, What is the impact of a yearlong instructional program that incorporates Graves's (2000, 2006) four components on the vocabulary development and appreciation of fifth-grade students?

The Study

We conducted the study in Donna's fifth-grade classroom at a low-income (65% free/reduced-price lunch), diverse (56% African American,

25% European American, 14% Latino/a, 5% other), elementary school in a medium-sized U.S. community. We gathered data on 20 students in Donna's class. We pretested students in August. From September through April, we integrated vocabulary lessons and activities into Donna's reading and language arts block, social studies class, and several other periods during the day (see Table 1). Posttesting occurred in May. Data sources included several published reading and vocabulary tests, student writing samples, student and parent questionnaires, student interviews, lesson plans, student work and logs, and researcher journals.

Donna provided most of the vocabulary instruction, with Jim and Elizabeth (university collaborators) teaching occasional lessons and assuming responsibility for much of the data gathering. In keeping with the formative experimental design, we used students' performance and our own reflections on the program to modify and refine the vocabulary instruction throughout the course of the study (Reinking & Bradley, 2004).

The Vocabulary Instructional Program

We selected vocabulary techniques and strategies compatible with Graves's (2006) framework from professional journals and user-friendly books such as *Words, Words, Words* (Allen, 1999), *Bringing Words to Life* (Beck, McKeown, & Kucan, 2002), *Teaching Vocabulary in All Classrooms* (Blachowicz & Fisher, 2006), *The Vocabulary-Enriched Classroom* (Block & Mangieri, 2006), *Vocabulary in the Elementary and Middle School* (Johnson, 2001), and *Teaching Word Meanings* (Stahl & Nagy, 2006). Donna's belief in the importance of writing in literacy development led us to integrate considerable composition into the four components.

Providing Rich and Varied Language Experiences

Research reveals that students learn words from linguistic context through immersion in a

Table 1
Classes and Periods Within Which the Vocabulary Program Was Implemented

Period	Instructional activities
Morning organizational period (15 minutes)	• Word-of-the-day activities • Word-play activities • Independent reading • Teacher–student reading and writing conferences
Reading and language arts block (90 minutes)	• Independent reading and writing • Read-alouds • Literature circles and literature response activities • Shared and guided reading • Instruction in self-selected and teacher-selected words from books read or compositions being written • Writing workshop • Minilessons on word-learning strategies • Teacher–student reading and writing conferences
Social studies class (50 minutes)	• Instruction in specific subject-matter vocabulary • Word-learning strategy instruction integrated into social studies lessons • Content-related read-alouds and trade book reading
After-lunch homeroom period (25 minutes)	• Read-alouds • Independent reading • Reader's–writer's chair

vocabulary-rich environment that includes books read independently and read aloud (Anderson, Wilson, & Fielding, 1988; Cunningham, 2005; Elley, 1989; Swanborn & de Glopper, 1999). Therefore, this component exposed students to the extensive vocabulary in children's literature (Hayes & Ahrens, 1988). We provided students multiple experiences with new and interesting vocabulary by reading aloud regularly, allocating considerable time for self-selected independent reading, conducting literature discussion groups, and exploring word choice and usage through writing activities.

Donna read aloud many chapter books (*A Long Way From Chicago*, Peck, 1998), titles that addressed the fifth-grade social studies curriculum of U.S. history (*The Blue and the Gray*, Bunting, 1996), poetry (Hughes's "Dreams," Rampersad & Roessel, 1994), and books that involved word play (*Miss Alaineus: A Vocabulary Disaster*, Frasier, 2000). She used picture books extensively, often to address specific objectives. For example, she read

aloud *Two Bad Ants* (Van Allsburg, 1988) and *Exploding Ants* (Settel, 1999) to contrast fiction and nonfiction genres. Donna infused vocabulary work into read-alouds selectively and naturally. For instance, when reading aloud *Maniac Magee* (Spinelli, 1990), Donna addressed a state language arts standard on parts of speech by reproducing a section of the read-aloud on a transparency and having students identify Spinelli's use of lively verbs (e.g., *jammed*, *sneered*, *jutted*, *blinked*, *shrugged*, *sighed*). Students then worked with partners to read a sample of text and identify "strong verbs" on their own.

Students selected books for daily independent reading, which exposed them to a range of titles, genres, and new words. In a section of her reading log, Jessica listed titles as diverse as *Tuck Everlasting* (Babbitt, 1975), *Where the Sidewalk Ends* (Silverstein, 1974), *Philip Hall Likes Me. I Reckon Maybe* (Greene, 1974), and *The Zebra Wall* (Henkes, 1988). Donna used literature circles (Daniels, 2002) regularly; for example, in one round students could choose to read *Dear Mr. Henshaw* (Cleary, 1983), *Because of Winn-Dixie* (DiCamillo, 2000), *Bridge to Terabithia* (Paterson, 1977), or *Crash* (Spinelli, 1996). Students kept various records and logs of new or interesting words they identified as they read books. For example, drawing from Daniels's (2002, pp. 113, 118) Word Wizard and Vocabulary Enricher role sheets, Donna constructed Word Finder Think Marks—cards in the form of book marks on which students listed novel words (see Figure 1). These words subsequently became

---

Figure 1
Samples of Students' Word Finder Think Marks

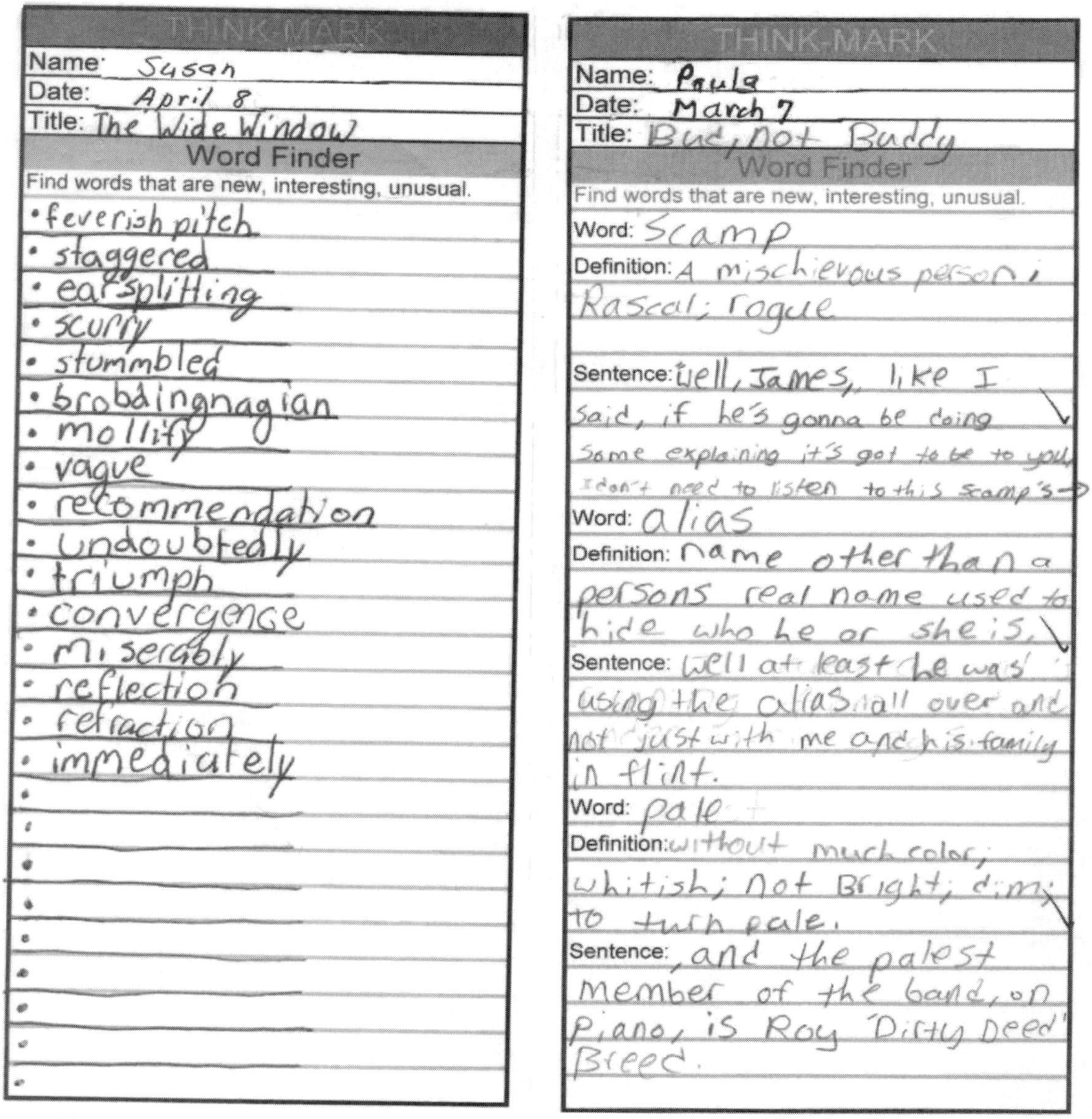

THINK-MARK

Name: Susan
Date: April 8
Title: The Wide Window

Word Finder
Find words that are new, interesting, unusual.
- feverish pitch
- staggered
- earsplitting
- scurry
- stummbled
- brobdingnagian
- mollify
- vague
- recommendation
- undoubtedly
- triumph
- convergence
- miserably
- reflection
- refraction
- immediately

THINK-MARK

Name: Paula
Date: March 7
Title: Bud, not Buddy

Word Finder
Find words that are new, interesting, unusual.
Word: scamp
Definition: A mischievous person; Rascal; rogue

Sentence: Well, James, like I said, if he's gonna be doing some explaining it's got to be to you, I don't need to listen to this scamp's→
Word: alias
Definition: name other than a persons real name used to hide who he or she is.
Sentence: Well at least he was using the alias all over and not just with me and his family in flint.
Word: pale
Definition: without much color; whitish; not Bright; dim; to turn pale.
Sentence: and the palest member of the band, on Piano, is Roy "Dirty Deed" Breed.

a source for group discussion and word study, and they found their way into students' written compositions.

Donna and her students maintained weekly dialogue journals (Hall, Crawford, & Robinson, 1997), within which they exchanged ideas about their independent reading. Donna introduced these at the beginning of the year by including a page in the students' journals (Fountas & Pinnell, 2001, p. 154) that explained the journal process and listed possible topics to address in their entries. Students' journal responses were varied and interesting. For instance, a student wrote, "I have been reading a book called [The] Pinballs [Byars, 1977]. I think that this book can teach us something about life: No matter where you are, you can control it." Donna responded, "You definitely picked up on what I think Betsy Byars was trying to tell her readers when she wrote this book." Dialogue exchanges often turned to word craft and usage. For example, in a reaction to The Watsons Go to Birmingham—1963 (Curtis, 1995), Gary noted, "I think that Christopher Paul Curtis used very good descriptive language in that chapter. Does he always?"

Daily writing workshop provided students opportunities to develop expressive vocabulary, and they often demonstrated intertextual links in their word choice. For instance, in a story titled "The Dreadful Elevator," Kenneth used the word interminable to describe a repeating elevator song that tormented his main character. Donna attributed Kenneth's usage to an earlier activity in which the class explored the meanings of interesting words Taylor used in Roll of Thunder, Hear My Cry (1976), with one of those being interminable.

Students demonstrated growth in word choice, as evidenced by a short story titled "Red Dust" that Sophie published. Sophie wrote her story after learning about the Dust Bowl in the social studies textbook that included an excerpt from Stanley's book (1992) Children of the Dust Bowl and after reading a selection in her basal reader about Dorothea Lange's famous photos of the Dust Bowl. The following is an excerpt from Sophie's story, in which the main characters, Erica and Jonsohn, find a young girl named Evan

they've befriended but who has died in a dust storm. Sophie demonstrates her growing sense of diction by including words such as crumpled, trickle, protruding, and embraced, as well as figurative expressions such as choking back tears, eyes flooded, and soar the heavens to express an appropriate mood and tone.

> I walked up and just stood there. I waited 'till Jonsohn caught up.
>
> "Oh, Erica, I'm so sorry...." Jonsohn said choking back tears.
>
> Evan. Evan Boot. Evan's lifeless body lay in a crumpled heap next to a wooden post.
>
> I could see a small trickle of blood protruding from her mouth.
>
> "No!" I cried. "She can't be!"
>
> "It's okay. Shh." Jonsohn embraced me, but I saw his eyes flooded with tears.
>
> I had just known her for four days. But those days came as four million.
>
> Evan. Come back.
>
> But I knew that [she] was gone. Gone to soar the heavens and never come back.

In summary, Donna's students demonstrated vocabulary growth through immersion in the world of books and through a variety of reading and writing activities.

Teaching Individual Words

Research indicates that students acquire new word meanings through explicit vocabulary instruction (Baumann, Kame'enui, & Ash, 2003; Beck & McKeown, 1991; Blachowicz & Fisher, 2000), and Donna provided lessons and activities that focused on specific words that connected to reading, writing, and subject-matter study. The class kept a Word Wall (see Figure 2) of interesting vocabulary (e.g., infamy, scraggly, alias) for discussion and writing, with students offering words from books they read (e.g., gargoyles from Night of the Gargoyles [Bunting, 1994] or skedaddle from Charley Skedaddle [Beatty, 1987]). Other Word Walls displayed content area vocabulary and words with affixes (Cunningham & Hall, 1998) that were used for teaching word structure.

Figure 2
Portion of a Word Wall Displaying Vocabulary That Came From Books, Discussion, and Writing

Note. Photograph by Donna Ware

We encouraged students to be Word Wizards (Beck et al., 2002), so that they developed the habit of noticing and sharing interesting words that they encountered in school and in out-of-school contexts. For instance, Dennis shared *rummaged* after explaining how he had seen highway workers rummaging around in a van. Students also acted out word meanings. One time, when Clevon offered *ajar*, William spontaneously went to the door and cracked it open. *Ajar* is an example of a "memorable word"—a word a student came to "own" (Beck et al., 2002). When Donna read aloud a section of *Roll of Thunder, Hear My Cry* (Taylor, 1976), Jim wrote in his field notes, "Donna reads on in the book and comes across the word *ajar*, and everyone perks up." Donna responded later to

Jim's comment, writing "It is amazing how many of the words do reappear in other contexts and how students pick up on them."

Literature was a rich source of vocabulary, providing students a means to mine words and bring them to the surface. For instance, before reading a section of *Bud, Not Buddy* (Curtis, 1999), Donna listed *devoured, paltry, knickers*, and *scrawny* on a paper and had students self-assess their word knowledge by checking one of three columns (see Table 2). Students then read to look for the words and discussed their meanings afterward.

Donna used other anticipation strategies, such as Nickelsen's (1998, p. 18) Predict-O-Gram, which requires students to hypothesize which words might fit within the categories of "setting," "characters," "action (problem)," "describing words," or "other." For example, prior to reading a chapter in *The Watsons Go to Birmingham—1963* (Curtis, 1995), Donna had students predict categories for *hostile place, vital, incapable, emulate*, and *intimidate*. Following the reading, the class revisited the Predict-O-Gram to check if their guesses were sensible. These kinds of activities sensitized students to think about and look for key vocabulary as they read.

Graphic organizers were key tools for learning specific word meanings, and Donna drew from various resources for ideas and examples (e.g., Allen, 1999; Blachowicz & Fisher, 2002). Donna and the students frequently created semantic maps (Heimlich & Pittelman, 1986) for fiction and nonfiction texts. For example, they mapped *imperialism* and *siege*, key terms in a social studies reading on early 20th-century U.S. history (see Figure 3).

Donna used a number of additional techniques for teaching specific words, often integrating them as brief word-study activities within the morning reading and language arts block. For example, following lessons on synonyms and antonyms, students compared words (e.g., Are you more afraid of a *vicious* dog or a *mischievous* dog?; Beck et al., 2002, Chapter 5), and they ranked lists of words according to intensity (e.g., order *sickening, distasteful*, and *revolting*; Johnson & Pearson, 1978, p. 163). Donna used a related strategy called "linear arrays" (Allen, 1999, pp. 52–53), which required students to place words on a continuum. For instance, beginning with the word *puny* from *Bud, Not Buddy* (Curtis, 1999), students created the following array: *puny → frail → weak → sturdy → strong*. In sum, students acquired the meanings of specific words, enabling them to learn entirely new words and to develop enhanced meanings for familiar words.

Teaching Word-Learning Strategies

Research supports the practice of teaching students strategies for analyzing word-structure clues (i.e., root words, prefixes, suffixes, Latin or Greek roots) and context clues (Baumann et al., 2002; Baumann, Edwards, et al., 2003;

Table 2
Students Self-Assess Word Knowledge Prior to Reading a Selection That Contains New Vocabulary

I know the meaning of....

	Very well	Somewhat	Not at all
Devoured			
Paltry			
Knickers			
Scrawny			

Note. Based on Dale and O'Rourke (1986) and Allen (1999).

Figure 3
Graphic Organizer Donna and the Students Constructed to Learn and Distinguish Specific Social Studies Concepts

imperialism: empire building

siege: a long lasting attack

profitible

acquire land

annex

take over control

imperialism

control

blockade

take over

siege

long lasting

armistice

battle

attack

Fukkink & de Glopper, 1998; White, Sowell, & Yanagihara, 1989) as ways to infer and acquire the meanings of unfamiliar words. Instruction in the use of resources such as the dictionary and thesaurus also promotes independent word learning (Graves, 2006). Drawing from our prior research (Baumann, Edwards, et al., 2003; Baumann, Font, Edwards, & Boland, 2005), we presented students with a chart of a general strategy, the Vocabulary Rule, which was adapted from Ruddell's (1999) Context-Structure-Sound-Reference strategy:

Vocabulary Rule

When you come to a word, and you don't know what it means, use

1. *Context clues*: Read the sentences around the word to see if there are clues to its meaning.

2. *Word-part clues*: See if you can break the word into a root and prefix or suffix to help figure out its meaning.

3. *Context clues*: Read the sentences around the word again to see if you have figured out its meaning. (pp. 151–152)

Jim introduced the Vocabulary Rule using excerpts from *The Pinballs* (Byars, 1977) to demonstrate how "twisted angry faces" provided context clues to the meaning of *gnarled* (p. 25) and how knowing the meaning of the prefix *un-* helped determine the meaning of *unpleasant* (p. 41). We then provided students more elaboration on word-part clues through the following chart (adapted from Baumann, Edwards, et al., 2003):

Word-part clues

1. Look for the *root*: the basic part of a word. It might be a whole word (e.g., *happy*) or a meaningful part of a word (e.g., *vis-*, *vid-*).

2. Look for a *prefix*: a word part added to the beginning of a word that changes its meaning (e.g., *un-*, *in-* = "not").

3. Look for a **suffix**: a word part added to the end of a word that changes its meaning (e.g., -**ness** = "state or quality of"; -**ible**, -**able** = "capable of").

4. Put the meanings of the root and any *prefix* or **suffix** together and see if you can build the meaning of the word (e.g., *un*happy, happi**ness**, *un*happi**ness**, *vis*ion, *vis*ible, in*vis*ible, tele*vis*ion, *vid*eotape, vi*vid*, e*vid*ent).

To provide a memorable structure for students to learn and recall high-frequency prefixes and suffixes (White et al., 1989), we organized them into clusters, or "families," which we displayed in the classroom (see Table 3) and taught through a series of lessons. For instance, in a lesson on the "Not Family," Elizabeth taught students to disassemble words, identify the prefixes and roots (e.g., *il-legal*, *ir-responsible*), and reassemble them to construct their meanings. Students then added the "Not Family" members to their "Affixionary" notebooks (Blachowicz & Fisher, 2002; Lindsay, 1984), within which they

Table 3
Prefix and Suffix "Families" Taught in Word-Part Instruction

Family	Prefix or suffix	Meaning	Example words
"Not" prefix family	dis-	not, opposite	dislike, disloyal, disentangle, disparity, disrepute
	un-	not, opposite	unafraid, unhappy, undefeated, unsympathetic
	in-	not, opposite	invisible, incurable, inappropriate, inedible, infallible
	im-	not, opposite	imperfect, impolite, imprecise, immobile, immortal
	il-	not, opposite	illogical, illegal, illiterate, illegible, illimitable
	ir-	not, opposite	irresponsible, irreplaceable, irresistible, irrelevant
	non-	not, opposite	nonfiction, nonstop, nonliving, nonviolent, nonverbal
"Position" prefix family	pre-	before	preview, predawn, prehistoric, prepublication
	fore-	before	forewarn, foreleg, forenoon, forethought, foreshadow
	mid-	middle	midnight, midair, midland, midlife, midterm
	inter-	between, among	intercity, intermix, interaction, international, intergalactic
	post-	after	postwar, posttest, postdate, postoperative
"Over" and "Under" prefix family	super-	over, high, big, extreme	superheat, superhuman, superdeluxe, supercompetitive
	over-	more than, too much	oversleep, overload, overheat, overqualified, overexert
	sub-	under, below	subset, substation, subcontinent, subtropical
"Together" prefix family	com-	together, with	compress, composition, compatriot, compassion
	con-	together	conform, concentric, conjoin, configure
	co-	together, with	coauthor, cosign, coequal, cooperate
"Bad" prefix family	mis-	bad, wrong, not	misuse, misread, misunderstand, mismanage, misquote
	mal-	bad, ill	maltreat, malodor, malnourished, maladjusted
"Against" prefix family	anti-	against	antifreeze, antibiotic, antisocial, antipollution
	contra-	against, opposite	contraband, contradict, contraindicate, contravene
"Number" prefix family	uni-	one	unicycle, unicorn, unidirectional, unicellular
	mono-	one	monorail, monosyllable, monogram, monotone, monocle
	bi-	two	bicycle, biweekly, bicolor, biplane, binomial
	tri-	three	triangle, tricycle, tricolor, triathlon, tripod
	quad-	four	quadrilateral, quadruplets, quadrennial, quadrangle
	penta-	five	pentagon, pentameter, pentagram, pentathlon
	dec-	ten	decagon, decade, decapod, decibel
	cent-	hundred	centimeter, centipede, centennial, centigram
	semi-	half, part	semicircle, semiyearly, semiprivate, semiretired

(continued)

Table 3
Prefix and Suffix "Families" Taught in Word-Part Instruction (*Continued*)

Family	Prefix or suffix	Meaning	Example words
Other useful prefixes	re-	again, back	redo, reorder, rearrange, reposition, reconnect
	trans-	across, through	transport, transatlantic, transmit, transfusion
	de-	take away	defrost, deforest, deodorize, deflate, deactivate
	ex-	out of, away from	export, exhale, extinguish, exclude, excise
	under-	low, too little	underweight, underachieve, underestimate, underappreciated
"Person" suffix family	-ee	person who	employee, referee, trainee, interviewee
	-er	person/thing that does something	writer, teacher, composer, reporter, consumer
	-or	person/thing that does something	actor, governor, dictator, juror, donor
Other Useful Suffixes	-ful	full of, characterized by	joyful, beautiful, successful, delightful, pitiful
	-able	can be, worthy of	valuable, comfortable, dependable, impressionable
	-ible	inclined to	terrible, responsible, reversible, compatible
	-less	without, free of	helpless, hopeless, bottomless, expressionless

Note. From Baumann et al. (2005).

listed prefixes and suffixes, their meanings, and example words and sentences.

We used the following chart to teach context clues and how to integrate them into the Vocabulary Rule:

> *Context clues*: Ideas or hints about the meaning of a word in the words and sentences around the word.
>
> - Look for context clues both *before* and *after* a hard word. Sometimes they are close to a word, but other times they may be several sentences away.
> - Some context clues will be strong or really obvious but others will be weak. Sometimes context even might be confusing or misleading.
> - Use the Vocabulary Rule: (1) use context, (2) look for word-part clues, (3) use context again to check meaning.

We taught five context clue types—definition, synonym, antonym, example, and general

(Dale & O'Rourke, 1986; Johnson & Pearson, 1978)—and presented them with examples (see Table 4). For each context clue type and other word-learning strategy we taught, we used an instructional framework that included verbal explanation, modeling, guided practice, and independent practice (Duke & Pearson, 2002; Hunter, 1982). For instance, when teaching synonym context clues, Jim explained the strategy using the following example: "Captain Jackson's uniform was *impeccable*. In fact, it was so *perfect* that she always had the highest score during inspection." Jim then modeled synonym context clues using an excerpt from the magazine *TIME for Kids* ("hieroglyphics" and "picture writing"). For guided and independent practice, Jim monitored students' work in groups, in which they had to (a) predict the meanings of *predators*, *invasive*, and *foreign*; (b) read an article to identify context clues for each word; and (c) write the meanings

Table 4
Five Context Clue Types Taught in Word-Learning Strategy Lessons

Context clue type	Example
1. Definition: the author explains the meaning of the word right in the sentence or selection.	When Sara was hiking, she accidentally walked through a patch of **brambles**, *prickly vines* and *shrubs*, which resulted in many scratches to her legs.
2. Synonym: the author uses a word similar in meaning.	Josh waked into the living room and accidentally tripped over the **ottoman**. He then mumbled, "I wish people would not leave the *footstool* right in the middle of the room. That's dangerous!"
3. Antonym: the author uses a word nearly opposite in meaning.	The supermarket manager complained, "Why do we have such a **plethora** of boxes of cereal on the shelves? In contrast, we have a real *shortage* of pancake and waffle mix. We've got to do a better job ordering."
4. Example: the author provides one or more example words or ideas.	There are many members of the **canine** family. For example, *wolves, foxes, coyotes,* and pets such as *collies, beagles,* and *golden retrievers* are all canines.
5. General: the author provides several words or statements that give clues to the word's meaning.	It was a **sultry** day. The day was very *hot and humid.* If you moved at all, you would *break out in a sweat.* It was one of those days to *drink water* and *stay in the shade.*

Note. Words in italic provide context clues for bold words.

Note. From Baumann et al. (2005).

of the words from the context clues. For *predators*, one group wrote "something that is weird" (prediction), "hungry, eat anything they could fit in their jaws" (clues from selection), and "an animal that hunts and eat[s] another for food" (word meaning).

We also taught word-part clues through the use of Cunningham and Hall's (1998) Nifty Thrifty Fifty—a list of words that contains examples of common prefixes and suffixes (e.g., *compos-er, im-possible, encourage-ment*) to promote word building and spelling. For additional instruction in context, Donna used Kiester's (1990) *Caught'Ya!*, a daily grammar activity that included a low-frequency word (e.g., *vilify*) that often contained useful context clues (e.g., *insulted*). In summary, we provided students explicit instruction and practice activities on how to use word-part and context clues to infer the meanings of novel words.

Fostering Word Consciousness

Word consciousness involves "an awareness of and interest in words and their meanings" (Graves, 2006, p. 7). Various inquiries document that when teachers engage students in word play and promote their metacognitive knowledge about word use, students acquire an interest in words, develop an appreciation of word choice, and expand their vocabulary (Graves & Watts-Taffe, 2002; Scott & Nagy, 2004). We implemented this category through activities that addressed word play and figurative language (Blachowicz & Fisher, 2004; Johnson, Johnson, & Schlichting, 2004). Our Learning About Words and Language chart (see Table 5) provided definitions and examples (drawing from Johnson, 1999 and Johnson, 2001) for 13 such items.

We relied on this chart for informal lessons. For instance, Donna's love of poetry led naturally to inquiry activities involving authors'

Table 5
Chart Used for Listing and Teaching Various Word Play
and Figurative Language Elements

Learning about words and language

Category	Definition	Examples
Synonyms	Words that are similar in meaning	fight, quarrel, argument, squabble, altercation, beef, feud, brawl, fray, scuffle
Antonyms	Words that are opposite or nearly opposite in meaning	hot/cold, night/day, warm/chilly, boisterous (loud)/placid (quiet)
Homophones	Words with the same pronunciation but different spellings and meanings	night, knight rode, road, rowed
Alliteration	Repeating the beginning sounds of words	Five famished foxes feasted on fifty fresh fish.
Slang	Informal words added to our language	chopper (helicopter), hacker (computer intruder), 24/7 (all day, every day), iffy (not certain)
Simile	Comparing two different things using the words *like* or *as*	*Ann* runs like a *deer*. The *cookie* was as hard as a *rock*.
Metaphor	Comparing words or ideas in a figurative way	*Josh* is a walking *encyclopedia*. The *tennis court* was a *griddle*.
Hyperbole	An exaggerated statement	Tommy ate a ton of pizza. It took me a million years to clean my room.
Idiom	A saying that does not mean the same as the individual words	It's raining cats and dogs. Now you'll be in hot water.
Oxymoron	Using words together that have opposite or very different meanings	Mom believes in *tough love*. Please grab me some *plastic silverware*.
Homograph	Words with the same spelling but different meanings and sometimes different pronunciations	the *bear* growled/could not *bear* it a *bow* tie/take a *bow conduct* the band/have good *conduct*
Acronym	Abbreviations using the first letters of words	USA = United States of America ATM = automatic teller machine
Personification	Attaching human qualities to animals, ideas, or things	The *kite danced* in the wind. My *report card beamed with pride* as Mom looked at my straight As.

Note. Adapted from B. Johnson (1999) and D. Johnson (2001).

use of alliteration. She shared examples with the students from Prelutsky's (1983) "The Hippopotamus" ("The huge hippopotamus hasn't a hair") and Tennyson's (1851) "The Eagle" ("He clasps the crag with crooked hands"). Students also composed their own alliterative sentences (e.g., "Alice Alligator ate another ant." "Lucy loves luscious lollipops."), and they looked for examples in books they read and included alliterative phrases in compositions they created.

Donna used read-alouds and shared readings to explicitly teach ways authors used language to help readers form mental images. For example, Donna reviewed figures of speech and demonstrated how Curtis's (1995) language in *The Watsons Go to Birmingham—1963* was more engaging than "plain language." She composed and wrote the sentence, "They went into the living room," and then had students compare it to Curtis's metaphorical text, "They danced into the living room" (p. 67). Donna wrote "Momma's voice got strange" versus Curtis's use of simile, "Momma's voice got strange, hissing like a snake" (p. 68). Donna reviewed other examples of figurative language, and students worked in small groups to find additional instances of similes, metaphors, hyperbole, onomatopoeia, and alliteration from *The Watsons*.

Elizabeth conducted several lessons on how language is enriched by the addition of informal words. In one lesson, she invited students to interview family members about slang terms. The class created a chart listing the persons interviewed, the slang terms that were offered, their meanings, and when they were used. Entries (see Figure 4) included one dad offering *far out* as *awesome* from the year 1974, and a grandma providing toodle-loo as *good-bye* from 1938. In conclusion, we promoted an appreciation for the color and elegance of language. For example, one student demonstrated this playfulness—and some obvious humor—by writing the following on a paper requiring students to create hyperboles: "This sheet is taking so long to do that I'm going to have a beard by the time I finish."

What We Learned

Quantitative results demonstrated that students' word knowledge grew. A comparison of pretest and posttest results of the Expressive Vocabulary Test (Williams, 1997) revealed that students' expressive, or speaking, vocabulary grew more than expected across the intervention period. Results from the Peabody Picture Vocabulary Test (Dunn & Dunn, 1997), a measure of receptive or listening vocabulary, suggested that the students initially below average in vocabulary

Figure 4
A Portion of a Class Poster Displaying Slang Terms From Family Members

Relation	Slang Used	Meaning	Year
Dad	far out	awesome	1974
Granny	far out	awesome	1980
Mom	groovy	awesome	??
Mom	what's up	How are you doing?	1980-85
Uncle	Hey, sweetie	Greeting for a female	??
Grandma	toodle-loo	Saying good-bye	1938
Mom	conflabbit	oh, shucks	1994
Mom	you-go-girl	When a girl does a good job	1975
Dad	cool	It's all right	1965
Sister	off the chain	very exciting	1999-2000
Sister	thick	a crowd of people	2002-03
Sister	dang	whoa	1995
Cousin	shoudy	what's up	2000
Mom	Pig Latin	talking funny	??
Grandpa	tooky-pook	term of endearment	1992-2002
Mother	out-of-the-loop	uninformed	1990
Dad	Yeah	yes	1974
Mom	crazy	wild	1979
Father	been there, done that, got the t-shirt	already been through that	1996

Note. Photograph by Donna Ware

may have benefited from the program more than students initially above average in vocabulary. Writing sample results indicated that students used 36% more words in the spring writing sample compared to the fall sample, and the number of low-frequency words they included in their essays grew by 42% from fall to spring. As per a written questionnaire, parents' spring ratings were higher than fall ratings with regard to their assessment of their children's vocabulary size and how often their children talked about learning vocabulary. Results from a student questionnaire revealed fall-to-spring growth on items assessing their self-reported interest in reading, writing, and vocabulary.

Qualitative findings revealed three main themes:

Theme 1: Students Used More Sophisticated and Challenging Words. Students selected novel words from various sources to add to the Word Wall (e.g., *ersatz*, *vinaigrette*). For instance, William offered *hypertension* and explained that a family member had "high blood pressure."

Students also identified novel or interesting words from books, listing, for example, *sinewy*, *dwarfed*, *formidable*, *gusto*, *tawny*, *ornate*, and *penetrated* while reading *Roll of Thunder, Hear My Cry* (Taylor, 1976). Donna noted in her journal that "Today Donald put a book back on the shelf, making the comment that the word *bewildered* was all though that book." She also commented that a student "shared with me that he used the word *urn* in his story. He encountered this word in one of his independent reading books."

Theme 2: Students' Interest and Attitudes Toward Vocabulary Learning Increased.

Gary informed Donna that he wrote *gab* in his Vocabulary Log after reading it in one of Brian Jacques's books. Overhearing this conversation, Richard noted "That's what we do—we gab a lot in class!" In response to the questionnaire item, "How important is it for a reader to have a large vocabulary," a student provided no response in the fall but wrote, "It is very important. Without a big vocabulary you wouldn't be able to read that well" in the winter, and commented in the spring that, "Without a large vocabulary I couldn't read the book[s] I read." Several parents noted changes in their children's vocabulary, writing, "Vocabulary has gotten better," "Enjoys learning new words," and "Shares words and books more often."

Theme 3: Students Demonstrated Use of Word-Learning Tools and Strategies Independently and Engaged in Word Play.

Students used vocabulary resources. For example, Donna noted, "we read the word *lethargically* and Dennis grabbed a dictionary to look it up." Catherine stated that the charts displayed in the classroom helped her, and Gary found that the Word Wall got him "in the habit of trying to find those words." Students also demonstrated word-learning strategies. Following a lesson on context clues, a student noted that the author used *sad* as a synonym clue for *melancholy*. Kendra reported that, "I learned some oxymorons, hyperbole, slang, and alliteration." Students engaged in word play. One student told Donna, "I have a word problem," and he wrote the word America in bubble letters with the word

made inside it, to which Donna responded, "Oh, 'Made in America.'"

Final Thoughts

It was our intent to explore the impact of a program based on Graves's (2000, 2006) four components of effective vocabulary instruction on students' word knowledge and appreciation. We found that by immersing students in a vocabulary-rich environment and providing them instruction in words and word-learning strategies, they developed greater breadth and depth of vocabulary knowledge, as demonstrated by Richard's statement near the end of the school year:

> Before I came to fifth grade, if I read a word that I didn't know, I wouldn't take the time to stop. I would just go straight through it. I'd read it and I'd just try to sound it out.... But now I don't have to do that. I use context clues and everything...so if I find a word I don't know, I stop and think about it for a while and then I go on if I figure out what the word means.

Richard also commented on his growth in writing and use of vocabulary resources:

> First I thought my stories were really good, but they were really plain because I...didn't have any new words in there.... [Now] if I want to change the word—like this is really plain and I want to find a new word that's better than this that means almost the same but is different—that's when I started using a thesaurus. When...I came to fifth grade I had no clue what a thesaurus was. I didn't know what an antonym was. I didn't know what a synonym was. I didn't know what a metaphor was.

In a recent theory-to-practice review, noted vocabulary researchers Blachowicz, Fisher, Ogle, and Watts-Taffe (2006) stated that "the current burgeoning interest in vocabulary, coupled with documentation of less-than-robust classroom practice, has left conscientious teachers with many questions about how to design and implement effective instruction" (p. 524). In our formative experiment, Richard and his classmates demonstrated an enhanced understanding of, sensitivity to, and appreciation for the nuanced uses of words in texts they read and wrote; they discovered, that is, the value of "spicy, tasty words that catch your tongue." We believe that our work begins to provide answers to at least some of the questions that conscientious teachers have about constructing and employing effective, classroom-based vocabulary instruction.

Notes

This research was supported by an Elva Knight Research Grant from the International Reading Association titled "Effects of a Comprehensive, Year-Long Vocabulary Instructional Program in Fifth Grade: A Formative Experiment."

References

Allen, J. (1999). *Words, words, words: Teaching vocabulary in grades 4–12.* York, ME: Stenhouse.

Anderson, R.C., Wilson, P.T., & Fielding, L.G. (1988). Growth in reading and how children spend their time outside of school. *Reading Research Quarterly, 23,* 285–303.

Baumann, J.F., Edwards, E.C., Boland, E.M., Olejnik, S., & Kame'enui, E.J. (2003). Vocabulary tricks: Effects of instruction in morphology and context on fifth-grade students' ability to derive and infer word meanings. *American Educational Research Journal, 40,* 447–494.

Baumann, J.F., Edwards, E.C., Font, G., Tereshinski, C.A., Kame'enui, E.J., & Olejnik, S. (2002). Teaching morphemic and contextual analysis to fifth-grade students. *Reading Research Quarterly, 37,* 150–176.

Baumann, J.F., Font, G., Edwards, E.C., & Boland, E. (2005). Strategies for teaching middle-grade students to use word-part and context clues to expand reading vocabulary. In E.H. Hiebert & M.L. Kamil (Eds.), *Teaching and learning vocabulary: Bringing research to practice* (pp. 179–205). Mahwah, NJ: Erlbaum.

Baumann, J.F., Kame'enui, E.J., & Ash, G.E. (2003). Research on vocabulary instruction: Voltaire redux. In J. Flood, D. Lapp, J.R. Squire, & J.M. Jensen (Eds.), *Handbook of research on teaching the English language arts* (2nd ed., pp. 752–785). Mahwah, NJ: Erlbaum.

Beck, I.L., & McKeown, M.G. (1991). Conditions of vocabulary acquisition. In R. Barr, M.L. Kamil, P. Mosenthal, & P.D. Pearson (Eds.), *Handbook of reading research* (Vol. 2, pp. 789–814). White Plains, NY: Longman.

Beck, I.L., McKeown, M.G., & Kucan, L. (2002). *Bringing words to life: Robust vocabulary instruction.* New York: Guilford.

Blachowicz, C.L.Z., & Fisher, P.J. (2000). Vocabulary instruction. In M.L. Kamil, P.B. Mosenthal, P.D. Pearson, & R. Barr (Eds.), *Handbook of reading research* (Vol. 3, pp. 503–523). Mahwah, NJ: Erlbaum.

Blachowicz, C.L.Z., & Fisher, P.J. (2002). *Teaching vocabulary in all classrooms* (2nd ed.). Upper Saddle River, NJ: Merrill/Prentice Hall.

Blachowicz, C.L.Z., & Fisher, P.J. (2004). Keep the "fun" in fundamental: Encouraging word awareness and incidental word learning in the classroom through word play. In J.F. Baumann & E.J. Kame'enui (Eds.), *Vocabulary instruction: Research to practice* (pp. 218–237). New York: Guilford.

Blachowicz, C.L.Z., & Fisher, P.J. (2006). *Teaching vocabulary in all classrooms* (3rd ed.). Upper Saddle River, NJ: Merrill/Prentice Hall.

Blachowicz, C.L.Z., Fisher, P.J.L., Ogle, D., & Watts-Taffe, S. (2006). Vocabulary: Questions from the classroom. *Reading Research Quarterly, 41,* 524–539.

Block, C.C., & Mangieri, J.N. (Eds.). (2006). *The vocabulary-enriched classroom: Practices for improving the reading performance of all students in grades 3 and up.* New York: Scholastic.

Cunningham, A.E. (2005). Vocabulary growth through independent reading and reading aloud to children. In E.H. Hiebert & M.L. Kamil (Eds.), *Teaching and learning vocabulary: Bringing research to practice* (pp. 45–68). Mahwah, NJ: Erlbaum.

Cunningham, P., & Hall, D.P. (1998). *Month-by-month phonics for upper grades.* Greensboro, NC: Carson-Dellosa.

Dale, E., & O'Rourke, J. (1986). *Vocabulary building: A process approach.* Columbus, OH: Zaner-Bloser.

Daniels, H. (2002). *Literature circles: Voice and choice in book clubs and reading programs* (2nd ed.). Portland, ME: Stenhouse.

Duffy, A.M. (2001). Balance, literacy acceleration, and responsive teaching in a summer school literacy program for elementary school struggling readers. *Reading Research and Instruction, 40,* 67–100.

Duke, N.K., & Pearson, P.D. (2002). Effective practices for developing reading comprehension. In A.E. Farstrup & S.J. Samuels (Eds.), *What research has to say about reading instruction* (3rd ed., pp. 205–242). Newark, DE: International Reading Association.

Dunn, L.M., & Dunn, L.M. (1997). *Peabody picture vocabulary test* (3rd ed.). Circle Pines, MN: American Guidance Service.

Elley, W. (1989). Vocabulary acquisition from listening to stories. *Reading Research Quarterly, 24,* 174–187.

Fountas, I.C., & Pinnell, G.S. (2001). *Guiding readers and writers, grades 3–6: Teaching comprehension, genre, and content literacy.* Portsmouth, NH: Heinemann.

Fukkink, R.G., & de Glopper, K. (1998). Effects of instruction in deriving word meaning from context: A meta-analysis. *Review of Educational Research, 68,* 450–469.

Graves, M.F. (2000). A vocabulary program to complement and bolster a middle-grade comprehension program. In B.M. Taylor, M.F. Graves, & P. van den Broek (Eds.), *Reading for meaning: Fostering comprehension in the middle grades* (pp. 116–135). Newark, DE: International Reading Association.

Graves, M.F. (2006). *The vocabulary book: Learning and instruction*. New York: Teachers College Press.

Graves, M.F., & Watts-Taffe, S.M. (2002). The place of word consciousness in a research-based vocabulary program. In S.J. Samuels & A.E. Farstrup (Eds.), *What research has to say about reading instruction* (3rd ed., pp. 140–165). Newark, DE: International Reading Association.

Hall, N., Crawford, L., & Robinson, A. (1997). Writing back: The teacher as respondent in interactive writing. *Language Arts, 74*, 18–26.

Hayes, D.P., & Ahrens, M.G. (1988). Vocabulary simplification for children: A special case of "motherese." *Journal of Child Language, 15*, 395–410.

Heimlich, J.E., & Pittelman, S.D. (1986). *Semantic mapping: Classroom applications*. Newark, DE: International Reading Association.

Hunter, M.C. (1982). *Mastery teaching*. El Segundo, CA: TIP Publications.

Jiménez, R.T. (1997). The strategic reading abilities and potential of five low-literacy Latina/o readers in middle school. *Reading Research Quarterly, 32*, 224–243.

Johnson, B.v.H. (1999). *Wordworks: Exploring language play*. Golden, CO: Fulcrum.

Johnson, D.D. (2001). *Vocabulary in the elementary and middle school*. Boston: Allyn & Bacon.

Johnson D.D., Johnson, B.v.H., & Schlichting, K. (2004). Logology: Word and language play. In J.F. Baumann & E.J. Kame'enui (Eds.), *Vocabulary instruction: Research to practice* (pp. 179–200). New York: Guilford.

Johnson, D.D., & Pearson, P.D. (1978). *Teaching reading vocabulary*. New York: Holt, Rinehart and Winston.

Kamil, M.L., & Hiebert, E.H. (2005). Teaching and learning vocabulary: Perspectives and persistent issues. In E.H. Hiebert & M.L. Kamil (Eds.), *Teaching and learning vocabulary: Bringing research to practice* (pp. 1–23). Mahwah, NJ: Erlbaum.

Kiester, J.B. (1990). *Caught'ya!: Grammar with a giggle*. Gainesville, FL: Maupin House.

Lindsay, T. (1984). The affixionary: Personalizing prefixes and suffixes. *The Reading Teacher, 38*, 247–248.

Nagy, W.E., & Scott, J.A. (2000). Vocabulary processes. In M.L. Kamil, P.B. Mosenthal, P.D. Pearson, & R. Barr (Eds.), *Handbook of reading research* (Vol. 3, pp. 269–284). Mahwah, NJ: Erlbaum.

National Institute of Child Health and Human Development. (2000). *Report of the National Reading Panel. Teaching children to read: An evidence-based assessment of the scientific research literature on reading and its implications for reading instruction* (NIH Publication No. 00-4769). Washington, DC: U.S. Government Printing Office.

Nickelsen, L. (1998). *Quick activities to build a voluminous vocabulary*. New York: Scholastic.

Reinking, D., & Bradley, B.A. (2004). Connecting research and practice using formative and design experiments. In N.K. Duke & M.H. Mallette (Eds.), *Literacy research methodologies* (pp. 149–169). New York: Guilford.

Reinking, D., & Watkins, J. (2000). A formative experiment investigating the use of multimedia book reviews to increase elementary students' independent reading. *Reading Research Quarterly, 35*, 384–419.

Ruddell, R.B. (1999). *Teaching children to read and write: Becoming an influential teacher* (2nd ed.). Boston: Allyn & Bacon.

Scott, J.A., & Nagy, W.E. (2004). Developing word consciousness. In J.F. Baumann & E.J. Kame'enui (Eds.), *Vocabulary instruction: Research to practice* (pp. 201–217). New York: Guilford.

Stahl, S.A., & Nagy, W.E. (2006). *Teaching word meanings*. Mahwah, NJ: Erlbaum.

Swanborn, M.S.L., & de Glopper, K. (1999). Incidental word learning while reading: A meta-analysis. *Review of Educational Research, 69*, 261–285.

White, T.G., Sowell, J., & Yanagihara, A. (1989). Teaching elementary students to use word-part clues. *The Reading Teacher, 42*, 302–308.

Williams, K.T. (1997). *Expressive vocabulary test*. Circle Pines, MN: American Guidance Service.

Literature Cited

Babbitt, N. (1975). *Tuck everlasting*. New York: Farrar, Straus and Giroux.

Beatty, P. (1987). *Charley skedaddle*. New York: Morrow.

Bunting, E. (1994). *Night of the gargoyles*. New York: Clarion Books.

Bunting, E. (1996). *The blue and the gray*. New York: Scholastic.

Byars, B. (1977). *The pinballs*. New York: Harper & Row.

Cleary, B. (1983). *Dear Mr. Henshaw*. New York: Morrow.

Curtis, C.P. (1995). *The Watsons go to Birmingham—1963*. New York: Delacorte.

Curtis, C.P. (1999). *Bud, not Buddy*. New York: Delacorte.

DiCamillo, K. (2000). *Because of Winn-Dixie*. Cambridge, MA: Candlewick.

Frasier, D. (2000). *Miss Alaineus: A vocabulary disaster*. San Diego, CA: Harcourt.

Greene, B. (1974). *Philip Hall likes me. I reckon maybe*. New York: Dial Books for Young Readers.

Henkes, K. (1988). *The zebra wall*. New York: Greenwillow.

Paterson, K. (1977). *Bridge to Terabithia*. New York: Crowell.

Peck, R. (1998). *A long way from Chicago*. New York: Dial Books for Young Readers.

Prelutsky, J. (1983). *The Random House book of poetry for children*. New York: Random House.

Rampersad, A., & Roessel, D. (Eds.). (1994). *The collected poems of Langston Hughes*. New York: Knopf.

Settel, J. (1999). *Exploding ants: Amazing facts about how animals adapt*. New York: Atheneum.

Silverstein, S. (1974). *Where the sidewalk ends*. New York: Harper and Row.

Spinelli, J. (1990). *Maniac Magee*. Boston: Little, Brown.

Spinelli, J. (1996). *Crash*. New York: Knopf.

Stanley, J. (1992). *Children of the Dust Bowl: The true story of the school at Weedpatch Camp*. New York: Crown.

Taylor, M.D. (1976). *Roll of thunder, hear my cry*. New York: Dial Books for Young Readers.

Tennyson, A. (1851). *Poems of Alfred Tennyson* (7th ed.). London: E. Moxon.

Van Allsburg, C. (1988). *Two bad ants*. Boston: Houghton Mifflin.

Questions for Reflection

- The authors describe a classroom with a particularly rich vocabulary environment and instructional program. What components described here exist in your classroom? In your colleagues' classrooms? Which components have proven particularly successful with children in your school? What can you do to expand vocabulary activities and word learning to create a similarly rich environment as described in this article?